LONDO

ALSO BY HILDA KEAN

*Animal Rights: Political and Social Change in
Britain Since 1800*

*Challenging the State?
The Socialist and Feminist Educational Experience*

*Deeds not Words: the Lives of Suffragette Teachers*

*Ruskin College: Contesting Knowledge, Dissenting Politics*
(with Geoff Andrews and Jane Thompson)

*Seeing History: Public History in Britain Now*
(with Paul Martin and Sally J. Morgan)

# London Stories

## PERSONAL LIVES
## PUBLIC HISTORIES

**HILDA KEAN**

RIVERS ORAM PRESS
London, Sydney, Chicago

First published in 2004 by
Rivers Oram Publishers Limited
144 Hemingford Road
London N1 1DE

Distributed in the USA by
Independent Publishers' Group
814 North Franklin Street
Chicago, Ill 60610

Distributed in Australia and New Zealand by
UNIReps
University of New South Wales
Sydney, NSW 2052

Set in Bembo by
NJ Design, Fordingbridge, Hants, and
printed and bound in Great Britain by
T. J. (International) Ltd, Padstow, Cornwall

ISBN 1 85489 148 0 (hb)
ISBN 1 85489 149 9 (pb)

# CONTENTS

For my current and former students at Ruskin
who have taught me so much

# LIST OF ILLUSTRATIONS

# ACKNOWLEDGEMENTS

I could have written a book about London lives without the help of those indicated here—but then it would have been a very different sort of book. Without the different contributions of those cited below *London Stories* could not have been written. I am most grateful for the input and advice I have received.

I thank all those individuals who have offered information and shared ideas, particularly: staff at High Down prison, Banstead; Glynis Morris; publicity officer at the Mildmay Mission Hospital; Paula Sallnow; Arthur Mankelow; Lily Mankelow; Beryl Hatton; Joyce Thain; Glenda Nelson; Ann Hughes; Winifred Kean; Gwen Neal; Dorothy Sheridan; Katherine Bradley; Anne Digby; Caroline Morrell; Ken Williamson; Jo Stanley; Alison MacNair; Marjorie Mayo; Ivy Popham; Robin Jenkins, Alan Mann; Brenda Kirsch; Laura Worsley; P&O Archivist; Felicity Harvest; Alison Oram; Sally J. Morgan; Linda Sullivan; Ivy Ebdon; Russell Burrows.

I also thank the staff at the following libraries and archives: London Metropolitan Archives; Family Records Centre; St Bartholomew's hospital; Tower Hamlets Local Studies library; Hackney Council archive; Bishopsgate Institute; Bodleian Library, Oxford; British Library; Essex County Council Record Office; Victoria and Albert Museum Archive; Guildhall Library; Geffreye Museum Archive; Shropshire Record Office at Shrewsbury; Staffordshire Record Offices at Stafford and Lichfield; Kent County Council Record Office at Maidstone; National Maritime Museum Library; Local Studies Library at Keele University; National Institute of Marine Engineers; Surrey Record Office; Southampton Record Office; Norfolk Record Office; and, of course, the wonderful staff at Ruskin

College library: David Horsfield, Chris Keable and Val Horsfield.

I am particularly grateful to those who have commented on various drafts: Dave Reeves, Jo Stanley, Russell Burrows, Paul Martin, Melanie Tebbutt, Keren Abse, Farhana Sheikh, and especially Ken Jones; my current and former MA in Public History students who always made me think again about approaches; Ruskin Certhe and Family History students for always making me look again at materials I thought I knew and sharing their breadth of knowledge and experience with me. I also acknowledge the value of comments received at different presentations of various drafts at conferences of the Women's History Network; Regional Identities conference, Manchester Metropolitan University; and at presentations given at the London Metropolitan Archives; London Guildhall University; University of Sussex; Bishopsgate Institute; University of East London; Institute of Historical Research, University of London; Women's Library; Department of Heritage and Culture, Wellington, New Zealand.

Images on pages 32, 48 and 73 are reproduced with the permission of the British Library; those on pages 28 and 55 with the permission of the Bodleian Library, University of Oxford, and those on pages 33, 36, 94 and 104 by the kind permission of the London Metropolitan Archives. Other images are from the author's archive.

# INTRODUCTION

## Collecting material

At first it seemed easy. Sitting in her hospital bed with a broken leg, Mum had already made a list of the furniture she wanted with her in the residential home. Other items had already been allocated for local good causes. The washing machine and fridge had been taken away by the National Children's Home to give to a 'deserving' single mother and her children. Jean from the Loughton branch of the Essex Handicraft Association had arrived and together we had lifted the heavy sewing machine complete with its own table into her estate car. Boxes of knitting wool, scraps of material for patchwork and piles of *Cross Stitch Monthly* had already caught Jean's eye and she loaded the boxes into her car with the anticipation of future pleasure. I had taken the heavy Victorian and Edwardian furniture hand-crafted by my paternal grandfather. My mother had wanted none of it. But a dressing table and tallboy, utility furniture made in 1946, the year of her marriage, she took with her. What remained seemed simple for me to organise and to process.

I just needed to make separate piles for the books, or so I thought. The needlework, tapestry, embroidery, patchwork and quilling coffee-table books had already been distributed to the ladies of the Essex Handicraft Association for their bring and buy stalls. In another pile I had put the hundreds of religious books: the Bibles in a series of editions—Moffatt, *New English Bible*, *Good News Bible*; the William Barclay commentaries; the homilies from Patience Strong. These would go to the Loughton Methodist church for a jumble sale. They would all be going to a useful new home; someone would find a place for them, just as Mum and Dad—Winifred Kean (née Mankelow) and Stanley Kean—had, in their own way.

The remainder of the books were mainly about the history and topography of London: these were old, often rare and invariably in hardback and I would take these. I too would use them, for researching and writing, these books that my father had collected over the years about his home town. As Stan, who was born in London Fields in Hackney, used to say, he was a Cockney, born within the sound of Bow Bells, if the wind was in the right direction. Books that Winifred deemed to be still 'useful' or of sentimental value would be going with her to the Methodist residential home in which she would now live. These included the prizes for good conduct at Sydney Road elementary school in 1920, the Bible presented on her conversion to Methodism, and music scores of *Messiah*, *Elijah*, *Creation*, and *The Crucifixion* that she had sung in the London Choral Society with her husband before I was born.

Sorting through the rest of the books and ephemera should have been a simple task of objective categorisation, a sort of Dewey system for house clearance, but it became more complicated than this. For here I was engaging with collections of things that were now simultaneously anchored in the spaces of a 'past, yet stubbornly present' domain.[1] Here were objects, things, material, which crossed time. I had thought the books were simply books but they were also receptacles of notes and jottings, artefacts that had belonged to people, people I had known, and had been used as part of their daily existence. The books had transformed themselves into testimonials of many lives: of my mother who wrote sermons and the order of services, drawing on her Bibles and religious texts, writing out every word neatly in spiral notebooks; of my father who had died ten years before and whose possessions had never been sorted (I only now realised) by his widow, since the slips of paper, the notes, remained sticking out undisturbed from the piles. But the books and ornaments also went back to at least another, earlier, generation. There was the example of the Walter Scott novel given to my father, as the inscription explained, by his mother Ada. It had been a birthday present in 1914 that neither of them—to judge by the book's good condition—had ever got round to reading. But my father had not thrown the book away; nor did I. As Sally J. Morgan has described, in the account of her own father leaving a selection of photographs to his children before he died, 'The raw place where "history" begins is in the fear of oblivion. Out of that fear we begin to look for immortality and for meaning in narrative…When my father gave me his photographs he was giving me his own narrative of his own life.'[2] What was surrounding (or was it overwhelming?) me in the jumble and mess of this tiny council flat on the London/Essex borders was material from the past from which a history might be made. These were not titles that I had called up in the reading rooms of the Bodleian Library in Oxford or scrutinised, carefully using just a pencil, in the Rare Books room of the British Library. The material here was stuff that I had probably lived with as a child (I could not have been sure amidst the quantities and mess), and which my parents had lived with at least since their marriage. However, many of the things went back beyond the twentieth century into at least the last decades of the 1800s. In her illuminating exploration of the art of writing history Ludmilla Jordanova has suggested that what is 'relevant' material in the creation of history is 'never straightforward'.[3] I was surrounded by artefacts from the past; were they things that would assist me in writing a history of the family within which such items had been held?

I did not just observe books, or scribblings in them. Here too were minutes of meetings: Toc H, Women's Toc H, a typed report of a National Trefoil Guild conference my mother had attended in 1958;[4] accounts of the day care centre she had run; reports of Islington council care meetings, for whom my father had done voluntary work on his retirement; running orders for concert parties given to old people's clubs, churches and day centres; jokes and quizzes with bits of paper marking the questions. In Stan's hand there were notes, bookfuls of them, garnered from systematic and regular attendance at London evening classes over a period of thirty years. No scholar, he always said of himself (he'd left school at 15), but he'd made up for it in other ways. Those who spend their employed hours as clerical workers are not supposed to engage in such activities in their leisure time; conventionally this is left to the middle classes, the students, the lecturers, the professionals. But here were History notes, mainly of London, notebooks listing slides taken throughout mainland Britain of famous buildings, interesting cathedrals, 'sights' rather than 'sites'; and philosophy too: Hobbes and Locke and *Zen and the Art of Motorcycle Maintenance*, set texts from classes at the City Literary

Institute. Here were notes on Religion, Comparative Religion, Islam, Judaism, Hinduism, all made by this life-long Protestant Non-Conformist. Although the evening class note-taker was dead, the sermon writer and Women's Fellowship class leader was not. If I had asked Mum what to do with these things she had not divested onto others, she might have said chuck them out, they are no use now; so I didn't ask and I chose what to keep and to 'use'—in my way, as historians (and probably daughters) always do.

My mother had never known when things might come in 'useful' and so plenty had been hoarded. Used stamps were carefully cut from envelopes and placed for safe-keeping in a jar, to be forwarded, at some unspecified future time, to a charity. Here too were custard-cream biscuits in a royal wedding tin from 1981, given away free, she said, by the milkman; kept untouched on top of the kitchen cupboard for eighteen years. There were drawers full of receipts for Christmas presents to my mother from my father for kitchen goods, which themselves were rarely taken from their boxes. Instructions, too, existed in carefully kept booklets for the unused sandwich maker, unused filter coffee funnel and unused foot spa. Here were never opened gadgets purchased in a heady moment at a 1940s Ideal Home exhibition, an indication of what might have been.[5] They stayed in their boxes—a reminder of the self-denial of daily life. Here were boxes of presents: presents received and putative gifts, often the self same items, a recycling of good intentions. Drawers of Avon talcum powder bought for others; tea towels from a Trefoil Guild penpal in Australia or from the Canadian couple met on a coach tour two decades before or from the church bazaar for missionary work. Over twenty such tea towels were kept, used neither for drying dishes nor display: never to be used by this couple. Their lives had not been 'good enough' to allow the extravagant use of bright tea towels or a choice of talcum powders and soaps for their own use. There would always be a 'best occasion' to wait for, a right time, a better time, which never came. The flat was full of such reminders of a bygone era: the unopened wedding presents—the tablecloths in their crinkly cellophane wrappers, being kept for some future 'best'; the wedding photos in their presentation folders never distributed to the guests. As I moved my 85-year-old mother's effects with her into a residential home, they were still there in her flat.

The ephemera of these lives lived in working-class London were kept and not thrown away. These were the traces of existences lived in some ways set apart from contemporary time, adhering to outdated Liberal politics or Non-Conformist religion, staying in jobs in declining industries. The possessions hoarded reflected a coming together of lives of different generations and times into one place and moment. The existence of a world of hoarded bits and pieces, fragments and shards—I never used to think of them as materials for the writing of history when I lived amongst them as a child—were of a familial world into which I was born but which always seemed to be of a much earlier time. When I was young I never quite understood the fuss about Miss Havisham, the woman abandoned on her wedding day, in Charles Dickens's *Great Expectations*. Living a life in frozen time, the appurtenances of a previous event not removed, seemed a normal part of present life, to me. We did not quite have mouldering wedding cake for decades but uneaten Christmas cake kept in the tin to the following year, slivers of piccalilli residing in a jar in the bottom of a cupboard, paper bags and string in their own kitchen drawer, or in later years washed plastic bags, part of a present, redolent of a past, were all part of a daily routine. Here, as the twentieth century was turning into the twenty-first, was an almost illegible George III penny with the accompanying note of an unspecified child antiquarian explaining its historicity; Victorian hand-carved furniture; tiny and repeated relics of Southend-on-Sea; the World War One blanket used by the Rayleigh guide camp in the 1930s. These traces of earlier times had been gathered in my parents' and grandparents' lifetimes: they were still there.

Although I had started researching my family's history several years before my mother's accident and my role as a house clearer, it was seeing this physical substance of different lives that had given me the impetus to start to write this book. If, however, I had found such material in a public archive I would have been more confident about what to do with it. Discovering ephemera, particularly bits of paper carelessly left in otherwise ordered bundles, tied with ancient string, I would usually be excited. It would suggest that I had 'found something' that no one else had read, or noticed. It would have been obvious that here were materials for the writing of history since they had been preserved in archives, libraries, repositories, museums, created specifically for this purpose. I would have got out my pad of lined file paper and started scribbling. If it had been in a venue maintained by English Heritage or the National Trust I would have kept the glossy leaflet with key dates and facts, probably talked to the staff to get their perspective or, more likely, to provoke an argument about the rationale for the restoration or presentation. It wouldn't have seemed a problem getting material for writing history. But a council flat on an ex-Greater London Council (GLC) estate in Debden is not conventionally the stuff of history. Ordinary homes in the past are not the usual repositories of historical material. The commonplace childhood homes of Beatles Paul McCartney and John Lennon have not been preserved because of any apparent architectural merit but because of who these 'ordinary' children had become. My parents' cultural milieu and influence was surely in a qualitatively different league.

Since at least the 1960s, it has been 'permitted' to write histories of ordinary people's lives. This was how writers such as E. P. Thompson with his ground-breaking *The Making of the English Working Class* made their living and reputations as historians. Such history, however, was usually based on documents in archives, rather than what was found tucked away in a cubby hole, or dumped into plastic black bin bags. What elderly women decide to keep—or discard—is still not usually the substance of academic history, although family historians may operate otherwise. However, as Tim Brennan has suggested in his exploration of his great-grandfather's diary, dates of births, marriages and deaths, census returns, memories and heirlooms, are used by the family historian to construct a notion of self and to reject 'conventional cultural institutions as the sole arbiters of legitimacy and value'.[6]

Such items are personal but the experience of keeping things, using them, making connections between the past and the present is one shared by thousands of researchers engaged in writing about the lives of their own families. When I teach classes about writing family history or public history, students always have things that they are happy to bring into the group to share: a wooden spoon owned by Scottish peasants whose cottage Queen Victoria visited; the posthumous medal of a now-dead father who had been a London fire-fighter in the Blitz; a photo of 1950s children eating ice cream from a van on an ordinary day on their estate; a rent book, a ring, a badge.

## Historians and their histories

Such ephemera are not usually indicative of lives conducted centre stage in a conventional political or a social historian's idea of important events. In my own family, there are no documents to link my East London ancestors with the 1880s dock strike or to indicate political agitation for weavers' jobs; indeed there are no traces to link the people of this book with either conventionally defined significant local or national events. No close male relative died in the trenches of the First World War nor in the Normandy landings in the second (indeed they conveniently managed to avoid direct participation in both of these wars); no one joined the Labour party (and certainly not the Communist party). These were lives conducted off-centre-stage in the margins, of what has been seen, even by progressive historians, as the sidelines of history. Social historians of the 1970s insisted that the lives of working-class people like my parents, or grandparents and great-grandparents and their parents, covering in my case a traced time of a mere 200 years (a mixture of late breeders and long livers), were hidden from history.[7] History as a set body of knowledge existed but there were omissions; the lives of working-class men and women were—they said—ignored, often because of historical indifference or because of who wrote history. Minute books of union branches, diaries of working men and women were found and used;[8] interviews were conducted in the 1960s and 1970s with those who had been born as the nineteenth century had turned into the twentieth.[9] Emphasis was placed on the value of the spoken word, its alleged authenticity, its warmth and character, for the history of working-class lives.[10] There was an assumption that working-class people spoke, perhaps more truthfully, more engagingly, than the middle class who preferred to convey their life experiences by the written word.

But less attention was given to the places in which people lived, the things people possessed from the past and valued, items which were personal but reflected broader times. When one elderly man, for example, in Wilmott and Young's famous study, *Family and Kinship in East London*, proffered papers of his family's past this was treated quite casually: '[He] brought out an old paper written in somewhat strange French in the year of the Revolution, which as far as could be made out was a petition from a man who was his ancestor beseeching the Governors of the French Hospital in Hackney to employ his grand-daughter.'[11] In such times histories were written of big—and certain—events: *The Making of the English Working Class, Hidden from History: 300 Years of Women's Oppression and the Fight against it; The Voice of the Past.*[12] The definite article, 'the', reflected the grand narratives and optimistic overview of working-class activity facilitated by the contemporary politics of those years of radical campaigns. The political world we live in now has changed; so have the concerns of historians. There has been a reaction to the positive broad sweep of class action or socialist-feminist tales. No longer are the Luddite croppers, the obsolete handloom weavers and followers of religious utopian Joanna Southcott being rescued from the enormous condescension of posterity, as E. P. Thompson first described it some forty years ago.[13] The experience of surviving through times of acute social disturbances and of trying to change the world now attracts little interest in, at least, mainstream history. Indeed, the idea of experience itself has often been debunked.

Certainly the work of the late Raphael Samuel, who attempted to write about ordinary lives in contexts designed to explore the way historical knowledge has been constructed, has been largely overlooked in the last few years. His collaborative collection *The Enemy Within*, that reflected on the miners' strike of 1984–5, was written as an intervention in political and public debate but also as a reminder of 'individual experience and imaginative perception'[14] and the way in which the strike was 'assimilated in popular memory...both in the pit villages themselves and in the country at large'.[15] Such examples of history making (and history writing) in the public political domain offered a practical example of the connection between lived experience and more formal kinds of learning.[16] As he described in his last book, *Theatres of Memory*,[17] this work was 'a project concerned with the unofficial sources of historical knowledge and the ways these are affected by ideas of progress and loss'.[18]

In contrast to admittedly difficult attempts to explore how past experience might be seen in the present, a slippery elision has instead seemed to develop between the knowledge of the impossibility of ever being able to re-create the past 'as it really was' and the idea that the past is of no relevance to the present. Keith Jenkins argues this position in his *Refiguring History*:

> The past contains nothing of intrinsic value, nothing we *have* to be loyal to, no facts we *have* to find, no truths we *have* to respect, no problems we *have* to solve, no projects we *have* to complete...'[19] (original emphases)

Jenkins is, quite rightly, criticising the conventional view of an historian seeking 'truth' and 'objectivity' whilst refusing to acknowledge the role of the historian herself in the making of history. However his approach begs the question, Why bother writing history? And, needless to say, Keith Jenkins doesn't. Although he has written a number of thought-provoking works on the nature of history he does not even attempt in practical ways to create a different sort of writing about previous times. The past, experience, the existence of everyday lives have become utterly irrelevant—at least to writers of this outlook in their professional work.

## My history

In this book I want to argue that while it is impossible to recreate the past as it really was we can nevertheless create meaning, understanding and, even, interest by drawing on the substance of past lives. The idea of 'materials', however, is also controversial. Writing in very different ways from Keith Jenkins, Richard Evans, who recently acted as an expert defence witness in the libel case brought by David Irving,[20] has declared, 'Argument between historians is limited by what the evidence allows them to say.' Evans treats the reader to a metaphorical comparison of historians acting like figurative painters sitting around a mountain, painting it in different lights or angles. However they paint, they will all be painting the same mountain. 'The possibilities of legitimate disagreement and variation are limited by the evidence in front of their eyes.'[21]

Of course, documents should not be deliberately falsified (nor erro-neously translated),[22] but Evans's argument assumes that there is a consensus amongst historians about what 'evidence' is. This, I suggest, is not a given. To notice that there may be traces of earlier lives in a cubby hole in a council flat in Debden also requires a recognition that such lives may be constructed by material other than material written by the state, philanthropists, or do-gooders. However, those who use artefacts other than that found in official archives are by no means dominant amongst historians.

In this book I use material that exists inside—and outside—archives, in the local streets of the present, in graveyards and cemeteries, souvenirs and trinkets, photos and maps, memories and stories. In doing so I am not trying the impossible task of re-constructing the past 'as it really was', but rather, as cultural commentator and activist Walter Benjamin described, to attempt to bring the past into the present, 'The true method of making things present is to represent them in our space, not to represent ourselves in their space...we don't displace our being into theirs; they step into our life.'[23] The traces that I draw on to write the stories in this book are, in some senses, about my family but they are also part of broader cultural and social histories. When I teach courses on public history or writing family history I am always engaged and fascinated by the ephemera, the traces of former lives that students choose to bring to class: a sailor's embroi-dered picture from the early nineteenth century, a saying 'all fur coat and no knickers', a photograph which evokes sad memories. Inevitably, the rest of the group can relate to these apparently personal materials because of the social, and shared, nature of the way in which historical and cultural knowledge is created. Those who bring such material to history classes have chosen what to bring; what is writ-ten in this book is what I have chosen to write. The materials make it possible, provide the basis, the underpinning, but the written history is that which an historian attempts to create.

### My family history—and family historians

This book is about a past characterised by traced and traceable ephemera, an archaeology of lives lived in particular places and spaces, but a history that is being written in twenty-first century London.

The 'protagonists' lived amidst the distressed weaving of early nine-teenth-century Bethnal Green, the furniture trade in Shoreditch in the late 1800s and early 1900s, the workhouse in Hackney, the lunatic asylum in Surrey, farmlands in Shropshire, the brickfields in Kent, the home for inebriates in Norfolk, the London Electricity Board (LEB) and the Inner London Education Authority (ILEA). Attached to the chairs, bricks, graves, ornaments and photographs are stories; in the state records of the census of birth, marriage and death certifi-cates are narratives of a different sort. By using them in the context of this book of the twenty-first century there will be further narra-tives, other types of stories. This history, then, is itself a story of the process of creating past lives for present times. These are lives which were ordinary enough, mapped out against the routine of every-day existence: a getting by, a pulling through, of things not being what they might have been, of wanting them to have been better. In these stories there are traces of living on a peculiar sort of margin never in the worst slums but next to them, teetering on the edges of respectability, but, for the most part, remaining the right side of upright. They are lives that can be constructed because of the traces that still remain.

For some, the nineteenth century was a time of imperialist expan-sion and emigration, of possibilities in other lands or even other towns or suburbs. While others travelled thousands of miles to look for a new life, mostly my paternal family stayed put, not exactly stationary but moving in circles, in a radius of a few miles round and round the streets of East London, particularly Bethnal Green and Hackney. I currently live a 30-minute walk away from where Esther, my grandfather's grandmother, lived. Unknowingly I used to drive down her street every day taking the short cut to Tower Bridge, crossing the river southwards for work. I'm not sure Esther and I would have much in common if we were to meet in some East London form of Aboriginal dreamtime. But we would share a knowledge of the same geographical area; although our lives are very different and separated by nearly 200 years we have in common a place, a place which has changed, but a place which phys-ically still exists. It is against this physical—and metaphorical—space of London and the south of England that I am seeking to create a contemporary map for the lives of these people.

## The self and history

What is it that we are doing, those of us who, as John Aubrey the antiquarian put it, go 'grubbing in churchyards',[24] rummaging in the archives or hoarding inherited photographs? Are we looking for a past, searching for an elusive fragment which will help us in detective-like mode to give us an answer about a different time? Or are we trying to use this material to create a particular present and imagine a future? As Raphael Samuel suggested:

> If history is an arena for the projection of ideal selves, it can also be
> a means of undoing and questioning them, offering more disturbing
> accounts of who we are and where we come from than simple iden-
> tifications would suggest.[25]

Certainly the absorption in the activity and the engagement with the bald material of 'family history' surpasses many of the practices of the scholars in the British Library. Unlike the British Library, which rations its books, especially during the summer when schol- ars really do want to read them, the materials in the Family Records Centre are readily available: no rationing here—and helpful staff. This is the heart of 'non academic' research into past families today in England and Wales. As the repository of records of births, deaths and marriages since 1837 and full census returns from 1841 to 1901, the Family Records Centre is an exemplar of autodidactism. In the Family Records Centre in Finsbury there is not just the activity of reading but simultaneous interpretation: the details of the family or street found in the census need to be picked over, usually at that very moment, to ascertain whether it is indeed the 'correct' one. In contrast to an academic reading intent on garnering as rich sources as possible, which, in the case of social and cultural historians, might mean nice stories, plentiful anecdotes, new sidelines, or, rarely nowa- days, grand overviews—the family historian while relishing material is also looking very explicitly for only certain information. The social historian might scrutinise the war memorial in the Hadlow church outside Tonbridge for 1914–19, looking at the numbers of young male dead and considering how many of the families in the small village lost a son, brother or father; the family historian might note the name of only one, either to be pursued as a son of another scion of the family or be discarded as the 'wrong one'.

Some might reject the work of the family historian as a form of regressive train spotting, simply filling in the boxes in the genealogical tree. Certainly some of the material is precise, but family history is a much less 'objective' practice than it first seems. Family historians, like those working in other historical fields are, whether they necessarily realise this or not, privileging the role of the historian as a maker of narrative. Tim Brennan has characterised this approach as one which jettisons modernist views of an unfolding historical process, 'in favour of a more internalised and intersubjective invention of the past'.[26] The historian of family—like the conventional historian—is not recording every detail, every piece of material, but only the ones which fit their purpose. There is indeed the fascination with the illusion of apparently 'discovering' what isn't known, to use this as a source of imagination. Some are looking in a vague way for a wider family, others for an educational hobby, some for filling in the gaps in family stories. Some seek the fantasy of connection with someone in the past in not dissimilar vein to the excitement expressed by Studs Terkel meeting Bertrand Russell and 'shaking the hand of the man who shook the hand of the man who shook the hand of Napoleon',[27] or as an historian of British homosexuality has described in wittier ways, 'I once kissed a man who'd once been kissed by Lord Alfred Douglas…a man now in his forties is thus only two pecks away from Oscar Wilde.'[28]

Traces of stories do already exist in census records, birth, marriage and death certificates, ledgers of the lunatic asylum and workhouse minute books. But such fragments are also re-fashioned through their juxtaposition in the present. The pages that follow will discuss aspects of the lives of ancestors but they will also explore how such lives can be given meaning in the present through engagement with materials now. This is both about the bits and pieces and how they are made into different stories. The subject matter is my own family (as I have chosen to define it) but the approach is equally well one which can apply to others seeking to write such an account. In the pages that follow you will find neither genealogical tables nor stories of the 'good old days' when you could leave your front door open and gangsters Ronnie and Reggie Kray would keep

London's streets safe (from the other criminal gangs). Here you will not find accounts of 'the golden age' as ascribed by Gilda O'Neill to the testimonies of hardship and getting-by she covers in her popular book, *My East End.*[29]

My immediate family and their predecessors covered with silence the difficulties, the pain of uncomfortable realities; they did not talk about them. Thus many of the starting points for my own exploration have been based on physical materiality, a material culture which does exist, and which is being pursued by those engaged creatively in museum, anthropological and cultural studies as well as those researching their own families' lives.[30] As Adrienne Rich evocatively described:

> These things by women saved
> are all we have of them
>
> or of those dear to them
> these ribboned letter, snapshots
>
> faithfully glued for years
> onto the scrapbook page
> these scraps, turned into patchwork.
> A universe of humble things—
>
> and without these, no memory.
> no honor to the past.[31]

The fragments of materials I use are connected to me through a notion of family: the gravestone inscription, 'I waited patiently for the Lord and he inclined unto me and heard my cry'; the strange photograph of a mother's son posting a letter; the certificate exempting his daughter from vaccination against smallpox; fashioned stools and turned candlesticks; the memory of desert islands on the kitchen windowsill, fluttering palms created from carrot tops.

The bits and pieces of personal lives can also be the subject matter of public histories, histories created outside university rooms and libraries, that emphasise the engagement with history now.

Public history can act as an umbrella, under which the historical mind can be brought to bear on areas of research and thought which are often seen as mutually exclusive…it relies on a collective and collaborative effort of people working in different fields. This very process, of itself, helps to avoid academic navel gazing.[32]

This book is about personal lives but also the process in which they came to be included within this book. As the acknowledgements indicate, this book could not have been written in the way it has without the input of those researchers of family, locality and place, most of whom do this for pleasure rather than paid employment. These pages contain London stories; they are stories of personal lives but in in the process of their construction they have also become part of a broader public history.

# I

## IN THE ARCHIVE, IN THE STREETS

### ESTHER MOUNTFORD, SPITALFIELDS SILK WEAVER

For a moment in the 1990s, 'House', the statement created by the artist Rachel Whiteread, was the most famous house in the streets just north of Victoria Park, the biggest park in East London. It had been constructed as a plaster cast from a derelict house in a nineteenth century terrace awaiting demolition. As Whiteread had speculated at the time, it became controversial.[1] Her plaster cast questioned ideas of place and home in East London; it made a statement about the everyday; it enraged the local Liberal councillors pre-occupied with value for money and particular nostalgic ideas.[2] The creator received an award for her efforts, but this work of art itself was soon destroyed to prepare a site for a new dog-walking area. Nevertheless, 'House' is remembered in different ways in the public domain. There are books and articles interpreting its significance. Cards can be purchased confirming to a buyer that even though the artwork no longer exists, the unreal house was in fact there—once upon a time.

Around the corner off Roman Road market in Medway Street at number 46 is another house, one without the need for apostrophes. First existing there some 120 years ago, it's still there today. As you can see from the illustration, it is architecturally unassuming and is not distinguished by a blue plaque signifying that someone famous lived there. But for me, as I write this story and trace the lives of my ancestors, it gains some significance because of a personal, rather than a public, connection. Although the street, and this house, has been there for over a century it has reached these pages through a very recent, personal, journey.

I bring 46 Medway Street into the present because it was here on 26 October 1880 that Esther Keen, the daughter of Edmund Mountford, widow of William and mother of six children, William, John, George, Edward, Lydia—and Charles, my great-grandfather—

died aged 61 of, if the death certificate is correct, apoplexy.[3] Esther Keen did not die there alone. With her at the end was her youngest son, of 20 years, Edward. And nearby, at number 9, lived Lydia, Esther's only daughter, with her husband and baby William, as the census records.[4] I had—eventually—traced the death of Esther in an archive, the Family Records Centre, the national repository of census returns and registers of births, marriages and deaths. As Carolyn Steedman has suggested, historians spend time in archives because convention-ally here is 'a place where a whole world, a social order, may be imagined by the recurrence of a name in a register, through a scrap of paper, or some other little piece of flotsam'.[5] But

*1* No. 46 Medway Street, Bethnal Green, 2003

Esther, of course, had not died in a document or record office: here in Medway Street is where she passed away.

Although the London Metropolitan Archives, the largest English record office outside the National Archive in Kew, contains thou-sands of photographs of London streets, it contains no image of Medway Street.[6] This is partly why I drove there and took this photograph—precisely because it does not exist in this archive. Of course, I wanted this image—and photographs of the other houses where Esther lived—to exist in a public archive, to confirm that my personal connections and interests were sufficiently socially based to be included within a public collection. But archives are not like that; they don't necessarily record the mundane, the everyday. Images in the Tower Hamlets council archives or those in the London Metropolitan Archives usually preserve a particular significant moment in the life of a street, freezing an instant in time before a road disappears in redevelopment or after aerial bombing in the 1939–45 war. Why, then, would there be a photograph dated October 1880 to say that this was a moment, an instant, when Esther, the great-great-grandmother of Hilda (who has written this book and who in 1880 was waiting some 70 years to be born) died?

Although a death certificate told me that this was where Esther died, and nineteenth-century records confirmed when the street was built, in truth this is not how I really 'know' about this street, or this area near the park. My particular knowledge of the area is not derived from archives or books. Like Esther, I am a Londoner, and I live in East London. Medway Street is about a mile in a different, southerly direction from where I have lived most of my life in the adjacent borough of Hackney. I have often passed near by on the way to Whitechapel Sainsbury's, taking the pleasanter route through Victoria Park, still—as in Esther's day—the biggest park in East London.

Ideas of the past, of meaning and understanding, can be created because of personal knowledge of a present place, or through stories handed down in families and communities, from material culture, things, detritus, streets and artefacts, that never find their way into an official archive or record office. Until I discovered that I had an ancestral connection with this specific place, I had never thought of taking this photograph. The house had 'always' been there in the public domain—but I had had no need to acknowledge it personally and certainly no need to freeze it in time, to remember it visually. However, now that I want to pull the past into the present, to create a story of people in particular times and places, I need this image to confirm to myself that this woman about whom I know little did actually exist. I also need to convince you, as a reader, that I have not conjured up Esther out of thin air, that she did indeed live here. And that I have done the research, the hard graft that historians are supposed to do. The photograph attempts to bridge the time of Esther's death and the writing of this book. It's a place that existed two centuries ago and that still exists. Here people continue to live, walk to the local market and, as the sign on the lamp post reminds us, jostle with each other for where they might park their cars. And here too people lived (and died) in the 1880s.

## An illiterate silk weaver's story?

Family history tends not to start in the streets, or on the way to the shops, but in state records. Thus family historians tend to emphasise extraordinary moments in an individual's life, the events that occurred but once—birth and death. Traces of the mundane, of the routine substance of everyday life, are more elusive. But sometimes it is an absence that attracts us, allows us to imagine a life—and so it was with Esther, the grandmother of my grandfather, Charles Kean. In my trawl through the archive she had grabbed my attention as the first 'family illiterate' I had found. This is not the same as saying she was the first—or last—illiterate within my family, but she was the first illiterate I had the illusion of 'discovering' in the archives. She seemed to present me with her illiterate marks of 'x' as a signifier of continuity throughout her life as they appeared on public documents: her marriage records, the birth of her children and the death of her husband. In England in 1840, the year in which Esther came of age, a half of all brides and one third of all bridegrooms could not sign their names during the marriage ceremony.[7] However, as David Mitch has suggested, being illiterate was not necessarily a bar to employment, nor did the acquisition of literacy guarantee improved chances of a better paid job.[8]

I read Esther's illiteracy as a form of 'normality'. I have fancied that it established her as ordinary, commonplace, 'typical' in contrast to her descendants whom I had known in the following century, who had sought to define themselves as anything but 'like everyone else'. Esther's descendants, a grandson and his son, familial men who had prided themselves on the value of the written (and religious) word, and who had posed in photographs with books and newspapers, seemed a sharp antithesis of this woman. It was this absence of literacy on which I had focused and about which I fantasised; this aspect of 'what was not there', had first drawn me in, complementing the bald 'facts' collected by the state.

From the detailed census returns from 1851 I knew Esther's place of birth (Hackney), address (in Bethnal Green ) and job.[9] As a single and then married woman, Esther had worked in the silk trade, as a silk weaver or winder preparing the silk, which would then usually be woven into set lengths by male weavers. Certainly there is plentiful material about the work and lives of East London silk weavers, usually called Spitalfields silk weavers, even if this material is not specifically about Esther. Located immediately adjacent to the City of London, Spitalfields had been the oldest industrial suburb of London.[10] By the nineteenth century the words Spitalfields and silk weavers had become almost synonymous, although most of the weavers had moved further north and east into an area now defined separately, Bethnal Green, in search of cheaper accommodation. Silk weaving in London had had its origins in a livery company within the nearby square mile of the city.[11] The trade had been revitalised, however, by migrant Protestant weavers who had been forced abroad from their native France after religious persecution first at the St Bartholomew's Massacre of 1572 and, subsequently, when the freedom to practise their religion was rescinded by the Edict of Nantes in 1685.[12] In the nineteenth century many contemporary commentators chose to emphasise the Protestant nature of the area, which the Huguenots had configured with their reputedly hard work and thrifty habits.[13]

I should have been pleased to have realised that Esther and her father Edmund were silk weavers, and in some ways I was. In family-history circles Spitalfields silk weavers are rather sexy, seen as somehow 'authentic' and part of a particular East London tradition. There is also much extant material on the trade from two main sources, that can give an illusion of being able to reach back into the past. The first is from the Huguenot community who flour-ished in Spitalfields, formed successful businesses and friendly societies, and established the French Protestant Hospital where many elderly women and men ended their days. By the late 1800s the Huguenot Society, keen to establish and preserve the community's own heritage, organised discussions, collected materials and published their findings.[14] However, despite the French sounding name, 'my' Mountfords seem to have arrived in eighteenth-century London from East Anglia rather than the more exciting France.

A second source is several parliamentary reports and royal commissions that explored the specific circumstances of the weavers' existence. The geographical proximity of Spitalfields to the centre of financial and political power had given the authorities specific cause for concern. Famous for direct action to protect the trade being undercut by cheaper French imports during the 1760s, Spitalfields weavers had marched in their thousands, rioted and smashed looms. As the Hammonds have pointed out, 'the journeymen weavers were bold, determined and strongly organised.'[15] As a consequence, both state repression and executions followed, as well as the Spitalfields Acts, initially of 1773, that protected the area as the key location for silk making in England. In the same period in which repressive Combination Acts outlawed trade union activity, here was a form of collective bargaining, through negotiation between 'masters' and weavers, being enforced by the courts. In contrast to the exclusionary position of male power-loom carpet weavers in Kidderminster,[16] Spitalfields female silk weavers were permitted to complete regular apprenticeships as weavers and to be paid the same as journeymen once their apprenticeships had been completed. Wage levels were legally controlled and—unusually for the time—this regulation of wages applied both to men and women.[17] This legal protection of wage rates remained in force until 1824, when it was removed 'in the first free trade budget of the century', despite much local vociferous protest.[18] However, even in the hard times of the 1840s, women continued to weave the finest velvets and jacquard brocades and to receive the same piece rates as men.[19]

But do these materials really tell me anything about Esther? Although the nineteenth-century reports and surveys might tell me something about silk weaving, they were documents for a national debate about the value—or not—of state intervention into the economy.[20] In the course of a century during which Whigs (and then Liberals) advocated the merits of free trade the Spitalfields weavers became a metaphor for the efficacy, or otherwise, of *laissez-faire* economic policy. It was this wider, national, debate—and not the interests of future family historians—that provided the context for much of the extensive official literature on the silk trade.

One of the parliamentary commissions was conducted in 1840, the year before Esther Mountford would marry William Keen. In part it was concerned with combating the national (and local) influence of Chartism, the militant campaign for the vote and political representation for working men, and with the problem of unemployed male hand-loom weavers in the north of England who had lost work through industrialisation.[21] This particular inquiry had been set against the earlier knowledge, on all sides, that Spitalfields had formerly been a regulated industry. A superficial reading of the Reports of the Assistant Hand-Loom Weavers' Commissioners might suggest that here was an opportunity for individual weavers to describe their own experiences and tell their personal stories.[22] The stories included in the pages of these long reports are full of motifs of hard work, dedication and low wages, told in response to the largely unstated questions of the commissioners. Government inspectors and investigators were concerned that women under-taking paid work, often in circumstances injurious to their health, were undermining Victorian ideas of femininity.[23] But the story-tellers—like their interrogators—were all male. Female stories, told by women, were neither wanted nor included in these reports. Esther's narrative is not here, nor is there the story of another young female silk weaver that would help me imagine her as a story teller explaining her life: even such a trace is absent. Fathers and husbands spoke about the work of their daughters and wives. As William Bresson, an experienced silk weaver, testified to the parliamentary inquiry, 'There are few trades in which a woman is able to earn as much as my daughter gets by working at the loom.' However, the women who worked at the loom were silenced from presenting themselves as articulate, as potential creators of their own life stories, in a public arena.[24] Despite constructing powerful mascu-line stories of hardship and industrious work, the 1840 commissioners concluded that the local silk weavers were in a more prosperous state than their colleagues in the north and needed no special help: the Spitalfields weavers, the commissioners concluded, had merely been better able to attract attention due to their loca-tion in the capital.

But even if women—if Esther herself—had been called upon to give evidence would this have been her story any more than the story of William Bresson was his? The framework for the evidence, the structure of the narratives, was that demanded by the remit of the commissioners. The investigators' concern was the macro-economic situation. These are not the stories 'of' silk weavers created as personal stories, devoid of context and wider forms of story telling, but tales structured as evidence to a public, formal inquiry. In addition to individual stories, the parliamentary reports contain a statistical breakdown of the number of looms being worked in different districts of Spitalfields and by whom—men, women, boys, girls (and a separate category of boy and girl apprentices). As a young unmarried woman Esther Mountford is likely to have worked alongside her father Edmund, weaving silk in Hoxton. At the time of the commission's survey, Esther, then in her early 20s, would have been working at home, rather than in a mill, using a drawloom and probably weaving plain silks. As George Dodd described the Spitalfields weaving process in 1844:

> The weavers work in their own houses, and employ the hand-loom for their silk goods. There are no large factories, no power-looms, no steam-engines, but everything (with the exception of the Jacquard machine) goes on pretty nearly as it did in times past.[25]

If Edmund was better off than his neighbours, he may have owned his loom (or looms) outright, although more usually they were rented from a manufacturer. The commissioners declared in their returns for 1838 that this part of the Spitalfields area possessed few looms—82—and even fewer weavers, a total of 43 weaving families. Within this group there were just 17 women and 1 girl. Some might read this as an acknowledgement of the hard work of women and their evident skill in this trade; but it might also be set alongside the contemporary idea that a reason for weavers' poverty was not the squashing of laws protecting the industry, but the very numbers of people, including women, seeking to eke out a living in a shrinking market.

I'd like to imagine that this solitary girl was Esther: it might confirm that she did indeed do the work the census had indicated and it would give me the pleasure of 'finding something', 'getting it right'. But the commissioners' report, the document itself, would not have been her history (it would not tell me—or you, of course—how Esther felt about her work, or her father, or mother, or the area she lived, or anything else we might really want to know…). As Carolyn Steedman has argued in her book, *Dust*:

> In actual Archives, though the bundles may be mountainous, there isn't in fact, very much there…nothing happens to this stuff, in the

Archive. It is indexed, and catalogued and some of it is not indexed and catalogued, and some of it is lost. But as stuff, it just sits there until it is read, and used, and narrativised.[26]

The fate of Esther, the task of writing about her, understanding or constructing her life, is still resting in my hands. Even if the one young woman in the parliamentary returns for Hoxton had been Esther it would still have been my decision to then create her as unique and distinctive—or typical.[27] But this problem has not arisen: despite my careful scrutiny—and longing—Esther's individual story is not in the pages of the parliamentary reports, however much I might want it to be. Although intellectually I recognise the impossibility of creating set meanings and clear parameters, emotionally I want to fill in the gaps, to make the connections, pull 'everything' together and make a jumble of stuff fit into clear and organised explanations. I want to write a story like that which Stephen Poliakoff created visually in his 1999 fictional television film *Shooting the Past*. Here photographs gathered across time and countries, but collected in one archive, were juxtaposed to create both a public history of twentieth-century Europe and a personal history of a refugee from Germany. But even with Poliakoff's symmetry and elegance the fictional story created by the archivists, played by Lindsay Duncan and Timothy Spall, was insufficiently convincing to deter an American businessman from dismantling the collection. Such precise, dramatic histories have no place in a monetarist framework. Nonetheless I still want to know, as 'Dress Rehearsal Rag', a favourite Leonard Cohen song of my past and present has put it, 'where all the elephants lie down'.[28] This search, this wanting to know has not gone away and the plethora of material on East London lives creates the illusion that such knowledge is indeed possible. However, as Leonard Cohen's song also reminds us, such attempts too often end in failure.

## Squirries Street: a place in the past and the present

Just before Christmas in 1841 Esther married at St John the Baptist church in Hoxton. This 'respectable behaviour' was the norm. As the parliamentary commissioners declared, 'The weavers do everything in their power to discountenance unlawful associations…[On marriage] there is seldom any external appearance of any previous imprudence.'[29] Her husband William Keen, whose bricklaying father was already deceased, worked as a hearth rug maker and lived at that time, like Esther, in Allerton Street in Hoxton. William too could not sign his name, nor could the witnesses George Devine and Sarah Mountford.[30] Soon William and Esther would move into Squirries Street off Bethnal Green Road and share a house with George and Jane Devine and their young family. Sarah (and Thomas) Mountford were also residents in Squirries Street at this time and within this street William and Esther would spend the first years of their marriage.[31]

For much of its nineteenth-century existence the absentee landlord of most of this street of 54 houses was George Warde, lieutenant colonel of the London Rifle Brigade—who chose not to live in this street, but outside Westerham in Kent, at Squirryes Lodge. The nearby streets—William Street, Robert Street and part of Orange Street—kept him in a comfortable lifestyle. Together with his brother Charles, an admiral of the Royal Navy, who lived in nearby Squerreys Court, and who was defined by the Westerham Post Office directory at least as 'gentry', George Warde had much material, if not emotional, interest in the area. The Wardes' connection with Squirries Street had been a long one—far longer than that of the Keens: successive members of the Warde family had been Lord Mayors of the City of London, and the local land had been in the family since 1703 and would remain so until the twentieth century.[32]

Before I'd ever thought about Squirries Street I had known of the existence of the Westerham house, Squerreys Court. I recalled seeing the heritage sign while researching for an article on squirrels and the similarity of the names had stuck in my mind.[33] Looking through the *Victoria County History* this time I made different connections, with East London. I had wanted to see what sort of home could have been furnished and maintained from the rent Esther and William and their neighbours paid, how the hearth rug maker and silk weaver had enabled the Wardes to live then—and now—in Westerham. So, in the Spring of 2002, having paid my entrance fee, I wandered through the house with 'T'. I jotted things down in my notebook conscious of being watched, tailed almost, for the custodians were clearly unused to such engagement. My background knowledge of the family's status in the City of London (and a business card with Oxford on it) allayed anxieties. 'We have to be so careful of thieves,' explained a volunteer apologetically before proceeding to elaborate affably on her own interest in history. The current owner was summoned and pleased to confirm my book knowledge that the family had indeed owned streets of houses in Bethnal Green. I asked whether any records of this remained within the family. They didn't. 'We were lucky,' he explained; the family had sold off properties during the war before the 1945 Labour government came in—a 'terrible time for landlords,' he remarked. I didn't tell him my family had lived there, had helped his ancestors decorate and maintain their mansion with its artworks by Stubbs, Poussin, Van Dyck and Rubens.[34] I doubt whether either of us would have seen much reason for renewing this 'familial connection' some 170 years later...

Today, if Squirries Street is known at all, it is as a thoroughfare, a black-taxi route from Hackney Road opposite the shamefully derelict Children's Hospital, cutting through to Whitechapel down toward the Hawksmoor church by the busy Highway and thence to Tower Bridge. When I used to whizz down it during the morning rush hour I was too preoccupied with time and traffic to notice that the new flats were called Silk Court, and I was not interested that the silk industry had spread so far east towards Bethnal Green. Now, as in the past, Squirries Street is not a famous street although the East End aficionado might better know the continuation of the street, Vallance Road, as the childhood home of the mythologised 1960s gangsters, Reggie and Ronnie Kray. In the 1840s Squirries Street was both a place of working—mainly in the silk and related trades—and of living. By then Bethnal Green had gained a reputation, with some justification, for low priced housing. No other district in London had so many low-rated properties. Over 93 per cent of housing in Bethnal Green was rated at under £20 per year. Even some 30 years later most of the property in Squirries Street was rated considerably below this meagre level.[35] Although some of the Bethnal Green area in the 1840s and 1850s continued to sport the neat gardens with dahlias and tulips much in evidence some 50 years before, Squirries Street did not.[36] In the 1860s, I realised from the large-scale first Ordnance Survey map, there were only seven

2  Squerreys Court, near Westerham

trees in the gardens of Squirries Street—and none seemed to be at number six, the Keens' home. The long and busy Bethnal Green Road, to which Squirries Street led, was full of food shops: cheese-mongers, grocers, butchers and bakers and small workshops of coopers, printers, and corn chandlers. Even then there was a pub called the Marquis of Cornwallis as there is today (on the corner of Vallance Road).[37] Although the main road in the 1840s contained shops and businesses, it had few sewers, and Squirries Street had none at all. Paved footpaths were non existent, street drainage was absent, and consequently the gutters were full.[38]

The parliamentary reports I discussed earlier did not mention Squirries Street by name, even though it was a centre for the silk trade. Rather its specific inclusion in contemporary works on sani-tation suggest a place of disease rather than work. Hector Gavin's lurid book of 1848, *Sanitary Ramblings* presents a different perspec-tive on the lives of Bethnal Green weavers from that portrayed in parliamentary commissions or census returns.[39] Gavin, the local superintendent of health, collated data meticulously, street by street (and in almost every case the absence of a sewer), in an attempt to persuade the local authorities to install sewers and a clean water

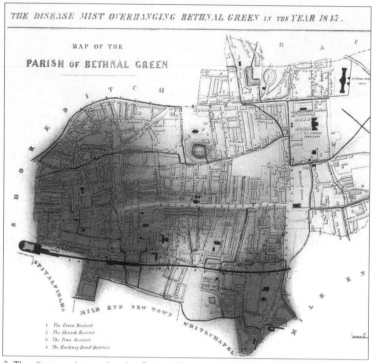

3 The disease mist overhanging Bethnal Green, 1847

supply. In tables, descriptions and melodramatic maps, he characterised this area of Bethnal Green within a framework of sanitation.
In Gavin's book Squirries Street was portrayed visually by dark
patches described as 'the disease mist overhanging Bethnal Green'.
Although caught by the diseases map, the Keen family nevertheless seemed to escape the perils of the pond at the other end of the
street. Bethnal Green ponds were no rural idyll but rather the repositories of dead cats and dogs—and sulphur gas.[40] On the same site,
'social housing' has now been built.

To look uncritically at Hector Gavin's plunging graphs and esti-
mates of local life expectancy one is surprised that *any* local children
lived to adulthood. But survive is what at least the little Keens did.
Esther's first child, William, was born four years after the marriage,
in 1845. There may, of course, have been miscarriages before (and
after) this, but all the children born to Esther survived childhood—

and the cholera epidemic. In September of 1849 there had been 10,000 deaths from cholera in London—mostly of infants and young children.[41] In one week alone of October of the same year, when young William was four and baby Lydia a mere two, in Bethnal Green there were 1571 cases of diarrhoea, an early symptom of cholera or typhoid which frequently led to death.[42] Esther and husband William also survived these epidemics—and Esther did not die in childbirth (to judge by reports on weavers, this was by no means unusual). The health of weavers as well as their employment was surveyed in contemporary state reports. In anthropological vein they were often depicted as a race apart. Those from weavers' families of more than one generation were reputedly small in stature, 'The whole race of them is rapidly descending to the size of Lilliputians. You could not raise a grenadier company amongst them at all,' commented Mr Redfarn to the enquiry of 1840 in an attempt to persuade unsuccessfully the commissioners of the hard times on which weavers had now fallen.[43] Even 50 years later, in a sympathetic, but odd, article in *The Graphic* of 1893 Spitalfields weavers were still depicted as 'other'. They were said to possess extremely small heads with a 'prevailing width of 6 1/2 or 6 3/4 inches in contrast to the average size of male heads of 7 inches in England'.[44] Despite the apparently small heads, difficult births were allegedly more common among weavers as they were conventionally seen as generally weaker and smaller than the rest of the community and mortality was high.[45] I do not know whether Esther (or William) had a large head (and what indeed would this tell me?), but she was certainly strong enough to survive to the age of 61 and to outlive her husband.

## Squirries Street: staying and not going

If the Keens seemed against the 'norm' in their resistance to disease, then Squirries Street as a whole appears defiantly against the conventional view of the time in the occupation carried out by most residents. Esther, like most of her female neighbours, continued to work, as she had done before marriage, in the silk trade. The Devines and Keens shared the same house: husband William and George Devine also shared the same job of hearth rug weaver. Rug making, unlike silk weaving, had never been a large local employer. Indeed in the 1840s there were only three local firms on the Hoxton, Shoreditch, Spitalfields borders.[46] Although William—like Esther—was not able to read and write, he did know quite precisely what he did for a living. He did not merely make rugs or floor coverings, but hearth rugs, so the public documents declared. William's job was making the floor covering of the cosy home, the house 'respectable enough' to aspire to the accoutrements of Victorian homeliness.[47] Originally based in the north of England the market for rugs and carpets also grew in London during the nineteenth century.[48] Certainly the firm of T. E. & W.W. Davis in Whitechapel, that made rugs, floor cloths, oil stair linens, mats and mattings, was thriving long after William himself had died.[49]

In 1851 Esther and William and by then their three children, William, Lydia and John were continuing to live in Squirries Street and Esther, like some 8,999 other women over 20 in London, continued to work in the silk industry, which, according to Sally Alexander, was less than 1.2 per cent of the total female workforce in London. Of these 9,000 women, 50 lived in this very street.[50] In Squirries Street, at least, weavers continued to ply their trade and silk continued to dominate the livelihoods of occupants. Of those men and women over 21 living in the street, 60 per cent of the jobs were in the reputedly moribund silk trade.

In 1851 this was not only an older person's job but a woman's job. While the silk trade represented just over half the jobs that men in the street carried out, three-quarters of the Squirries Street women were employed in this trade. For young people in the street, however, silk represented less than 30 per cent of jobs. Nevertheless the trade was not merely an older person's job, for weavers moved both in to and out of the trade.[51] Many worked in the textile trade, making fringes or trimmings, or hoods and cloaks. The street also possessed its own resident lay missionary, from the London City Mission, paid to bring the word to those capable of benefiting from it.[52] And there were two cow keepers, Thomas Roberts and George Robinson, both born locally; the usual practice would be to keep cows out in sheds at the back of the houses—without sewers.[53]

Some ten years later in 1861 jobs in Squirries Street were still dominated by silk. Certainly many of the inhabitants were the same residents of 1851 working in the same job. In 15 of the 64 houses not only was silk weaving still the main occupation but the self-same families were working in the trade as they had done a decade before. The street as much as jobs seemed to mark out the lifespan of local individual families.

If we simply accept standard histories of the silk trade and assume the generalisable is the same as the particular then Esther should not have been doing this. She should have weaved no more. The scrapping of the Spitalfields Acts and changes in the tax on silk imports had led to an overall downturn in the local industry. Those who continued to weave were frequently portrayed as out of time and living in a pre-industrial era. This depiction was often found in nineteenth-century visual images which contain common iconography. They usually show women, men and children working together in the trade: they defy later written accounts such as those by Manchee or Clapham that ignored the presence of women.[54] The image reproduced on the next page from *The Queen* in 1861 depicts a couple and their oldest daughter working together at their looms, while the moon shines and the youngest children sleep alongside them.[55] This is a picture of a particular sort of hard work. It has an emasculated quality: it is not the space of 'male craft'—heavy manual work—but of a 'female' domestic space, a home, but one in which men were also included. The plants on the windowsills recall the earlier flower-growing hobbies of the Huguenots; the bird cage reminds us of their bird-breeding reputation.[56] The inclusion of a clock, chairs and pictures on walls help create a particular image of respectability: the domesticity suggested by plants, birds and pictures is in sharp contrast to the new industrial factories of the north of England.[57] If this posed image is intended to represent hard work it is not back breaking: all the workers sit with straight backs—literally and metaphorically upright.[58] This is an image that looks back to an earlier time: those who continue in this job may be hard working but they are no longer part of the forward-moving industrial age. The illustration is neither new nor unique. Some ten years earlier, a similar image had been published in Godwin's *Builder*, designed to arouse concern for these curious relics of a former age. Here we have the clock on the wall, the sleeping children, the parental work late into the night.[59] Similar images, albeit in photographic vein, continued up into the

4 Home of the Spitalfields Weaver, *The Queen*, 1861

1930s, always defining the workers as of an earlier age, or the 'last weaver'.[60] Journalist and chronicler of London life G. Holden Pike described his walk through Spitalfields in 1892 as a journey out of time, 'The weavers, who are fewer in number now than they have been for some generations…may possibly become extinct before very long.'[61] In similar vein *Pall Mall Magazine* of 1905 represented an apparent conversation with an old silk-trimming weaver proud to create very expensive trimming for opera cloaks. The response of the journalist's companion is to admire the skill and 'true humility' of the elderly woman preserving, 'between the pages of a dog-eared hymn-book a little piece of silk fringe, very elaborate in pattern and exquisitely wrought'. But amazement is reserved in

5 Weavers' Room, Spitalfields, *The Builder*, 1853

anthropological vein for the very existence of this elderly woman and others like her: 'surely their day has gone!'[62] Even if one believed that sketches and photographs were simply representations of historical reality, surely the observant would notice the common iconography of these images over a time frame of decades, and speculate on a continuity of meaning.[63]

Historians such as L. D. Schwarz have endorsed this picture of silk weavers on the margins between domestic labour and industrialisation, between destitution and survival, and have depicted the weavers' story as one of perpetual decline and withering away. David Green, for example, has suggested that by the 1840s the area had become synonymous with impoverishment.[64] Certainly it is the case that weavers were obliged to apply to the Board of Guardians for poor relief. Esther and her husband would have been eligible for poor relief having lived and worked locally, like their parents before them, throughout their lives. But, according to the rough examinations books of the parish officers from times of downturn in the industry, they did not apply. In this snapshot of moments of destitution, they are absent. They were never 'poor enough' to have to tell 'their story' to the local officers to enter the workhouse or get 'outdoor relief'.[65] In the late 1840s the rough examination books of the local Boards of Guardians contained stories of weavers who had fallen on hard times. These were different stories from those told to the parliamentary commissioners: these stories demanded a particular knowledge of place in order for the 'right' story to be told. To be worthy of money the poor would need a life narrative—one that would explain where they and their father were born, where they had lived, how much rent had been paid, where an apprenticeship had been served and for how long, and to whom they were married. All of this needed written evidence, apprenticeship indentures, marriage certificates, or precise, local, geographical knowledge such as particular details of where the parental home had been situated. 'Next to Mrs Rudd, the cat's meatshop,' says one.[66] Ironically if you were obliged to enter the workhouse then stories were no longer required, instead silence was the norm during meals and work.[67]

I have mixed feelings reading these poor-relief documents in the London Metropolitan Archives. Part of me is willing Esther and William and their young family to be poor enough to be recorded as destitute—for my benefit as a historical researcher. But they have disappointed me, and yet again I am guilty of the condescension of posterity.[68] The physicality of the records themselves disturb me. The ledgers' leather covers are crumbling and need careful handling. The books are cherished: spongy lecterns support soft brown cushions and the document is placed on top like a dozing cat. These documents seem almost cosy in their immediate placing. This is in stark contrast to their contents, which do not suggest a warm embracing, but interrogations, testimonies in response to questions, stories of the 'deserving' poor, records of those who could not cope and were not 'protected'.

Some weavers took up other work locally in the wood trade making cheap goods for the West End stores; others emigrated. *The Queen* pronounced, 'The sooner the hand-loom ceases to be regarded as a means of existence the better.' Emigrate to 'pastoral districts and colonies', *The Builder* urged with tales of weavers 'who have done well as shepherds'.[69] But Esther was not among those who had moved into another job; even when the total abolition of duties on French imported silk was scrapped in 1860. If she had been able to read she could have read in *The Times* of the behind-the-scenes negotiations that Liberal MP Richard Cobden had undertaken. Today Cobden is perhaps known as the father-in-law of the painter Walter Sickert, dramatised as a notional Jack the Ripper.[70] In the nineteenth century, however, Cobden was best known for his opposition to the Corn Laws earlier in the century that had protected landowners' profits by keeping flour and bread prices artificially high. Apocryphally, on this occasion, his advocacy of free trade had led Cobden to allegedly declare, 'Let the silk trade perish and go to the countries to which it properly belongs.'[71] The parliamentary discussion and new treaty was reported and endorsed in *The Times*, 'Protection, expelled from palaces, has been lurking in comfortable corners, among people…standing out each for his own little craft.[72] But Esther, of course, being illiterate would not have known this; or rather she would not have known through the press that her work in 1840, or indeed in 1860, was apparently no more. For Esther, alongside thousands of her neighbours, continued with the same job she had always done despite what the men in Westminster had decided.

In 1861 George Devine, the Keens' marriage witness from twenty years before, was still living in Squirries Street, at number 6, and now sharing the house (and the same job of making hearth rugs) with Joseph Clark. Both their wives, Jane and Betsey, were washing clothes for a living: one washed, the other mangled, probably in laundries which proliferated through London. Such work necessitated similar long hours to domestic silk weaving: 14–16 hours a day, which, unsurprisingly, drew the attention of trade union activists and legal reformers alike to the need for reform and change.[73] Joseph was somewhat of a rarity in this street and locality having come into Bethnal Green from his birthplace of Hertfordshire, for in these streets to the north of Bethnal Green Road inward migration was unusual. Even by the last decade of the nineteenth century over 80 per cent of the local residents had been born in local parishes—and this was a figure that had remained remarkably constant since the mid century. Across the Bethnal Green Road going south towards Whitechapel and thence the docks, it was a different place in the late nineteenth century, a place of immigrant communities, particularly Jews fleeing from pogroms. Within a few hundred yards of Squirries Street there was a different mapping of the area, with the Bethnal Green Road providing a frontline of

6 Squirries Street, Bethnal Green, 1938

sorts between various geographies of Bethnal Green.[74] Unsurprisingly, as Christopher Husbands has put it, 'It is incontrovertible that during the nineteenth century some of the residents of the area developed a laager mentality about their neighbourhood.'[75] Or, as an early diary of the 1830s suggested of Bethnal Green, 'They are all weavers, forming a separate community: there they are born, they live and labour, and there they die.'[76]

Local families—and not just the Huguenots—intermarried and stayed here. In movement as well as working there was a sort of standing still; in some senses providing a continuation with earlier times despite the rupture present in the surrounding metropolis.[77] Even in the 1920s and 30s there were still traces of common surnames from those earlier times—the Agombars, Hayes and Holloways—and the vestiges of the cows who lived in Squirries Street.[78] For it was in a former cow shed at number 64 Squirries Street that Mosley's British Union of Fascists had their local headquarters.[79] A dying industry had not impelled some residents to leave—nor had a dead one. Although, by 1861—unlike their former friend George Devine—the Keens had moved from Squirries Street, they had not gone far, moving into Princes Court, off Tyssen Street, the name by which the north end of Brick Lane was known. This street too had a history of silk weaving: here in the 1770s at the Pitt's Head pub a weavers' benefit society, the Norman Society, had been formed and continued until the 1960s.[80]

## Dying and continuing

The Keens' move was probably not a sign of improving times. Rather than sharing one house with just one other family, here at 24 Princes Court were three families—still all involved in different ways in the silk trade—with eight children under the age of ten between them, several adolescents and a total (on the night of the census at least) of 22 human beings in this one house.[81] Their new landlord was a man of God, vicar Reverend Jas Brown, who owned many cheap properties here and in nearby Shacklewell Street.[82] But the Keens continued in some senses much as before: William, now 41, continued to weave rugs, and Esther, silk. Young John joined his mother in the silk trade working as a trimming spinner, 14-year-old Lydia worked as a sempstress and William junior, the oldest child, supplemented the family income by running errands for a living. As for Charles, he went to school. For me it is now the schoolboy Charles, aged nine, rather than his mother, who becomes the most important person in this family, for it is he who connects Esther and William to me in his future role as my great-grandfather.[83]

The neighbours worked in similar ways in silk, in the local wood trade, making cabinets or chairs, or in the small workshops of the local shoe trade.[84] Overwhelmingly they came, like the Keens, from Spitalfields and Bethnal Green. Lydia—Esther and William's only daughter—also stayed. Her future husband was from the locality and the couple married in 1867 in a church, at the back of Bethnal Green Road, called St Jude's, the saint invoked in desperate situations.[85] A couple of years later, in November 1869, still weaving hearth rugs, William died aged 49. His father John had also died young; when William had married, nearly 30 years before, he had been fatherless: now William was leaving his own children in a similar position—Charles was still only 17. The cause of death, the certificate said, was 'bronchitis'. It could, of course, have been bronchitis without the inverted commas; but too often it was not. As Thomas Dormandy has suggested, tuberculosis or TB, the feared white death, brought on by working in small, unventilated workshops, was the underlying cause of such categorisation. After 1890 bronchitis emerged, Dormandy argues, 'as a meaningless but popularly acceptable cause of death in childhood and mortality from this cause doubled almost from one year to another'. Although it was recognised that consumption was five times higher among the poor than the rich, the terminology for the disease was vague. The fear of TB and its hereditary effects often led to its rewording on the supposedly authoritative death certificate.[86] Esther, now a widow, outlived her husband by 11 years, still working, still living, in Bethnal Green albeit further away from the city and nearer Victoria Park.

I find creating meaning about Esther from available 'personal' public documents—certificates and census returns—problematic. The meagre materials that exist about her life encourage a story of constancy and lack of change: same husband, same area, same job, same illiteracy. This is in sharp contrast to Lynda Nead's recent description of nineteenth-century London: 'Change in London was happening so quickly that it seemed by enchantment rather than man-made.'[87] Census returns—mere moments recorded every ten years—can suggest a more mundane picture than rapid decline and change. Here is a potential story of continuity, the passing of ten years condensed in a brief moment. For historical narratives are not only models of past events and processes but also metaphorical statements, which suggest a relation of similitude between such events and processes.[88]

By looking at census moments ten years apart, complemented by contemporary reports of a declining industry and visual images of a pre-industrial past, I am seeing traces of a time that already seems outside the period in which the documents were created. This scant material for her life, such as it is, is never contemporaneous. The birth of children, or the registering of death after the demise of a husband or even the record of the marriage are (obviously) recorded after the event itself has happened. Census returns were written up from enumerators' logs after the night in question. Nothing of Esther's past to which I have access is truly contemporaneous. The bits of paper, certificates, that I can physically touch now, are not even from the nineteenth century but newly produced for me by civil servants in Southport on receipt of the set fee.

I have only one thing knowingly in the present that belonged to Esther or William. I had seen the anonymity of Esther's illiterate 'x' as a personal signifier of constancy against wider social developments. But it is through this illiteracy, the inability to know the variations of spelling 'Keen', that the family surname changed: my own surname is not that of the London-based name but of the Irish/northern English version, although there are no family connections with these places. Through familial illiteracy I have been disassociated with the phrase 'keen as mustard' deriving from the Keens' firm selling mustard at Garlick Hill in the City of London from 1742; instead I am' linked' to the actor Edmund Kean, or, if spelling is not a strong point, the footballer, Roy Keane.[89] Esther's absence of literacy when registering her son Charles did indeed give me something I still have, the 'wrong' surname. This discovery, this personal direct connection to Esther or William, seduces me into the role of detective, the piecer not of silken strands but traces of archival material tempting me into telling a story of times in the past I cannot recreate. There is more that I could write about Spitalfields silk weavers, and their involvement in socialist campaigns. Alternatively I might discuss at length Bethnal Green poverty. However, Esther, as far as I can ascertain, was neither radical enough to be recorded as a Chartist activist, nor poor enough to be a destitute applicant to the workhouse. In such stories of melodrama she has no personal place. The scant materials for her life, that do exist, caution me against the conventional stories of East London lives, the melodrama of Jack the Ripper, the religious rhetoric of lives destroyed by alcohol or lives stunted by insanitation and over-crowding. In choosing to write an individual life, I am wary of the excitement of such a social context unless I can find traces of this broader experience in the personal. I have indeed looked, trailed Chartist studies for particular names, examined the samples exhibited behind glass cases in the Victoria and Albert museum for evidence of Esther's expertise. But in these places there is nothing specific. In the archive, however, and the streets of Bethnal Green there are personal traces, albeit of a particular kind. The streets she walked are still there; so too is the park, perhaps safer then than now. There is a wider context, one of place, rather than politics, and this continues, at least in some form, into the present. Rachel Whiteread's 'House', 'one of the most captivating sculptures ever made,' is no longer there in Bethnal Green;[90] but Esther's house is still there, a potential repository of imaginings and dreams.

# 2

## OUTSIDE THE ARCHIVE AND INSIDE A MEMORY

### SARAH EICKE

### Finding the 'right' Eickes

Sarah Eicke, my mother's grandmother, like her father and grandfather before her, had been born over a hundred miles away from
London on the borders of the Black Country beyond
Wolverhampton, in what some locally call the white highlands of
Tettenhall.[1] She died, aged 77, in February 1914 in what was then
working-class Chelsea in West London. Sarah had suffered for many
years with spinal degeneration, and a brain haemorrhage had finished
her off. Sarah's daughter also lived in London; while mother Sarah
was in her last weeks of life, her daughter Mary was giving birth
to her latest child, Winifred, my mother. Here was a moment of
continuity between the generations; the first outing of baby
Winifred in the wider world, or so she had been told and remembered, was to her grandmother's funeral. The London district of
Chelsea, like the descendants of Sarah, also continues. The streets
that Sarah and her husband Tom Davies had known during their
married life are still there but the class topography has changed.
Perhaps the most famous local landmark is the gym frequented by
Princess Diana. College Place, the terrace in which Sarah died, still
stands but is now part of a fashionable gated development, designed
to protect the residents from their neighbours. This is not and was
not the area of Sarah's childhood, which had been spent in the
Staffordshire and Shropshire borders, but the place to which she had
moved as an adult after her marriage to Tom.

My starting point for this chapter, for this attempt to drag the
past of Sarah and her grandparents into the present, could not be
a physical place that I might know through personal connections
in contemporary London, as the villages of Oaken, Codsall and

Tettenhall off the Holyhead Road are not part of my own topography. Driving to the north I usually try to avoid the nearby M6 as it curves around the West Midlands; for me this is an area characterised not by villages and country paths but by motorways, and by the convergence of the M5 and M6, where traffic congestion becomes even worse. In the distance the flags of Wednesbury IKEA fly giving the illusion that the cars are aiming there (and many are). In the future I too would journey beyond Wolverhampton not for cheap furniture but in search of a past, but first I needed to know

7   College Place, Chelsea, 1999

in different ways where I was going and what I was looking for.

I do not have difficulty writing now with some confidence that Sarah and her Eicke ancestors came from the Shropshire/Staffordshire borders beyond Wolverhampton. It was neither the place itself nor the archive that provided the rationale for such authority but the practice and scholarship of family historians who, in different ways, had shared their knowledge with me. As Raphael Samuel declared in his book *Theatres of Memory*, if history was thought of as an activity rather than a profession, then the number of practitioners would be legion.[2] Those researching their own families are part of an interest group of millions, as the Public Record Office found to its cost when it severely under-estimated the numbers who would log on to read the census returns of 1901 when released in January 2002. The simultaneous logging-on of seven million people caused the service provider to withdraw the service temporarily as its servers were unable to cope with the massive demand.[3]

Certainly Samuel's promotion of historical practice as a shared activity, making links between lived experience and formal kinds of learning, is embodied in the work of family historians like 'Y' who had first helped me in my research.[4] On starting this activity several years ago it had seemed sensible, easy even, to commence my researches with an unusual name. In my desire to make connections, to make logical deductions, to create siblings for the Eickes that I had ostensibly traced in nineteenth-century London, I had contacted 'Y' and 'P' through the East London Family History Society who also had Eicke ancestors. We had shared facts, copies of census returns, and 'Y' had generously told me of her discoveries. Taking up her suggestions, I had enthusiastically visited a putative family grave in Raleigh in Essex, where my mother Winifred had spent some of her teenage years—thinking that this would be a good story, of me the historian making a family connection, where older participants had known none, despite being physically in the same place as their ancestor. I had picked the ivy off the gravestone 'Y' had told me was there and I felt I had found 'something'. At that time it had been a Louisa Eicke who I was tracking down: not a 'close' ancestor I later realised, but someone whose existence had seemed to possess symmetry, being apparently in a right place, Essex, near to London, rather than in an intangible Midlands. There had also been a trip to Prittlewell outside Southend, a venue for my childhood Sunday school outings, for another, I subsequently realised, still unconnected grave. In due course, apologetically, I did acknowledge the error—my mistake, my insistence on making things fit—to 'Y' who had already included me on a draft family tree, installing me as a distant relative. However, 'Y', being more thorough in her genealogical researches than I, had realised that there were two branches of the Eickes in the 1500s, one in the South East, the other in Shropshire; somewhere there would still be a place for me and 'my' Eickes in a larger, still-to-be-finished, Eicke tree. Both of us keep in touch, exchange the little we have found, correspond through Christmas cards. 'Absolutely no research achieved this year!!' says the latest one, but I don't quite believe her.

Of course, it would be good to say that I had found the Staffordshire/Shropshire connection myself, but it would not be true. Historical research is not an exact science; it is finding—and then using—what you might come across, but not necessarily knowing what it is you are looking for, or where. The material might be a photograph, an heirloom, a conversation with a colleague—or a stranger. I thought I might have found 'my' Eickes in the Midlands; but Tatenhill or Tettenhall, both in Staffordshire census returns, mean little if you are short-sighted and a Londoner. In Tatenhill, an upmarket Georgian village, outside Burton-on Trent, I had scrutinised the graveyard surrounding the fine ancient church hypothesising that in this rather nice village I would be unlikely to find a trace of 'my' Eicke, and I didn't. My tramp around the Tatenhill graveyard with no Eicke names at all simply suggested to me that this was the wrong place. I doubt, however, if I would have located the traces that I now have of the Eickes in south Staffordshire if a chatty researcher at the Family Records Centre had not helped. I had met an unnamed middle-aged woman at the 1881 census indexes who had heard my deep sighs sympathetically and put me right. 'You've misread it', she said, 'it often happens. It's probably not Tatenhill really, but Tettenhall, Wolverhampton. A dump, I know, I grew up there.' It was from such sharing of local knowledge outside the archive, although in this case located within it, that I traced at least the right place in which Edward Eicke, his son John, and grand-daughter Sarah, had been born.

## Placing the Eickes

I had no personal connection in the present with the area and scant life experience—day trips to Ironbridge Gorge open air museum hardly compete with local knowledge acquired from everyday life. But as a historian I did have a book knowledge of the locality, depicted as a special place, as the birthplace of the Industrial Revolution. In the period between roughly 1760 and 1860 British industry and the economy changed from domestic production to a factory system. Steam as a source of power and the development of new machinery transformed working lives and landscape alike—and by no means all for the better. By the 1790s, when Sarah's grandfather, Edward, was still a young and unmarried man, two-thirds of the population of nearby Staffordshire were already earning their living through manufacturing, commerce or mines.[5] Large areas of South Staffordshire were included in the Black Country, a nomenclature that had origins in the material

8 The Iron Bridge at Ironbridge, May 2004

circumstances of a working environment. The name Black Country is broadly applied to the area surrounded at its perimeters by Wolverhampton in the north east, Halesowen in the south, West Bromwich in the east, and Walsall in the north east. As the nostalgic Black Country Society proudly declares today:

> The 'Black Country' is defined by geology; it respects no human boundaries. Beneath the Black Country lies the 30 foot coal seam. This is Britain's thickest and richest seam of coal... [6]

Edward Eicke had been born c.1770 in Sheriffhales, in Shropshire, specifically in Benthall, that today is possibly known for Benthall Hall, a National Trust property with a special pewter collection. However, more important is the proximity of Benthall to the Ironbridge Gorge where new blast furnaces at Coalbrookdale transfigured the River Severn valley in the 1700s. As a child of nine Edward might have seen the building of the first bridge to be made of cast-iron, from the nearby furnaces, that traversed the river in 1779. Earlier still he might have witnessed as agriculturalist Arthur Young described, 'the noise of the forges, mills…with all their vast machinery, the flames bursting from the furnaces with the burning of the coal and the smoak [sic] of the lime kilns'.[7]

It is not difficult for me to present such visual depictions of this place, because of the material that still remains from the time. For Esther's life in Spitalfields I was obliged to use the written word of state commissioners or journalists like Holden Pike who ventured into the area in search of stories of destitution and poverty. However, for Edward Eicke and his son and grand-daughter, Sarah, comparable state material or investigative journalism does not exist. The Shropshire and Staffordshire borders did, however, hold a fascination for other outsiders, travellers and sightseers, who visited the area, not to interview the people, but to wonder at the machines. When Edward Eicke was a child, Coalbrookdale, near where he was born, became a tourist attraction, alongside Snowdonia and the Lake District.[8] Guidebooks gave performance times for coke making and iron smelting and the ironmasters commissioned a London scene painter to depict the Iron Bridge framing the Severn Gorge, 'like a theatre's proscenium arch'.[9] Examples of visual depictions of the contemporary industrial landscape are not difficult to find: the eighteenth-century engravings of the works at Coalbrook Dale, or woodcuts of Benthall, a painting of an explosion at Shifnal, or the more famous image by Philippe Jacques de Loutherberg of *Coalbrookdale by Night* are still reproduced and analysed.[10] It is no surprise that it was a radical film maker, Humphrey Jennings, who compiled a collection of images on the coming of the machine; nor that the collection, called *Pandaemonium*, includes several examples from the area.[11]

Apocalyptic accounts also exist particularly those drafted by a local Methodist preacher, John Fletcher, who described the noise of the forges, furnaces and mines, observing a 'confused noise of water falling, steam hissing, fire-engines working, wheels turning, files creaking, hammers beating, ore bursting and bellows roaring'.[12] For James Nasmyth the industrialisation of the area also presented a pessimistic outlook:

> Amidst these flaming, smoky, clanging works, I beheld the remains of what had once been happy farmhouses, now ruined and deserted... They had in former times been surrounded by clumps of trees but only the skeletons of them remained, dilapidated, black, and lifeless. The grass had been parched and killed by the vapours of sulphurous acid thrown out by the chimneys; and every herbaceous object was of a ghastly gray—the emblem of vegetable death in its saddest aspect.[13]

Whether the Staffordshire/Shropshire borders were observed as a site of a brave, new, industrial world, or as a hellish image of destruction, the dominant discourse of much of the contemporary material is the industrial landscape. It is relatively easy—and seductive—for a historian to construct a past of steam and machines. Thus I started this section by suggesting that Edward Eicke might have seen the building of the Iron Bridge, that 'quickly became one of the wonders of the world'.[14] This hinted at a conscious incorporation of individuals into important events, grand narratives, 'we all know about'. But I cannot really know whether Edward would have seen his childhood environment in this way. Rather than focusing on the Iron Bridge, Edward's own map and parameters of place might rather have centred on Sherriffhales, within which Benthall was also situated, a small area of cottages, gardens, crofts, stables, yards and meadows, owned, as the apportionment (a precursor to the Ordnance Survey Map) declares, by the Leveson-Gower family.[15] They had acquired titles in Staffordshire and owned much of Wolverhampton including part of the Birmingham canal and parts of Tettenhall and Bilston.[16] Today the descendants still own Trentham Gardens outside Newcastle-under-Lyme, and a reputation for cricket. A descendant of the nineteenth-century Gowers had been an advocate of country-house cricket and captained the Marylebone Cricket Club (MCC) tour to South Africa in 1909–10; another had run his own team against the Australians in the 1930s.[17] But in the nineteenth century they had acquired different reputations particularly in North-East Scotland when George Granville Leveson-Gower, the third Duke of Sutherland, summarily cleared poor Highlanders from his land. The remaining tenants were subjected to a levy for a statue in his memory that, still, controversially, dominates the Golspie skyline.[18]

Edward Eicke might have well have turned away from this new world, much like the peasant ploughing his furrow in Bruegel's painting, *The Fall of Icarus*. The main moment, the disaster happening in the sky, is the key 'historical' event, but for the ploughman the design of his furrow demands his total concentration. His work on the land is more important to him than strange goings on in the ether. As Auden commented on the image in his 'Musée des Beaux Arts':

The ploughman may have heard the splash…
And the expensive delicate ship
That must have seen something amazing,
A boy falling out of the sky,
Had somewhere to get to and sailed calmly on.[19]

Edward Eicke did not work in the furnaces, the canals, the mines or the Tettenhall lock industry. Throughout his life he worked on the land, engaged in agricultural work or working with animals as a husbandman; like Esther Mountford in Spitalfields, he occasionally moved home, but never far and never away from the land. As an anti-revolutionary pamphlet of 1792 epitomised the farmer's lot,'His property is invested in the soil he cultivates;—he has no power of movement;—he must abide the beating of the storm be it pitiless as it may be.'[20]

A survey of agriculture in Staffordshire in the last decade of the eighteenth century by the Tettenhall agronomist, William Pitt, noted that most of the cultivated land was enclosed; wheat, rye and barley were the main arable crops, and the cows that were to be found were 'fine, large and good'.[21] In Oaken, adjacent to Tettenhall, where the Eickes were farming in the 1850s, most of the largely arable land was owned by Sir John Wrottesley, former Whig MP for Lichfield,[22] whose estate also contained considerable woods of ripe timber.[23] At this period market gardens and nurseries developed in Oaken; the tradition continues there today with the firm of Hommers, a wholesale seller of bulbs.[24] Vestiges of the earlier times also remain in the restored Oaken manor farmhouse and coach house—and the restored row of workers' cottages. In the 1870s and 1880s such cottages were occupied by families of coachmen and waggoners, agricultural labourers and dealers in provisions. The current condition of the properties, as the photograph indicates, suggests a different type of inhabitant. In the adjacent Oaken house lived a succession of members of the titled Wrottesley family, wealthy enough to be described as possessing 'no professional occupation'.[25] In death too, the Wrottesleys made their mark on the landscape. In St Nicholas Church, in nearby Codsall, I would struggle with notebook and umbrella in the spring rain, transcribing inscriptions on the gravestones of the Eicke neighbours in Oaken village. Buried

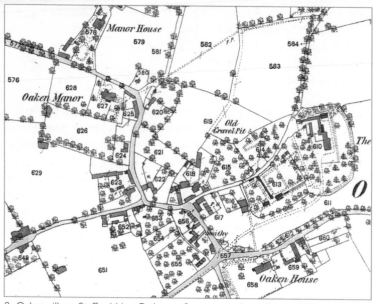

9 Oaken village, Staffordshire. Ordnance Survey map, first edition, c.1860s

here were James William a weaver, Edward Davis, John Marigold, Thomas Sheppard and Lucy Ford—for 45 years the 'faithful servant', the gravestone tells us, of the Wrottesley family.

David Hey reminds us that although people in the nineteenth century commonly moved beyond their original parish boundaries during their lifetime, they did not move very far. In 1851, 80 per cent of the population of England and Wales were living in their county of birth.[26] Certainly the villages around Tettenhall—Oaken and Codsall—where John and Edward lived for most of their adult lives, were linked to the neighbouring conurbation of Wolverhampton and became a venue for day-trippers from the town during the latter part of the nineteenth century.[27]

It may well have been towards Wolverhampton and the Black Country that the Eickes constructed their own mappings rather than back into Shropshire, Ironbridge or the town of Shrewsbury some 27 miles away. On Edward's marriage to Mary Peploe, a local woman, on 30 September 1800, he had moved nearer to Wolverhampton, to Tettenhall, and thereabouts he stayed for the rest of his life, chris-

tening his first son John there
on Christmas Day 1808.[28] In
due course, son John would
stay in the nearby villages of
Oaken and Codsall, marrying
Hannah. By 1851 the couple
had raised at least two children, Ann, and Sarah, my
great-grandmother. John, like
Edward, would continue to
work on the land, doing 'his

*10* Workers' cottages, Oaken, 2002

own work', farming 12 acres, that the whole family worked
together.[29] By 1871 John and Hannah were still working their land
and as late as 1881, John, by now a widower, continued in his lifetime's work even though his farm had shrunk to a mere eight acres.[30]
The Eicke farm had never been large and was smaller than those
of the neighbouring Oaken farmers such as Shadrack Hickman who,
in 1871, was farming 130 acres and employing 3 men and 2 women.
But although a 'small' farmer, John was sufficiently 'big' to be included
in the local Kelly's directory as a farmer who lived in Oaken alongside Shadrack Hickman, George Morris and James Till.[31]

## Continuity and local histories

To find documentary traces of such a continuing rural past, in which
there are neither sudden nor apocalyptic moments can be elusive,

for this is not the content of
historical works based on
moments, changes and disrup-
tion. The everyday, the usual, the
typical, can be more elliptical
than the momentous. The
Eickes of Oaken and Codsall
were not part of the new industrial age but neither were they
part of a past that was deemed
sufficiently evocative to be
summoned up in pastoral

*11* Graveyard, St Nicholas' church, Codsall

images: for that they would have needed to live elsewhere—in the paintings of Constable or Gainsborough or the fiction of Thomas Hardy. In the first decades of the nineteenth century, however, Codsall, like other localities in the Midlands, was famous for bull and bear baiting. It was by no means accidental that terriers bred for fighting bulls took the name Staffordshire bull terriers, nor that the bull ring took pride of place in central Birmingham. The village of Codsall organised its own wake in the years before the so-called sport was finally banned.[32] I do not know whether Edward and John were typical in their behaviour or whether they shunned such customs. But I realise that my interest, my noticing of such material from the available records, probably says more about my own interest in the history of animals, than the actual lives of Edward or John.[33]

A story of continuity, of working, surviving on the land that a narrative drawn from decennial census returns and local directories implies, seems also to be endorsed by the very absences within the local workhouse returns. Nowhere within a thirty-year period covered by the admission and discharge records of Seisdon, the local workhouse, are there records of the Eickes. For this Staffordshire workhouse there were no rough examination books containing stories of poor-relief applicants, as had existed in Bethnal Green; instead only scant records containing a handful of names, suggesting cyclical poverty and within particular, local families. Time and again, for example, the Beddoes or Madeleys are admitted, discharged and re-admitted when times get too hard again. These are potential narratives of husbands deserting wives, of women leaving the workhouse with their children only to return weeks later, and of the same children, with their workhouse admission number appended to their workhouse clothes, absconding from the institution when sent on errands. There are also the old, the infirm, the destitute scraping by in a particular way.[34] But no Eickes; the land seems to have provided them with a way of getting by.

Local history was written in nineteenth-century Shropshire and Staffordshire, but has been scant help as a source for imagining the lives of the Eickes. Certainly the gazetteers of antiquities, and natural history provided an antidote to an industrial present.[35] Historical merit was created by placing the local area in a national story.

Tettenhall thus became historically important, a local history concluded, when Edward the Elder defeated the Danes there in 911.[36] By the last decade of the 1800s the selfsame area was portrayed as enduring, unchanged in contrast to neighbouring Wolverhampton, 'Tettenhall has plodded quietly along during many centuries of village life' and was allegedly little altered from 1000 years before.[37] The emphasis on unchanging aspects of life in contrast to industrial rupture is also exemplified by the plethora of books on local arms, and the flourishing of genealogical societies committed to transcribing and publishing records of local parishes.[38] Shropshire, for example, was one of the earliest counties to publish parish records, an action still appreciated by modern family historians.[39] Colonel George Wrottesley would spend the last years of his life editing *Collections for a History of Staffordshire* and promoting the Salt library in Stafford, that still exists today, with the hope that it might, 'be the means of giving to Staffordshire a County History unsurpassed in England'.[40] But the concept of history embodied in these publications took scant notice of the tenants and employees living on Wrottesley's land. They might give us a picture of Wrottesley's interests but little of the histories of his Oaken neighbours.

### Being there

The description on the census returns of Codsall, Oaken, Tettenhall, Sheriffhales and Benthall—all places connected with moments in the Eickes' lives—had suggested localities that were different, separate and distinct. However, the counties' borders shift, the places connect and elide, the routes of transport cut across the county names. These are geographical borders but places at the centre of the Eickes' personal histories and movements. As David Hey has argued, people in the past—as in the present—identified with particular places, a wider neighbourhood, or 'countries' bounded by market towns: 'identifying such "countries" is a basic task for local historians.'[41]

So, how might I try and identify such places? As an outsider, like those who gaped at the blast furnaces or the Iron Bridge, I go and visit. I attempt to make some sense of the words I have read, finding traces in the daily routes, the roads, the paths that connect villages. I want to understand a mapping of a locality that is not my own.

As a Londoner I will see things differently from those who know the area through everyday experience. (I might also be more observant than in London.) It's doubly vicarious driving around a place you know only through records: every bit of 'colour', of 'information' in the streets you seem to notice. The villages of Codsall and Oaken were—just—within the Staffordshire borders, reached by Stafford Lane; the wheelie bins were inscribed South Staffordshire council, and the parish council notice in Oaken village was for the parish of Codsall with a Wolverhampton postcode. Encompassing Tettenhall is fashionable—of sorts. There was the Majestic wine warehouse (cases only) on the Wergs road and house prices of £250,000 upwards (in Spring 2001) and a pleasant lower green. Outside on the A41 towards Codsall and Oaken there was an advert for Elysium (disappointingly a private health club) and signs for equestrian stables. On the same fast road I passed the Foaming Jug, a pub, that I 'recognised' from my book knowledge. I wondered whether I should stop, talk to the landlord, ask him, Did he know, as I did from the 1871 census, that here had lived one Alexander Meredith aged 43, a potato dealer by trade? But what would this tell me or him?

Outside a shut newsagent on my first Sunday afternoon visit a flier of the local *Wolverhampton Express and Star* gave a flavour of the place I only knew from documents: 'W'ton golden girl pregnant'. Returning some months later at the height of war in Afghanistan and Israeli government outrages against Palestinians, the Friday headline was 'skin cream con'. Such 'stuff' might be one way of creating a micro-picture of an area…If I had lived in the West Midlands this 'basic task', these observations might have been different. Driving in London I had not looked at the streets Esther had inhabited in the same way because I had passed them every day driving to work. Here it was different. The journey I had made was special, undertaken precisely to observe, to traverse similar roads to those eighteenth-century observers of the Industrial Revolution. However, I was not aiming for a particular, spectacular destination, rather I was hoping to find things to help me imagine what I could not from documents alone. Visits to archives in Stafford, Lichfield, Shrewsbury and Keele University local studies library had been invested with much importance, for I needed 'stuff' to try and create the illusion of a personal connection that I could write about with the same confidence I might bring to stories of my London protagonists. I knew that I could not 'discover' 'what it was really like' but the proximity of Bethnal Green had created the idea that it was possible. Here the illusion was less tangible.

## A memory and a raspberry kiss

I cannot use the same materials to bring the Eickes into the present in the same way that I was able to do with Esther, the Spitalfields silk weaver. But there is something passed down to me, a snatch of a story—a glimpse connecting Sarah and Tom, to the present—a trace I did not possess for Esther. My mother Winifred could tell me a snippet passed on by Sarah through her daughter, Mary, Winifred's mother.

'Sarah's husband Tom used to say that when he kissed her she tasted of raspberries'. This is, perhaps, the only personal fragment I have had passed down to me, within the family, of this woman's life. I feel a duty to use this, to explore the meaning, to make connections across time and place. My mother had been told this as a child, held it in her memory throughout her long life and had passed on this snippet of a woman she had never met. It seemed an unusual comment to have been passed on and perhaps that is why it was remembered. Romantically, I conjured up the strawberry fields that existed around London, the market gardens in Chelsea,[42] and raspberries as a special treat in summer. I had difficulty connecting this to an idea of history based in documents, of materials in archives, or of places in the Black Country borders. Here was 'something'— a woman's memory of being loved in a particular sensual way by a man; it is a story in part about a personal history: Sarah's relationship to her husband, Tom.

This story told by a woman, explaining a woman's kiss as a fruit, something to be consumed, also seems to say something in different ways about time and place. For Sarah had seemed to use it as an important symbol of her worth, her lovableness: since this was a moment that had been passed on from her life over a distance of decades and is now being repeated publicly, perhaps some 140 years on. This description is of a particular time in the mid-nineteenth century when raspberries did not suggest small, expensive, super-market plastic punnets flown in from abroad with sell-by dates and special offers. What did raspberries signify in nineteenth-century west London where Sarah and Tom raised their family? And can I create any meaning through this tiny personal anecdote? Although this is a personal story does it have wider contexts too?

Chelsea was a traditional site of market gardens.[43] Fruit and vegetables for the London market were grown in Chelsea and Fulham, but few raspberries reached the Covent Garden whole-sale market. More usually the summer fruit was bought for preserving or by jam factories.[44] Earlier in the nineteenth century cultivated raspberries and strawberries—a large fruit with good flavour—had been promoted by a Mr Keen of Islington. As William Cobbett described it, 'The London gardeners have found that no other strawberry will sell, and in fact, there is hardly any other now brought to the markets.'[45] Perhaps then in the 1800s the taste of raspberries was not of the countryside but a much more modern, urban, context.

But in some ways, soft fruits provide a connection between places—Tettenhall and Chelsea—and the people who kissed each other. I do not know why Sarah Eicke, a farmer's daughter, and Thomas, a joiner from Shrewsbury, who had married and lived on the Staffordshire/Shropshire borders, moved to London. I find it unlikely to believe I can ever know this. But I do know of other migrations, every summer, of women from Shropshire to West London. Hundreds of women, transitory migrants to the great wen from the nearby Holyhead road, were employed to carry fruit in baskets from the strawberry beds at Hammersmith Bridge Road, in West London, to Covent Garden. This was described by the *Illustrated London News* as a task carried out for the most part by 'Shropshire and Welsh girls, who walk to London, at this season, in droves, to perform this drudgery, just as the Irish peasantry come to assist in the hay and corn harvests'. As the reporter continued, 'these women carry upon their heads baskets of strawberries or raspberries, weighing from forty to fifty pounds…these industrious creatures carry loads from twenty-four to thirty miles a day…'

The season of the carrying work was 40 days and after that the

12 The strawberry and raspberry girls from Shropshire, *Illustrated London News*, 1846

same women worked at the task of gathering and marketing vegetables for another 60 days at lower wages. They then customarily
returned home to Shropshire: 'With this poor pittance they return
to their native county, and it adds either to their humble comforts,
or creates a small dowry towards a rustic establishment for life.' This
was depicted as a romantic picture of 'virtuous exertion' and of
women with 'exemplary morals'.[46]

No reference is made in this lyrical account to the work apparently usually undertaken by such women, the daughters or wives
of colliers, used to hard, manual labour.[47] Allegedly performing their
work to support aged parents or to keep their own children from
the workhouse these 'nymphs of Arcadia', as the *Illustrated London
News* chose to describe them, 'live hard, they sleep on straw in hovels
and barns, and they often burst an artery, or drop down dead from
the effect of heat and exertion'.[48]

This account, however, is not a story 'about' Sarah, who did not die from youthful raspberry or strawberry exhaustion but survived into her 70s. Sarah and Thomas Davies married in Wolverhampton at St Marks church in December 1860.[49] The couple did not stay in Wolverhampton, or move further into the urban Midlands towards Birmingham, but followed the path of the Shropshire soft-fruit sellers to West London. Was this, I surmise, consciously following the path of the raspberry and strawberry girls and had Sarah been one of these women? I recognise that it was probably not the case for this would be a neat, tidy story, and it fits too easily with my earlier fantasy that there had been scandal and Sarah and Tom had run away to the metropolis to hide. This particular fantasy had been squashed by the 'facts' of Tom and Sarah living in a legal married condition at her parents' house in 1861.[50]

So why do I feel the need to include this story here? It is, in some ways, another and different story, but it is a story also centred on soft fruit, that makes connections between the metropolis and the Midlands. The stories share some common features—raspberries, places—and romantic notions. They are stories both of traversing places and uniting them, through a common motif. If I saw Sarah simply as a 'typical' woman from Shropshire I might feel less hesitant making these comparisons. I would embrace this 'source' wholeheartedly and advise you that, 'this is what women like Sarah did'. But, although I now have a degree of certainty about the facts of Sarah's birth, marriage and death, I feel unable to pronounce authoritatively upon her life; that I persist in including this story, however, suggests that I haven't completely giving up on wanting, in some way, this broader picture. In similar vein if I was not so cautious I might have embraced the story of the decline of Spitalfields silk weavers to suggest that Esther had died in poverty and distress, a victim of market forces. I am not convinced, however, that the stories of Esther, Sarah and other ancestors in my (or your) family, are necessarily simply hidden in the archives, in the 'sources', just waiting for a historian, like me, or you, to discover them. It would still be the case that I—or you—would need to fashion the material into a narrative for today. But when there are traces of earlier times if we do not bring them alive in this present then they will surely disappear.

## A story—and a different view of Sarah's husband

Of Tom Davies I 'know' more, but not much more, through maternal stories. He had—allegedly—come from Shrewsbury and 'done
things with wood'; when he died he had left money in 'his will' for
his two youngest grand-daughters to have dresses—and mum had
a red one. Suffice to say I can find no traces of a will of an impe-
cunious joiner in the Family Records Centre. But there was also
another handed-down story that did not portray a loving nor kindly
man, who romanticised his wife's kisses. This was a story I had known
for most of my life; it had not arisen from recent requests for information, and my attempts to mine my mother's memory. When Tom
and Sarah's daughter, Mary (my maternal grandmother), was in late
of an evening she had to be punished. The punishment was 'combing her father's hair' on a Sunday. I had remembered being told this
story very clearly (and on more than one occasion) during my own
childhood. My mother told the story with gestures of disgust. I
remember I used to interpret this story in one way. I imagined, when
I was told this as a young child, that his hair was dirty. If his hair had
been clean it might have had a different connotation, I remember
feeling. As a small child I somehow 'knew' his hair was dirty, greasy,
lank, and it was this, I was convinced, that made the act of combing abhorrent. I do see now that this was my childish naiveté, assuming
that this particular idea of 'dirtiness' was indeed the reason for my
mother's disgust. This is indeed a family story, and that this patriarchal act was even discussed and conveyed by Sarah's daughter, Mary,
to her own daughter Winifred and thence to Mary's grand-daughter (me) suggests an act that was sufficiently distasteful to allow for
a re-telling of the event as abhorrent but perhaps not too shameful
to be totally hidden. Or rather was it that this was the only way the
nature of an inappropriate relationship between father and daughter could be discussed? And how was it heard? I certainly did not
hear this as a young child as a story of sexual abuse. Was my mother
telling me an adult story or one that she too her learnt in childhood and had not reconfigured in her adulthood?

In European folk stories and legends female hair is a common
motif—Rapunzel, Snow White, the Lorelei. As Frigga Haug has
suggested in her memory-work project that encouraged women to

remember personal stories involving hair,[51] 'hair appears as something as once desirable and dangerous, as something magical and mystically powerful'.[52] Haug's work has encouraged the sharing of individual stories ' since it is as individuals that we interpret and suffer our lives…'[53] In some ways the repercussions of the act behind the story were embedded in the memory of a female line of the Eickes and Davieses. So repulsive had been the act that my grandmother Mary had been obliged to perform on her father Tom, that, psychological damage aside, a shrinking from touching hair had continued down the maternal family line; this was an odd inheritance to pass on to descendants but an inheritance, nonetheless. As a young adult (and middle-aged woman) my mother had disliked touching even her own hair; she shrank from going to the hairdressers and kept her, unsurprisingly, poorly conditioned hair in long weak strands before coiling it into a prematurely ageing bun. In turn she tried to avoid touching my hair as a child; my father's mother urged her to put papers into my straight hair to make it curly and 'pretty' but this was too much for her to stomach. And as photos of me from an early age show, the attempt at prettification attempted by my father's mother was soon abandoned for puritanical straight lines, that avoided touching and fussing. As a teenager and young adult I was quite happy to dye my hair, and even on a couple of occasions wash it with vinegar and plait and then unplait it for a pre-Raphaelite look, as long as it was done quickly. Fiddling, preening, tweaking, playing about with brushes, hairdryers—and time—has never been a realistic option. If my surname seems to have had origins in my paternal great-great-grandmother's illiteracy, then my own hairstyle (such as it is) might be imagined to have traces dating back to an inappropriate relationship between my maternal great-grandfather and my grandmother in the last decades of the nineteenth century.

This story about Tom, my great-grandfather, and hair, is not about a specific geographical place, although the acts occurred in late nineteenth-century Chelsea, but it is of a particular time, a specific patriarchal moment. It epitomises a certain abusive power that can demand a daughter's duty and compliance through physical loathsome touch. This handed-down story of Thomas Davies, the husband of Sarah Eicke, was not something I would have been likely to find in an archive. Certainly I have delved in the archive; I have experienced it in the way described by Carolyn Steedman as a 'kind of place, that is to do with longing and appropriation with wanting things that are put together, collected, collated, named in lists and indices'.[54] I too have rummaged and immersed myself in the documents, although I seem to have had more fun doing it than Carolyn Steedman suggests, who complains about tossing and turning in narrow beds of cheap hotels in strange towns.[55] For me, research in an archive is an opportunity to stay with friends, catch up on news, spend some relaxing time away from the chaos of the inner city or the pressures of work. In the Staffordshire record office I have put on white gloves to safeguard the documents from my contaminating hands. I have protected the documents from my incursions but not the lives of the people they ostensibly represented. I have read the relevant (and obscure) journals and contemporary accounts of travellers to the Black Country and its industrial environs. I have paid my dues in the Steedman caricature of the historian's hard graft. I can list the books, the articles, the documents in long footnotes; turn the pages to the end of this book, check for yourself. But does such endeavour, such scholarship, tell me what I want to know? Does it really tell me—or you—'how it was'?

As Sally Alexander has described in her work on mid twentieth-century memory, she is interested in the ways in which,'the individual life-story might engender a deeper historical present, and in the inseparable dialectic of individual and historical memory'.[56] In her study, Alexander analyses a young woman's story rooted in the geography and landscape of London, with its tension unfolding through the changing significance of her body.[57] Alexander argues that the traces of a generation are remembered and figured in different ways—through legislation, statistics, social policy, as well as fiction, film and family story—to produce a particular structure of feeling of a generation.[58] The story of the raspberry kiss and the hair-combing, farming land and joining wood, might also suggest different ways of creating histories of the lives of those migrating into London in the second-half of the nineteenth century. A memory implies the past living on into the present, transcending historical time. The memory of the raspberry kiss is rooted in a particular time and place. In transcending time its meaning might change; it can also become a memory of what is no more.

# 3

# GRAVEYARDS AND BRICKS IN KENT

## THE MANKELOWS

### Graveyards in the heat

My wanderings, like those of the Eickes, had moved on from my Midlands explorations of the autumn and spring months. Now it was time to explore nearer London, to seek out traces of ancestors of my mother's father. It was summer and proved to be the hottest day of the year so far. In hindsight the heat of 80+ had not been the ideal weather in which to trek up a steep hill to a Kent church in the vague hope of finding dead Mankelows. Earlier in the day I had already visited two churchyards in Pembury, further south along the Maidstone Road, since this village had featured in the family's eighteenth-century itinerary. In the old church of St Peter, Pembury, there had been the opportunity to photograph the grave of engineer and Liberal MP Sir Morton Peto, the first Non-Conformist to be buried in Anglican ground,[1] and the unusual gravestone image of the New Testament story of Mary and Joseph's flight into Egypt I'd read about previously; but there had been no grave of any Mankelow—however one spelt the maternal surname. I had also been unlucky in the graveyard of the church of the Holy Trinity in nearby East Peckham. Perhaps this walk to a disused church would prove to be another false trail, caused by wandering in places I did not know.

Fortunately, the woman in the supermarket where I'd replenished my bottled water pointed me in the direction of the other, older, church, St Michael in East Peckham, while warning me about the uphill walk. But, she advised, it was worth it: although the church itself was closed (and now run by the Churches Conservation Trust) it was a good visit and she had enjoyed it on the annual open weekend. This church was clearly a local landmark, as the owner of the

*13* The flight into Egypt, St Peter's church, Pembury, Kent

garden centre subsequently confirmed when I lost my way. He too had researched the history of his family and was happy to point me in the right direction (together with four plants for the pond).

The ascent from the hamlet of a few houses, the former centre of the East Peckham village before it had translocated into the valley floor, was not unpleasant but tiring in the 80s heat, reminiscent of walks in the Apennines rather than rambles in the Home Counties. In the shimmering afternoon heat the view too was almost northern Italian. From the summit of the hill I could see parcels of fields and villages in the distance faded by the sun: Hadlow with the distinctive landmark of the castle folly; Pembury, where I'd started the day; and the newer settlement of East Peckham, with its supermarket, down the hill. Hidden from view by the ancient pines, to the north east, would be my last destination of the day, Yalding, a confluence of the Medway, Beult and Teise rivers.

These villages I had noted had not been selected randomly in my panorama but ones I had known existed because of my—and others'—digging in the records. My mother's paternal family had lived in this part of western Kent, on the borders with Sussex, for over 350 years from the 1650s—and some still lived nearby and had researched the family's long history in the area. William Mackello had been born in Pembury in 1658; his married life took place where his children were raised, further east in Yalding, a settlement recorded in the Domesday book.[2] Subsequent generations had moved via East Peckham and Yalding to Hadlow where in 1795 my great-great-grandfather, also called William, but now with a surname spelt Mankelow, was born.

The summary here of names, places, and years, in just a few sentences does not reflect, of course, the years of collective effort it has taken to unravel the basic genealogy; a result of my own efforts and of others researching the same family and those met when, as John Aubrey the antiquarian put it, I go 'grubbing in churchyards'.[3] Here, those who prefer family history as a day-out-in-the-coun-tryside to being stuck in front of a computer screen, might find words on a stone which chronicle a lifespan. Often the gravestone might describe familial status and, sometimes, the nature of the individ-ual's work or the esteem in which they were held. At most there might be words enough to suggest elements from which a researcher might make a history for the present. The complex of symbols— names, dates, relationships—certainly suggests material for the making of family stories. As Hayden White, an historical philoso-pher has suggested, we place value on story-telling in the representation of real events, 'out of a desire to have real events display the coherence, integrity, fullness, and closure of an image of life that is…imaginary'.[4] And on this hot July day this was what I had been attempting to do: find material for my story.

However the helpful woman in the supermarket had been wrong: it would have been possible to drive to the lychgate of the church-yard and park—and cars were already there. Within the ancient burial place surrounded by trees, many of which were even older than the graves, there was the sound of an electric lawn mower and a hot, excited, dog. A young man naked to the waist emerged from behind the closed church apologising for his state of undress to this soli-tary, middle-aged woman swathed in clothing, sensible hat and barrier suncream. The man was not, he was at pains to explain, the regu-lar gardener, but he was, it was clear, someone who knew the nearby land in particular ways. He had local knowledge of the landmarks which he shared with me: the folly at Hadlow owned, he said, by a German who made porn movies; the village of East Peckham which had itself translocated and grown, down in the valley; and the course of the river, which he picked out amidst the trees. The contours of the land, the Weald and the Downs, were a framework for his visualisation of this locality that I, as a Londoner and driver, tended to see through the A21 and A26 roads that skirted the Sussex and Kent borders. From the vantage point of high ground and seeing the villages I had read about through the unofficial gardener's eyes, the land seemed different. The distance between Hadlow, Peckham and Yalding was small if they were seen in relation to the Medway river. The movement of the Mankelows between villages, I could now see, made a different sense. Over generations they had followed the course of the river to new villages, a traversing of the river valley now seemed logical and coherent in a way that merely plotting data from documents had not.[5]

In his recent book on graveyards, Mark Taylor has argued that what one thinks is deeply conditioned by where one thinks—and certainly standing on the top of a hill provided a different perspective to poring over a map.[6] A conventional historian is thought to know about things 'because you have been there', there being an archive.[7] But 'being there' can also mean being here in the present, in actually existing places in the contemporary landscape, where objects created in the past can transcend time and be with us here in the present. Landscapes created centuries ago remain visible today, at least in traces, if we have the eyes to see it.[8] Unlike a so-called objective historian, who seeks to engage in a supposedly unmediated way directly with the archive, family history research also seeks to involve others in an exploration and construction of a past. In contrast to the solitary note-taking observed in the British Library, many visitors to the Family Records Centre are accompanied by a spouse, partner or elderly mother who is prodded to remember family stories, to guess ages or places, to hypothesise about the apparent disappearance of an ancestor from the registers. Others choose to make contact with researchers through the Rootsweb website or regional family history groups, posting questions on internet message boards—and receiving answers.[9] And here in the graveyard of St Michael's in East Peckham this social construction of historical knowledge, as historian Raphael Samuel would describe such a process, involved discussing the landscape and exploring the movement of people with a sweating young man and his hot dog.

The headstones at St Michael's were interesting—I'd guessed that before I'd visited from a book outlining some striking examples.[10]

An initial walk through the yet-to-be-mown-grass revealed lovely angels, skulls acting as memento mori, an hourglass with shifting sand and a horse bending its head in grief, but not, at least not in this hot wandering, any ancestral graves. A subsequent, cooler, September visit would confirm the absence of Mankelow graves. My family's connection with the place may have been confined to a happier occasion—the wedding in 1794 of John Manktelow, the great-grandson of William Mackello, and father of William Mankelow, before his move to Hadlow. This seemed, then, a landscape through which they had passed rather than one that suggested the permanence of settlement associated with death and family gravestones.

## Gravestones in Hadlow

Wandering around in St Mary's church Hadlow, near Tonbridge, some years before, on the first occasion I had gone looking for dead Mankelows in Kent, it had been different. The impetus for that visit had been my mother's recollection that the family of her father, Fred Mankelow, had come from there, although she had never visited the place nor known his parents nor, indeed, any of his family. Before that visit I had never been to this part of Kent. Although, as a child, I'd spent most summer holidays in Kent, or the 'garden of England' as my parents told me, this was usually in Broadstairs. The environs of Tonbridge had never been on our itinerary in those times—our own mapping and travelling through Kent had been very different.

These had been the first of 'my' dead people who I had supposedly 'found', recorded on a gravestone, and I had the emotional illusion that the discovery was itself significant. Although it was not the case that there was new knowledge here as such about the Mankelows, in an analogous way to that described by Victor Seidler holding in his hand the notarial deed outlining what happened to one of his uncles shot by the Nazis in Warsaw, 'The materiality of the document somehow helped me feel the reality of what had happened.'[11] It gave an additional meaning to previous researches. For me, being in this place, Hadlow, was a way of reconfiguring fragments of the past in the present and making more of them than simply words on a microfilmed parish register.[12]

Surrounding the Hadlow church of St Mary's is a closed churchyard. As Hilary Lees has explained, a churchyard, as opposed to a cemetery, has the feeling of antiquity, indeed many stand on prehistoric sites pre-dating the churches they surround.[13] As this headstone was the first gravestone I had 'found' belonging to an ancestor it seemed important to commemorate the discovery in a visual image. I needed to create an additional layer of permanence and record, perhaps to confirm to myself that I had, at last, found 'something tangible'. But on the first occasion it was too dark to photograph the gravestone clearly, so further visits became inevitable.

*14* The grave of Mary and William Mankelow, St Mary's church, Hadlow, Kent

The stone had first been erected to remember Mary Mankelow, née Hayward, born in the last year of the eighteenth century, who had died aged 60 in August 1859. *Morbus cordis* the death certificate had declared—Latin for straightforward heart disease. Under her name was recorded that of 73-year-old William, her husband of nearly 40 years, who had survived his wife by a decade. The brick-maker and farmer had, his death certificate declared (in English), passed away due to 'general decay'. The stone itself had also suffered decay in the intervening 140 years and it was difficult to read the inscription clearly. Although the names of her seven surviving adult children were listed,[14] the quote from Psalms 40 was more weath-ered: 'I waited patiently for the Lord and he inclined unto me and heard my cry.'

The sentiment expressed on the stone was different from the warning I would see on an 1840s stone in Pembury, 'Learn to die'; in contrast a different sort of homily was being offered to visitors here, which may have been deliberate. In a rural churchyard manual of 1851, Kelke had specifically advocated the inclusion of a biblical text so that stones themselves could become an effective medium of conveying religious instruction and improvement. Texts from the Psalms were particularly recommended for those suffering from a long illness (however, unfortunately, he does not cite this one). He also suggested the motif of assuming the character of a voice from the tomb. Thus, he continued, there could be a permanent lesson with gravestones 'perpetually teaching from generation to generation'.[15] In some ways he was proved to be right, although teaching family historians about facts in their ancestors' past was surely not what he had in mind. For those like Mary Mankelow, who in life was illiterate,[16] there was a particular sort of transformation in death. Her 'voice' became both articulate and literate, and one that still remained in the landscape of her native village nearly one and a half centuries after her death. As Jacques Ranciere has analysed, 'The availability of writing—of the 'mute' letter—endows any life, or the life of anybody, with the capacity of taking on meaning, of entering into the universe of meaning.'[17]

At one time the stone would have provided a recording, in the then present, of former lives known to those who had erected the stone; but, as Mark Taylor has suggested, a graveyard is where we keep the dead *alive as dead*. (original emphasis)[18] I cannot 'remember' a person, outside the public domain, whom I never knew. But churchyards themselves are embodiments of memory; they are places which make explicit the passing of time. Now it is the grave itself that is 'remembered' and which I photograph, making this new artefact a conduit of meaning.[19] In the materiality of the stone the past connects with the present; it remembers for me someone I do not know. There is no relative either I, or my mother, would have ever known who knew the woman that this stone remembers. However, by its very existence the gravestone suggests that once there was a woman who did indeed exist—and one who should be remembered and commemorated. It also suggests that a story can be told in the present.

The last verse of the chapter of the Psalms used on Mary's gravestone defined the psalmist thus, 'I am poor and needy; yet the Lord thinketh upon me.' However, by local standards, these Mankelows were neither poor nor needy; after all, they had money for the headstone and jobs which would sustain them throughout the year. William Mankelow, Mary's husband, had worked as a brickmaker, and farmer, and from the 1820s developed a carrier business, running a daily service transporting goods—and people—to and from Tonbridge. Their oldest son, also called William, would join his father, in the carrier business, moving, eventually to London and taking a younger brother, Thomas, my great-grandfather with him. Other children had continued working on the land or as a dressmaker or carrying goods. The men, at least, were of sufficient status to be mentioned as those with trades worth recording in the local directories.

Although I was pleased to have found my 'first' ancestral grave-stone even I realised that this was neither the most interesting nor important stone in the churchyard. The commemoration of this death was indeed a small moment compared to the bigger event recalled in the far corner of the churchyard in the shade. Here was an obelisk dating from October 1853 commemorating 30 migrant hop pick-ers—from London—drowned when the horse and cart capsized on a nearby bridge while taking them back to their campsite near Tudeley, known today as the only church in England which possesses a stained-glass work by Marc Chagall. For me this has personal resonances too, for this was the church where James Mancktelow, the grandfather of William and Mary Mankelow, had married Ann Richards from Yalding in 1767. Hop picking was labour intensive and much of the harvest was carried out by women and children from London, or Ireland, who came down for the summer work and some sort of holiday, returning every year to work for the same farmer.[20] Hop pickers were often criticised for excessive drinking or petty theft and there are also stories of their supposed extravagance. As a local woman commented on the hop pickers' penchant for buying flowers to take back home, 'We told them time and time again that chrysanthemums would travel better, last longer, but they loved the brilliance of the dahlias.'[21] Local residents had testified to the inquest that they had complained about the poor state of the bridge for many years and the jury returned the verdict of accidental drowning entirely due to the defective state of the bridge. The dead included 16 members of one family.[22]

15 Obelisk in memory of the thirty
drowned hop pickers, St Mary's church,
Hadlow, Kent

This event was bigger and locally more important, as befitted the size of the memorial stone, than the lives I was tracing in the same graveyard. In the normal course of events those who picked hops would have been unlikely to be able to afford to commemorate in stone those relatives who died of natural causes.[23] Rupture and disaster had given these transient hop pickers a permanent place in the Kent landscape. In contrast to a time of movement or even migration for work the hop pickers' memorial is about a specific time and place, a moment which changes the course of the London hop pickers' lives.[24] In contrast to the Mankelow stone, this was not a commemoration enacted by, or for, the families of the dead—in several instances whole families from babies to grandparents had perished and there were none left to remember in this way. Rather it was a way of a community recording an event out of the ordinary in their own locality, creating a mark on the local landscape of an important occasion.[25] This recording of names was not the same as those on the gravestone of the wife of the brickmaker; there was no encouraging verse from the Psalms here. The obelisk was not to a single (nor related) family but—confronting the norm—to 30 individuals buried together in one grave on successive days united in death because of their work, rather than familial bonds.[26]

I do not know whether the event in October 1853 or the subsequent erection of the memorial impinged on the daily lives of the Mankelows. Did they carry on harvesting their hops? Did they make their bricks as usual? Did this bigger event affect their lives in any way? I could not state categorically whether Edward Eicke, growing up in Shropshire, had—or had not—seen the cast iron bridge.

Similarly, I cannot make a clear connection between the bigger event and 'my' Mankelows in 1850s Hadlow. In death, however, they share the same place of commemoration within the same village. Together—the hop pickers and the Mankelows— they have made a particular mark on the landscape.

## Stones in Yalding

On the same hot July day in which I had seen the layout of the villages of the Medway with the eyes of another, I also visited the graveyard of St Peter and St Paul church in the

*16* Mankelow graves in the church of St Peter and St Paul, Yalding, Kent

village of Yalding—a place that had been dismissed by a gazetteer of 1834 as 'a place of little importance', declaring the church to be old 'with a square tower but [which] possesses nothing worthy of notice'.[27] My perception was rather different, for here to the left of the side path of the churchyard was a group of seven stones almost sheltering together near a side wall, and all sharing the same surname of Mankelow. In life these people had shared at least a common name through descent or through marriage.[28] But it was not just the common surname which suggested a closeness. The stones were of brothers and sisters, husbands and wives, cousins as well as those more distantly related. The gravestones' physical location in a distinct group almost suggested an emotional closeness and a particular sort of familial bond for which there are no other fragments or traces. The very material of the stone seemed to suggest an affective, human condition because of the juxtapositions of the graves.

However, it was not only the existence of graves which had linked the Mankelow family of the past with the present landscape. Some years before the research of this sweltering day, when I had returned to the Hadlow church in light good enough for a photograph, I met

'H', a local historian, who was explaining to visitors the history of the thirteenth-century church of St Mary.[29] As a local woman she had known descendants of the Mankelows in the graveyard; she told me about a bomb falling on their pub, a child who was disabled, and directed me to the Mankelows' land. 'H' also knew the name of another descendant of the buried Mankelows. He too was researching his family history. She said she would contact him and then write to me once she had checked this with him. And this she did.

## Bricks

'A' still lived locally, and I realised through our correspondence that we shared great-great grandparents in common, William and Mary Mankelow, who were buried in Hadlow—and, of course, an interest in history. 'A' is a careful researcher and has compiled detailed charts which trace back, as far as he can, the lineage of the Mankelows, emphasising the line which leads directly to him. The more recent family tree is recorded in a chart that has pride of place on his dining-room wall alongside the ancient pipes and objects which he and his wife have found at low tide in the Thames estuary on the north Kent coast. For several years he has collected material on the Mankelows including maps and photos, which he willingly shares. An aspect of his research is a means to an end, of getting back further in time. We meet and talk about our respective explorations; this confirms for me again that this isn't my main rationale. I don't want to go back into the past; I want the Mankelows to come forward into the present.

'A' possesses and values an annotated map inherited from William Mankelow's son, George (his great-grandfather), born in 1827, who had continued to work the land after one of his younger brothers, Thomas (my great-grandfather), had moved away. The framework of the map was the ownership and renting of land, rather than natural topography. It noted the different types of land used for hop gardens, orchards, cottages with gardens, roads, the processes for brick-making—kilns and faggot yard, pond and brickearth, brickyard—as well as a cricket field. Brick-making (like cricket) was a seasonal activity: brick earth dug in autumn was left over winter to be broken down by frosts before being fired in the spring and summer.[30] A source of fuel was needed for firing the bricks: hence the area, outlined on the map, set aside for faggots.[31] Conventionally brick-making was hard work needing unskilled and skilled labour, a trade learnt within a family.[32] Certainly some familial handing-down of skills can be surmised. In the 1700s, when based further south in Pembury, William Mankelow's father had worked as a collier, probably as a charcoal burner.[33] The Kent Weald had been famous for its use of wood in iron making and the first modern blast furnace in the area had been established in Tonbridge in the 1550s, ensuring that by the late sixteenth century the Tonbridge parish was an important focus for ironmaking in the Weald.[34] However, the overuse of timber had led to its lack of availability and, in turn, an increase in the price of charcoal: the owners closed down the works and many relocated to Aberdare and Merthyr Tydfil in Wales.[35] The Mankelows had not gone away. However, in order for them to remain in Kent, they themselves had needed to change their ways of earning a living.[36] Or, as Lampedusa, the author of *The Leopard*, phrased it more elegantly, 'In order for things to stay the same, things will have to change.'[37]

The Mankelows, who had come to Hadlow most recently from Yalding, stayed, working the brickfield, renting the land from some of the 2,400 acres owned by the local worthy Sir William Geary, the former attorney general in Accra on the then Gold Coast.[38] Staying—and not going—was a new feature of the Industrial Revolution. Previously, itinerant brick-makers had traversed the country testing the local clay and then working it until the building, for which the bricks and tiles were needed, was completed.[39] Locally, brick-making skills stretched back to the Tudors with the clay of the Weald maintaining an excellent reputation for producing some of the finest bricks available.[40] Some Kentish bricks were destined for London, the largest single market in the country, but most bricks fashioned around Tonbridge were for local use.[41] In 1836 alone there were over 5,700 brick-makers in England,[42] and Tonbridge itself boasted six.[43] The Mankelows' brick-making venture may have been successful. The brick tax, that had been introduced in 1784 to help pay for the wars with France, was repealed in 1850. This led to a general expansion of the industry,[44] which had been further assisted from the 1830s by the railway boom: a turnpike road over a railway, for example, would require 300,000 bricks.[45]

Hadlow Common where the Mankelow brickfield (and the cricket field) existed, was—and still is—part of rural Kent. As 'H', the Hadlow local historian, had indicated, although the cottages where William and Mary Mankelow and their children had spent their days were gone, the site of their former brickfield—with a local cricket pitch in front—was still here. According to 'A', who possessed not only documents but local knowledge, the present cricket field was a former large clay pit, that had been an integral part of the Mankelow business.[46] When 'A's' great-grandfather George had finished digging clay he had apparently filled it with faggots and seeded it to make the current cricket field. It was slightly lower, 'A' had observed, than the surrounding fields because of the rotting of the faggots over the years causing subsidence.[47] Neither the map of the landholdings nor my viewing of the land would have revealed this: the small changes in the landscape, that an outsider can neither know nor see, would only be observed by one who knew the place, who lived in the same place but in the present. As Raphael Samuel noted in an article published nearly 30 years ago, though still timely and relevant:

> Local history demands a different kind of knowledge than one which is focused on high-level national developments, and gives the researchers a much more immediate sense of the past. He meets it round the corner and down the street…[and can] follow its footprints in the fields.[48]

I can, however, at least in some way, interpret maps. The entire rented land as covered on 'A's' document was calculated as 'A r p— 21.0.13'. In those far gone 11-plus days we were taught to know what this meant (and forgot once the exams were over) but at least I know the initials stand for acre, rod and perch. This, I realised, was a bigger area than the 12-acre farm occupied by the Eickes on the Staffordshire/Shropshire borders (and considerably larger than the houses that Esther and William Keen inhabited in Bethnal Green). However, when I look at this document and the large-scale Ordnance Survey map of the same land I see shapes, possible build-

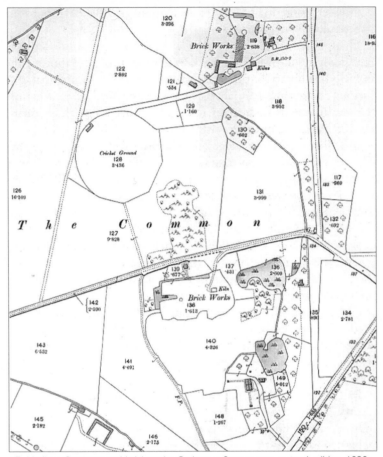

17  Hadlow Common and brickworks. Ordnance Survey map, second edition, 1890s

ings, but I have difficulty imagining people or signs of activity. Others see it differently. One of my MA students sees the Ordnance Survey map in other ways when I try out this chapter on them for feedback. As a professional surveyor 'M' is able to calculate the size of the brick kilns, add up the square footage and estimate the numbers of people who could have worked there:

There are some outbuildings so perhaps you could assume a maximum of 30 employees, not all there at the same time, including the manager. As the area had lots of these works and kilns, this may be an overestimate on numbers.

He apologises for not going back to research this more thoroughly in his office library but he does know, in a way I do not, that 'the various cricket fields are approximately two thirds of an acre and the measurements are in acres, rods and perches…a perch is a quarter of a chain…about five yards I think'.[49]

'A's' documents also suggested that the Mankelows grew hops. The local directory had stated that not only was Hadlow known for its clay and loam soil, but for its fruit, wheat and hops. Hadlow was seen as a brewery village and unsurprisingly William and Mary's son, George, developed beer-making as a sideline.[50] In its nineteenth-century heyday more than 330 of the 400 rural parishes in Kent boasted hop gardens.[51] But few hop fields remain today. In Yalding where an earlier generation of the Mankelows had lived and died there are still remnants of hop fields; and along the Maidstone Road, linking Pembury and East Peckham villages, tourists can pay for the 'experience' of a hop field with a hop garden country park. In 'A's' modern house on the outskirts of Tonbridge he points to the trees, at the back of the well-maintained garden, that formed the perimeter of the local hop fields of his childhood and on which his house and garden were built.

Brick-making, like hop farming, was part of an earlier Mankelow history. By the late 1800s brick-making had become a large-scale industry: publications such as the *Brick and Pottery Trades Diary*, published in the first years of the twentieth century, became primers of technology, gadgets, calculations and contract management.[52] This was a new age of steam and engines; bricks fashioned on the land were part of an earlier time. In the same way that the Eickes had carried on farming and the Keens weaving, the descendants of William and Mary Mankelow had continued the trade into the twentieth century with George's son, also called William, continuing to work as a brickmaker.[53] George himself had kept the business going through diversification. As a flier in the possession of another Mankelow descendant asserts:

George Mankelow
Manufacturer of
Bricks, Tiles, Drain Pipes and Pottery
Hadlow Common
Tonbridge
Birch and Heath Brooms always on hand
Orders Respectfully Solicited[54]

But, these distant relatives advise me, the solicitation for work was not entirely successful. George, so the story goes, drank away the family's money.

## Thomas the carrier: moving through the landscape

On the gravestone in Hadlow churchyard had been listed some seven children of William and Mary. They included the eldest son, William, running the carrier business, George, of whom 'A' was the direct descendant, and Thomas, my great-grandfather born some 15 years after the first child, in March 1835. However, unlike his brother George, Thomas did not work on the land, but instead moved through it, delivering parcels. The seasonal nature of brick-making and hop farming alike did not provide sufficient income for survival throughout the year. As bricks tended to be used locally and the conveying of bricks was part of the production process, brick-makers often developed a sideline in transport.[55] For some this meant work as coal merchants, but the Mankelows developed a transport business delivering goods. Three of William's sons—William, Thomas and John—ran a daily carrier service for parcels, goods and people to and from Hadlow to Tonbridge.

The trade of carrier, providing a parcel and goods service run at particular times on particular days, had existed for centuries. Carriers were a certain sort of traveller. Those who drove from London, usually based in the Strand or Holborn, into the surrounding counties often went no more than 20 or 30 miles a day, stayed overnight and returned, on the same route, the following day.[56] Particular inns as well as the turnpike roads mapped out the routes which the carriers followed. The way from South London to Rye on the coast, through Lewisham and then Bromley, Sevenoaks,

Tonbridge and Lamberhurst was established as early as the seventeenth century; it is still a way to get to Tonbridge today, if you are keen to avoid motorways.[57] Far from declining with the advent of railways, the job of carrier changed and expanded. The railways had facilitated transport of goods (and people) to towns served by railway stations; but the carriers provided a link between the villages and the towns.[58] Even when the post office parcel service was introduced in 1883 the upper weight limit of 11 pounds ensured that demand was still high for the unregulated carrier service of large items. Throughout the second half of the nineteenth century the numbers of those working as carriers, carmen or carters in England and Wales rose to well over 270,000 by 1901. It was this same period which saw the increase in offices—and profits—of London based firms like Carter Paterson or Pickfords.[59]

Alan Everitt has suggested that carriers, 'will always remain shadowy figures, although it is clear from the impression they have left in the memories of elderly people that they were often men of marked individuality'. His justification for this characterisation is that written records in the form of carriers' notebooks remain rare even though, he argues, it is unlikely that they were illiterate since they did deliver goods correctly. Unsurprisingly, a written source for Everitt's study of carriers in Kent is the ubiquitous local directories.[60]

In some ways, of course, Everitt is right. Those who work for a living moving through existing landscapes rather than making new ones—either making bricks, creating faggot fields, planting cricket fields or carving headstones—make their mark in different ways. They do not change the earth but merely map it, configure it, differently. The Mankelows were involved in marking out a link between Hadlow and Tonbridge—although the county town of Maidstone was roughly equidistant, they helped create a route westwards away from Maidstone, towards Tonbridge. This route followed the direction of the river Medway. Indeed during the 1700s Tonbridge had become the 'port of the western Weald' and so extensive was the trade along the river, with carts and wagons waiting for barges unloading at Tonbridge, that the town outstripped Sevenoaks, Cranbrook and Westerham in importance.[61]

Within country districts carriers continued on well-trodden routes, marked out over the years, delivering food, goods and transporting people, acting as a rudimentary country bus.[62] The Mankelows' carrier business also thrived. William junior drove to the local town from the village twice a day. As his self-publicity in the local directory declared this was a London service with the rest of the journey being completed by rail. In time the service would be continued by a younger brother, Jonathan.[63]

As the nineteenth century turned into the twentieth, many of the Mankelows stayed locally; others moved to London or to Canada or New Zealand.[64] In the 1870s brothers William (junior) and Thomas moved the business in different forms to London. William established a base south of the river Thames at the Nag's Head in Borough High Street receiving goods for the Tonbridge area; and his younger brother, Thomas, set himself up in the Beaufort Street area in working-class Chelsea.[65]

## Different histories of the same family

When I met 'A', a fellow researcher and distant relative, in his Tonbridge home I was slightly taken aback. He was older than me by some years and looked both like a long-dead aunt of mine and a man whose appearance I only knew from a photograph, my grandfather, Frederick Mankelow. I'd brought his photograph with me to display, in a sense, my credentials—to show that I was who I said I was, a descendant of the Mankelows—which would give me some sort of right to research the family, to ask questions of people I had never met, and to accept their kind hospitality. Such 'proof' of probity, of belonging to the same family, seems to carry far more weight with family history researchers than a printed business card outlining academic qualifications. You need to give 'proof' of your actual research, of the different ancestors you have tracked, the certificates you have accessed (and purchased), the census returns you have photocopied. Such ephemera indicates that you are no outsider to this form of historical practice and therefore able to be included within this particular community of researchers. I had a fantasy that 'A' being local, and rather older than me and thus closer to 'the past', could tell me 'what the Mankelows were like'. I found he could, indeed, understand the landscape differently but he could no more pronounce authentically on their inner lives, or on 'what the past was really like', than I could. However, I did relish the anecdote, the personal snippets and note that the Mankelows he knew 'were Tories and drinkers' in contrast to my Liberal and abstemious grand-father, Frederick Mankelow.

I am not sure that 'A' and I are looking for the same things, nor that we are looking for them in the same way. 'A' scrutinises the docu-ments, especially during a wet winter; I prefer the outdoors, the artefacts, the places—history as a day out away from London. Nor are we particularly interested in the same line of the family—at least from the 1830s when our respective great-grandfathers were born—but we continue to exchange material. It is through 'A' that I meet 'B', one of his cousins, who, he recalls, has a quantity of photographs handed to her many years before by an old aunt. Noting that the addresses of the photographers on the back included Chelsea and other London addresses, and remembering my interests in the Mankelow carriers who had moved to that part of London, 'A' suggests a possi-ble connection worth pursuing.

'B', a founder member of her local history society in East Anglia, also has her own interests. She describes herself as having 'a passionate interest in history', and when she replies to my initial letter she explains that we are second cousins once removed, 'It's lovely having a relative one didn't know one had.' She is interested in the census returns for the village in which she now lives, which are difficult to access there and in due course I forward photocopies of the microfilm in the Family Records Centre. She is also hoping that I might be able to help her discover more about a mystery woman from her childhood past: a Lucy Jones who visited her family in Hadlow and arrived by motor cycle from Portsmouth and was either married to (or the daughter of) a ship's engineer. But despite our mutual interest in completing a puzzle of a common past neither of us can join together these places, these names, these stories. Although we appear to have parts of the same jigsaw that does not apparently fit we realise that we do have in common a knowledge of London and a love of Benjamin Britten's operas. As a young woman 'B' had queued all night for seats for *Peter Grimes* when it was first performed at Sadler's Wells on 7 June 1945 and we find ourselves talking enthusiastically about recent Britten productions.[66]

I was more optimistic than 'B' about her photos, passed on to her from another relative. Neither she nor 'A' had recognised any of the people or the places. She viewed my hypothesis that these could be part of the Mankelow family who moved to Chelsea to work as carriers extremely sceptically (although she was generously prepared to photocopy me both the images and backs of the cards which displayed the names of the photographers). 'No', she pronounced authoritatively, as we looked through them in turn— 'they don't look like Mankelows.' As 'B' suggests, I do realise intellectually that these unlabelled and unnamed images could, of course, be of anyone; however, I do not want them to be thus. I want them to have a connection, to contribute to meaning, to help explain a move from Kent into London. I speculate on who the people might be, the common aspects of their features, the locations of the photographers. I consult the post office directories for the names of photographers in London to correlate obsessively the dates of the photographers' businesses with Thomas Mankelow's move to Chelsea. I want to make the images fit to 'my' Mankelows, my story. And certainly there were matches between the locations of photographers and the streets in which Thomas lived. I showed the photo that I wanted to be Thomas and his son to my mother and my aunt Lily in the vain hope that they might have seen a similar image when they were children—and had remembered this. But it meant nothing to them; it was just an old-fashioned photo. Notwithstanding the fact that the child in the picture is in a dress, I recalled that both boys and girls wore similar clothes when very young and hoped— without substance—to convince myself that this was indeed my maternal grandfather Thomas, with his baby son, Frederick.[67] But, I cannot make such connections with my photographs, however much I might desire it; the material just is not there. 'B' is right: I cannot achieve such a knowingness any more than she can make connections with a mysterious Miss Jones on a bike.

'G' in Canada, who I contact thanks to 'A', has also been researching the Mankelows. We seemed to share a great-grandfather, Thomas Mankelow. As 'G' wrote, 'I have really enjoyed doing family research. The ways families are connected is history and finding distant relatives is a joy.' By the time I wrote to 'G' she had already researched her family extensively, jotting down details of ancestors, traces of memories, oral stories, and written a history. A motto of one of her great-grandfather's sons, a Christian, had been, 'do a job and do it well', a sentiment that had also been handed down to me as a philosophy of life. In a way such nineteenth-century Protestant ethics were personal but also, I realised, sentiments held by many of that generation and outlook. 'G' had also noted a snippet of a story of the same man who had emigrated to Canada. He has been a 'quiet man', working as a stonemason and 'as a small boy he knew the loss of a father'.

This seemed to suggest a more personal story, and a sad tale of the hard-working, honest Christian whose quietness as an adult was 'explained' by a childhood trauma. 'G' had been frustrated at not finding records of Thomas's death but had assumed that the story passed down in the family of a childhood loss was a story of a child orphaned through his father's death. However, I did not share 'G's' assumptions that this had been a loss through death. 'G' had thought that there may have been omissions from the records to explain a failure to find Thomas's elusive death certificate. And certainly she had been diligent in her researches, scrutinising the Mormons' world-wide digest of births and deaths, known as the IGI,[68] photocopying me details of the apparently relevant pages. But on this occasion, the state records had been neither wrong, nor missing. The supposed marriage between Thomas and Sarah Mankelow was an illusion. There had been no such first marriage—and there was no missing death certificate for Thomas. Although 'G' and I certainly shared a great-grandfather in Thomas Mankelow, the carrier, we did not share a great-grandmother. Thomas had deserted his partner Sarah and his five children for another woman, Ann. 'G' had indeed had an ancestor who, as a small boy, knew the loss of a father; but this had not been through death but abandonment.

A new life in a new country, Canada, might have beckoned for children of Thomas and Sarah, but a new start for Thomas himself had begun, nearer to home, in Chelsea in London. Within his new, second, family, of which I was a direct descendant, nothing existed of this earlier part of Thomas's life in Hadlow other than the handed-down knowledge to his grand-daughter Winifred, long after his death, of the titbit of information that he had come originally from Hadlow. In London he had traversed the streets in his cart, taking, I'm told, the only child of his marriage to Ann Gardener, his new partner, with him. His son Frederick, I'm informed, knew the streets of London well because of this. But if son Frederick was ever told about his father's life in Kent he did not pass this on to his own children. They, like his descendants in Canada, had known nothing of this particular part of his Hadlow past. Thomas, like one of his abandoned children, had also become a quiet man about his earlier life. Because of this silence, this lack of vocalised memory, or familial stories, other material has had to suffice to create a history. The landscape, and the gravestones have had to substitute for stories that were never told. But silence too has a history and a continuity across time. The silence of omission and absence would continue to influence in various ways the married life of Thomas and Ann and their only child Frederick, my grandfather.

# 4

## OUTSIDE THE ABYSS

### THE EAST LONDON OF ADA SALLNOW AND CHARLES KEAN

In her nostalgic romanticisation of East London lives, professional Cockney Gilda O' Neill dedicates her book, *My East End. Memories of Life in Cockney London*, to her family 'who filled my head with wonderful stories.'[1] Although I have, I suppose, Cockney forebears I do not have such memories of wonder, nor do I have childhood memories of stories of my grandparents' London past. As a child I did regularly visit my paternal grandparents, Ada and her husband Charles, but I do not remember any stories about Esther, the silk-weaving grandmother of Charles Kean, nor about Rebecca Mansfield and John Sallnow, Ada's parents. I was not told stories of 'what it was like' in the 'good old days'. I did pick up, however, in the way that children do, that God-fearing grandfather Charles had disowned his family 'because they were drinkers' and I knew that 'we' did not talk about this. The material I do have about this couple comes from my activity in the present, as a contemporary historian of family, as one who draws on found material as well as memories of my own childhood in their presence.

In some ways it should be easier writing a history of people that you have met, socialised with, even lived with for some time when you had nowhere else to live, rather than those known only through an epithet on a gravestone or a name on a census return. But is it possible to develop meaning, simply based on a memory of a couple I only knew for about 14 years at the end of their long lives and at the beginning of my own? Although the illusory ties of familial immediacy might suggest this as a possibility, there is not the commonality of emotional space arising from sharing personal chronologies in similar ways at the same moment in our lives. My grandfather Charles, the grandson of Esther and William Keen, the Spitalfields weavers, died aged 86 in December 1964, outliving his wife Ada (née Sallnow), who had died aged 83, by some three years. Ada was already over 70 when I, her first and only grandchild, was born. Although we shared a common external time of the 1950s our personal chronologies were starkly different. Ada Sallnow, like her future husband Charles, had been born in the seventh decade of the nineteenth century; I am now writing about her in the first decade of the twenty-first century. I am not convinced that it is possible to bridge this gap of time by simply suggesting an unproblematic, personal meeting of two individuals of different ages. This would suggest that I 'know' what their lives were 'really' like because I had 'been there' over 40 years ago. Were Ada and Charles the same people at the end as at the beginning of their lives, with the same views and experiences? Didn't the grandchild of the 1950s and the middle-aged adult of this new century experience and see things in different ways?

In the same way that I needed images from the past that could be recognised and grasped now to write about the Mankelow brickmakers, the Eicke farmers and the Keen weavers, I also need similar starting points to write about Ada and Charles. However, because of the shorter span of years, different materials might be available to help write such an account. An impetus could be household objects which, as Chicago sociologists Csikszentmihalyi & Ruchberg-Halton argue, 'constitute an ecology of signs that reflects as well as shapes the pattern of the owner's self'.[2] I want, then, to begin with objects, rather than people: the chairs, stools, candlesticks, lampstand and chess set that Charles Kean made for his own family. Some of these items were probably fashioned for his own wedding in 1899; the chess set carved later for his son, Stanley, my father. As I write, these artefacts of a former time when furniture really was made of wood (and not synthetics), that people did produce locally in workshops (rather than self-assembling the plastic for themselves from IKEA), are with me in my current home. As Grant McCracken has suggested, goods can serve as bridges to different times and spaces, enabling individuals and groups 'to recover displaced meaning'.[3] Many items I possess are now over 100 years old. They have not been thrown away, nor have they fallen apart. Like the maker's descendant, they are still here.

## Charles and the chairs

Charles Kean, who was born in 1879, was, like his father Charles, the son of the weavers, a worker in wood. He was a wood carver and maker of chairs, and spent his adult life in workshops around Shoreditch and the Hackney Road. In the nineteenth century, East London was both a place in which the furniture trade flourished and a locality in which the iconography of furniture gained a particular significance in the writing of social and religious anthropologists and philanthropists. Much written material exists about the London furniture trade, but does this necessarily tell me anything about the life of Charles? Images of furniture as possessions were employed to epitomise lives of either respectability, or destitution, within the genre of 'East End explorers'' narratives. To those such as Andrew Mearns, the Congregationalist minister, or William Booth, the founder of the Salvation Army, who created melodramatic narratives of the poor in their respective, *Bitter Cry of Outcast London* and *In Darkest England and the Way Out*, the 'motif' of the possession of furniture, and of particular kinds, was used to signify the respectability (or not) of East Londoners.[4] As Mearns recorded, amongst the standard questions asked by the missionaries of the London City Mission to the malnourished families they fed was, 'Is your husband in work now?' followed by, 'Is the furniture yours?'[5] A changing status from that of non-believer to religious convert was frequently depicted by reference to a changing relationship with furniture. According to the Salvation Army, conversion quickly led to an improved material change epitomised by possession of furniture:

> When (a sinner confessed his sins) his furniture consisted of a soap-box for a table and starch boxes for chairs. His wife, himself, and three children had not slept in a bed for three years. He has now a happy family, a comfortable home.[6]

Strikingly no attention was paid in such stories to those who actually made the chairs: the carvers, turners, chairmakers and upholsterers who had the skill to produce articles worth buying—and keeping. Chairs and objects made in wood, however, might help create different stories from those handed down by the philanthropic outsider. That such objects exist at all might suggest different stories from those conjured up by a reading of Henry Mayhew on the slop trade of East London, or Charles Booth on the poor quality of the work of East London wood workers.[7] Such writers emphasise unskilled workers producing badly made work in unsanitary work-shops. In different vein is the interesting catalogue, *Furnishing the World*, which accompanied a 1980s exhibition at the Geffreye Museum, the furniture museum in Shoreditch. It covered the lives and oral testimony of mainly Jewish cabinet-makers in East London and, in particular, their trade union activities.[8] But such materials seem unhelpful here: Charles was neither Jewish, nor a cabinet-maker, and certainly not a trade unionist. Further, given that the furniture he made (or at least some of it) has not fallen apart then it also suggests a different story from that of oppressed unskilled workers making insubstantial goods with a short lifespan.[9]

My interest in the chairs carved by Charles was stimulated vicar-iously by some family photographs, taken in the 1920s, that I found after my father, Stanley, had died. In them I recognised not only the people, a younger Stanley and his father, Charles, but also the chairs. In the first years after the Great War in which, as some commentators would argue, there was a bursting of modernity into the homes of the respectable, here was Charles Kean sitting in his self-crafted Queen Anne style chair adjacent to the hearth.[10] Here too was Stanley, his son, the young photographer, posing studiously as if reading a *Cruden's Concordance*, the Non-Conformist key to the *Bible*, on the carefully turned, upholstered dining chair.

Photographs and furniture share at least one common feature. Although both are fashioned at particular moments in time they possess a potential longevity that can span generations. The chair-making father and photographer-son were dead; the chairs (and the photographs) had outlived them both. It was the photographic images rather than the artefacts themselves, which I tended simply to use, that engaged my attention as a historian. In the creation of such images the furniture, it seems, is as much part of the family as the people sitting on them.

Trying out a new camera probably with a flash, which was rare in working-class homes of this date, seemed the first and simple explanation, for Stanley was into gadgets and a keen amateur

18 Charles Kean posing in his own chair

photographer. But this was no one particular occasion: on closer scrutiny the suits and ties change—and so do the chairs. The younger Stanley depicts himself reading on a dining-room chair; the slightly older Stanley in pin-stripe trousers and clean shoes sits in the patri-archal chair, vacated by his father for the occasion of the photograph, and takes a more expansive gesture than his care-fully restrained father. Is it the people themselves who are significant in these images? Rather it would seem that the act of creating a photographic image indoors is important and a part of that particular compo-sition is the furniture. The envy of his father's craft—or was it admiration?—was not articulated verbally by his son, but visually through such images. The skill of making things in wood which had also been practised by Charles's (and also Ada's) father finished in this family with Charles: Stanley did not follow his father into this dying trade. Even if jobs had been available Stanley lacked the expertise. He kept the larder cupboard he had made in school woodwork until his death, but he also knew that the pencilled mark he received for the work, still visible on the back, was not good enough. His interest in the craft of Grinling Gibbons as he took me around Wren churches in post-war London was not of a tradition he shared, but which he had broken.[11]

These are photographs which embody skill: the objects of the photos as well as the act of taking the photograph itself. The skill displayed by Stanley's father in making his chairs is strengthened by the conceit displayed in Stanley freezing the furniture and their occupants as moments in time. For cultural theorist, Roland

Barthes, a photograph does not necessarily say what is no longer, but only, and for certain, what has been.[12] Although much of his *Camera Lucida* concerns the interpretation of photographs of people, Barthes also notes that the photograph embodies the absence of the object while simultaneously acknowledging that the 'object' has indeed existed.[13] While it is true that in the images reproduced here the dead and thus absent people become authenticated, the furniture does not, at least not in the same way. Both the maker of the objects and of the image are dead. Yet the very existence of this portraiture situated against the still present chairs reinforces the

*19* Stanley Kean posing on a dining-room chair

absence of the people. The photograph alone does not create this meaning. It is not just the image which continues to exist but, as if they were valuable heirlooms, the furniture as well.[14]

In contrast to Barthes' example I already knew, and could see, what had been and, indeed, what still existed: the objects, the chairs, were in my house and used daily. But I had not seen them before as subjects of domestic photography. Through reading the photographs I could, perhaps, also understand why, when going blind, my grandfather Charles had refused to go to occupational therapy, weaving baskets, at a local Methodist church. 'I can't see to do it,' he would exclaim in frustration, the man who knew how to make useful things, whose hands could still move, and who could frighten his middle-aged son by running across the road with his white stick aloft as some sort of magic talisman to protect him against the Hackney drivers. He had crafted things worth making in the past; basket-weaving was no substitute.

20 Stanley Kean in his father's chair

Some writers have suggested that by thinking of a chair one can remember the person who sat in it: it summons up pleasant memories.[15] But I'm not sure I remember Charles sitting in these chairs, had they become 'best chairs' by the time I knew him? Nor do I remember Charles as a wood carver; our crossing of different personal chronologies in the same external time meant that when I knew him he was no longer able to make such artefacts. To me as a child he was always an old, very old, little man. The continuing existence (and use) of furniture made by him—something I would never have the skill to produce myself—has, however, suggested a person whose manual skills might tell me something about him, that my memory cannot. In some senses this story of the chairs and Charles is a personal story, but, as I discovered when corresponding with, and interviewing, others who were descendants of workers in wood, it is not unique.

People sent me photocopies of photographs of prized furniture an ancestor had made; told me stories of the furniture they had inherited. As one interviewee declared of the nineteenth-century furniture made by her Hackney ancestor, 'It's family history…I like it, I keep it. I wouldn't get rid of it.'[16] Being part of the present as well as the past, furniture and other crafted goods were both useful and practical items as well as symbols or reminders of a known relative or a name heard in family stories. The very act of keeping or inheriting things, and not having to buy new goods was also significant. In some sense this emphasis on practicality seemed to echo the sentiments of the makers themselves. This was also a rather different slant on the famous put-down by Tory MP Alan Clark against self-made millionaire, Michael Heseltine, namely that he was a man who had had to buy his own furniture.

## Summoning up Ada

If writing about a major part of Charles's life has seemed possible by thinking about the practical artefacts he had passed on, writing about Ada, his wife, and my grandmother, has seemed less easy to grasp. Certainly I possess some of her ornaments (which I will consider in the next chapter), fish knives and forks, a wonderful double saucepan I have used for melting chocolate, and photographs; but Ada didn't make things, at least not in the same way as Charles. She was in domestic service as a young woman, but she 'never worked' after her marriage, as she proudly declared. To summon up an image of Ada in the present suggests the need for different approaches. A contemporary work on domestic economy for girls suggested that if a mother understood the management of a home, 'she will work more wonders than a fairy'.[17] Even this exemplar of domestic rectitude admitted, with reference to Ecclesiastes, that such diligence might come to naught: although there should be 'study by your wisdom, your love, your purity, your unselfish domestic economy', it acknowledged that, despite this activity, 'no one may remember you'.[18]

Like her future husband, Ada had come from a family who had lived in Bethnal Green and Bow in East London since the late 1700s. At the time in which the now widowed Esther Keen, the silk weaver, was living with her adult children and their own families on the south side of the Roman Road market, Ada's parents, John and Rebecca, were living in various houses to the north of the same Roman Road towards Victoria Park.[19] John Sallnow was a descendant of George Sallnow ('Gentleman') who had settled in East London during the late eighteenth century, probably from Germany. It was from this immigrant that those possessing the Sallnow name owe their sojourn here. Unlike those possessing the surname of Eicke, Keen, Mountford or Mankelow, whose ancestors had been living in England for several centuries, these were newcomers to the country, and to East London. And here George's immediate descendants had stayed—not as 'gentlemen' but as hatters, cabinet makers, porters, painters—in the growing industrial eastern districts, out on the edges as London turned into Stratford and West Ham. Ada's great-grandfather, had lived in Pelham Street in Spitalfields in the early years of the nineteenth century when it was still a locale of silk weavers although this had not been his job—he had worked as a porter. Ada's grandfather had also lived locally and worked as a cabinet maker and her father, John, continued the facility with wood in his employment as a carpenter.[20] Her mother, Rebecca Mansfield, was the daughter of James Mansfield, who made mathematical instruments for which London was renowned at the time.[21] Rebecca and John had probably known each other from childhood since the families were neighbours in Abingdon Street, off the main Cambridge Heath Road.[22] Ada, then, had been born into a union of skilled Bethnal Green families. The Sallnow women worked in typical female jobs: Rebecca worked as a dressmaker; in her teens Ada's sister Minnie helped her at home;[23] later, after employment as a domestic servant in East Ham,[24] sister Annie stayed at home looking after her parents, Rebecca and John, in their old age, before finally marrying at the mature age of 45.[25] Ada was in service, working for the founders of the Mildmay Mission hospital, the first mission hospital in London, in Shoreditch behind the Shoreditch church: by the end of the nineteenth century many of its patients were those injured at work in the nearby local furniture workshops.[26] The impetus for the founding of the hospital had come from the Rector of St Philip's church, on the borders of the nearby Nichol (or fictionalised Jago) during the cholera epidemic of 1866. Although this was not the church nearest their homes, this was where John Sallnow and Rebecca Mansfield had married in 1859, perhaps suggesting regular attendance at the church. I wonder whether this familial connection may have led to Ada's subsequent employment with the deaconesses, attached to the church, who ran the hospital.[27] On this, however, the archive is silent. Early records of the hospital, the archivist of the still functioning hospital informed me, no longer exist.[28] If they did, I'm not sure that they would record much about a young woman working as a domestic servant. According to Anna Davin, 'East End or Irish girls had no hope of the "good" jobs in households of higher social status."[29] But Ada, at least, saw her former employment differently, and was proud to have undertaken this work. When she married she both relinquished her job—and her distinctive surname.

None of the material in the last paragraph about Ada's ancestors is known to me because of my relationship to Ada as a grandchild; rather it is because of material I have explored in recent years and snippets I have exchanged with other researchers. The collection of such material had started from a bored moment in the Bodleian library, a British telephone directory on CD installed before the library had internet access, and the typing in of the name Sallnow. This revealed only a handful of Sallnow surnames, sufficiently few to make contacting individuals a logistical possibility. Letters were posted, replies received, snippets were sent. I heard from 'D' hoping, not altogether seriously, for ancestors with French vineyards: 'I did once find a record of a Duke of Normandy called Salnoe who was titled and owned land back in the fourteenth century.' Others mentioned a grandfather who was a time-keeper in Beckton, another who had been an innkeeper, and one who in the very distant past had worked as a surgeon. Several correspondents led me to 'P' who— several Sallnows correctly advised—was researching the entire family, compiling a 'one name study' as family historians describe it. 'P' had researched and was carefully constructing a detailed family tree which she has generously shared. It revealed both that the nine-teenth-century Sallnows were long lived and had a tendency to produce more female than male offspring.

The paucity of modern names leading backwards to just one family had surprised me. I had not realised previously that my grand-mother's own surname was so distinctive (I had not even thought about it). It had not occurred to me that it was possible to trace back to 'a' beginning in populous London.[30] A simple starting point of a name and phone book had created a different perspective on the ordinary, the commonplace. Even the 1881 census national surname index contains only 30 instances of the Sallnow surname. This 'fact' was seductive, it was history displaying its Scotland Yard badge, a suggestion of the possibility of showing things 'as they really were'. It was indeed, narcotic.[31] However, of the 30 names, 21 were female. The surname that had marked out young female members of this family was frequently obliterated, disappearing on marriage. The extra-ordinary was wiped out.

## On the margins

But if the female names of the six Sallnow sisters, the daughters of
Rebecca and John, had been obliterated, the place in which they
had lived was not. It had been possible to walk the streets which
Esther the silk weaver had trod and to track her movements eastwards into the Roman Road. It was also possible to trace the
topography, the personal maps of the Sallnows whose geography
centred on the far east of what is now Tower Hamlets, in Bethnal
Green and Bow. After their marriage John and Rebecca Sallnow had
moved from the Cambridge Heath Road eastwards, following the
Bethnal Green Road as it changed its name first into Green Street
and then the accurately named Roman Road, that had been the main
road from London to Colchester.[32] By the 1880s, John and Rebecca
Sallnow with their six daughters and one son were living even further
east on the very fringes of the 'Hertford Union' canal and the
Hackney cut navigation,[33] in Wyke Road, and then the adjacent
Monier Street.[34] In some ways, as the details of occupancy in the
census suggest, this move seemed to indicate improved circumstances—most of the houses in Monier Road were occupied by just
one family; in contrast, in a former house in Usher Road, two households often shared the same house, occupying three rooms each.

In different ways this Hackney Wick industrial estate was defined
as a place on the margins both of geographical boundaries, and, for
many writers, those of respectability. As Charles Booth had characterised this area around the canal:

> It would seem as though the rejected from the centre had been flung
> completely over the heads of the rest of the population to alight
> where no man yet had settled, occupying ill-built houses on the
> marshy land that is drained or flooded by the river Lea.[35]

Acknowledging the dominant characterisation of the area, Crory
attempted to counter this image in his almost eulogising work, *East
London Industries*, arguing:

> Every attempt to make the locality seem the plague spot of the
> metropolis is unjust…Were I influenced by current literature alone, I

21 The former Bryant & May factory, 2002

might feel disposed to regard East Londoners as Yahoos. But I have met with no such people, in fact, no good reason for applying such an epithet is to be found in all the bounds between Aldgate and Beckton, and from Bethnal Green to the Isle of Dogs—or Ducks—respectively.[36]

Most of Rebecca and John's new neighbours, the relevant census returns indicated, were manual workers—labourers, machinists, glass blowers, employed on the local industrial estate.[37] According to trade unionist Will Thorne the local gas and chemical works provided 'fairly constant work'[38] although unsurprisingly residents petitioned against the smell.[39] As a local headteacher recorded, staff and children in the Smeed Road school for girls on the industrial estate complained of being sick because of bad smells seeping into the classrooms.[40] Here lived the foreman at the waterproof works, a lighterman on the barges, a young man who washed ostrich feathers and still, even though it was towards the end of the nineteenth century, a couple of silk workers, surviving against the odds.[41] Despite the environment, Ada and her five sisters all physically survived the 'unfragrant character'[42] and rigours of this aspect of East London life well into adulthood. The only child of Rebecca and John to die in infancy, from meningitis at three years old, was Fred, Rebecca's last child and only boy, born when she was in her late 40s.

The streets are still there on the eastern side of the approach road to the Blackwell tunnel, which is built over the former sewer outlet.

22 Monier Road in the 1950s

From the walkway across the motorway there is a good view of the former Bryant & May factory, where the young women won their strike for better wages in 1888. The factory is still standing but has been transformed into gated lofts with a swimming pool for residents. But in Monier Road and the other roads abutting the canal, signs of human habitation have now gone; instead industry—and learner drivers practising three-point turns in deserted evening streets—fills the space. I had guessed as much from looking at photos of the road in the London Metropolitan Archives. The very existence of such images of almost empty streets of houses, taken by the photographic unit in the LCC design department, suggested that the buildings were the significant feature (rather than the people who lived in them). It also suggested that such architecturally undistinguished houses needed to be commemorated photographically as they would soon be no more. This is ostensibly a functional image, but the symmetry of the drawn curtains, regular windows and chimneys evokes a similar sadness to Edward Hopper's famous painting, *Early Sunday Morning*. It suggests a street both captured in the moment of the mid-twentieth century, but one which endures from an earlier period. There seems to be almost a knowingness that this indeed was an important moment in the story of the inhabited street: its future obliteration would destroy many potential stories of the inhabitants.

In the summer of 2002 at 30 Monier Road, the main address of the Sallnows, I found a new, bright industrial complex. The new schools that had been opened in nearby Smeed Street in 1885 had gone. However the nearby manufacture of reproduction furniture and the roasting of Percy Dalton's peanuts still survived in the original nineteenth-century warehouses. In Ada's childhood this had been a place where London turned into industrial suburb, Bethnal Green into marshes, here into there. The area still borders the water and is still a mixture of different places. Wandering around on a Summer Friday evening, smelling the sewerage, I observed the abandoned television studio and a barge transporting machinery slowly through the lock while walkers and cyclists made their way along the towpath towards Stratford. There were also herons elegantly swooping to feast on the debris. The place still seemed to be on the margins, at the end of something: now a meeting point of post-industrial and almost rural landscapes.

**The general and the particular**

Conventional descriptions of the lives of East Londoners as the nineteenth century turned into the twentieth have concentrated on dramatising the area around St Philip's church where John and Rebecca Sallnow had married. The vicars of St Philip's and nearby Holy Trinity churches had helped create an image of the 25 streets of the adjacent Nichol as a place of destitution and infamy in order to encourage philanthropy in those living outside East London.[43] It also helped encourage a fear of the unknown, the idea of the enemy within lurking in the very capital of the nation. This actually existing place became both dramatised and fictionalised, emblematic of a much wider East London. An earlier vicar from St Philip's had gained a particular publicity for his views, being quoted by Frederick Engels, the colleague of Karl Marx, in his polemical *Condition of the Working Class in England*. Speaking of his parish, the vicar had declared dramatically, 'I believe that…people at the West End knew as little of it as of the savages of Australia or the South Sea Isles.'[44] From the 1880s this mythology of an 'Outcast

London' was further developed by socialists and evangelising Christians alike. Visiting tenants in her work for the Charity Organisation Society in 1880s, Beatrice Webb described her clients as 'the aborigines of the East End'.[45] American socialist Jack London, who adopted the persona of an unemployed, homeless man to document the locality, described local women as 'screaming harridans or broken-spirited and doglike [who] lost what little decency and self-respect they have remaining from their maiden days, and sink together, unheeding, in their degradation and dirt'.[46]

I have difficulty in thinking that Jack London's lurid account, *The People of the Abyss*, describes Ada even though before her marriage she had worked nearby in domestic service (and Charles too had lived locally near the Columbia Road market and also worked near the places described by Jack London). Physically Ada and Charles were living and working on the edges of the place imagined as Jack London's abyss or the Jago, as the streets of the Nichol were so fictionalised. Affectively they were somewhere else. My difficulty in personalising such accounts of East London to 'fit' Ada and Charles does not emanate from a need to defend their fierce pride in their respectability (as they might have seen it), after all many family historians boast quite romantically of ancestral destitution and Jago origins.[47] But such a story seems to ignore other possibilities, different—less dramatic—narratives of the people of Bethnal Green. It denies differences in the experience of a locality and it fails to understand that by using different materials an historian might create different stories. As Raphael Samuel discussed in an article on local and oral history, 'By using a different class of record…the historian can draw up fresh maps.'[48]

### Personal memory and public stories

Ada and Charles married at the young age of 21, just months after Ada's father John had died, in August 1899 at St Mark's church at the eastern end of Victoria Park, the nearest established church to the Hackney Wick estate. After their marriage the couple moved away and kept on moving, first into Bethnal Green and thence to various addresses in Hackney including a sojourn near the marshes and the River Lea renting rooms or floors in houses, but never even acquiring the space of a whole rented house. For most people a home is not just a utilitarian shelter but a repository of things whose familiarity and concreteness helps organise the consciousness of their owner. As Bachelard analysed, 'Our house is our corner of the world…it is our first universe, a real cosmos in every sense of the word.'[49] Objects within the home cross time from youthful possessions to repositories of memories perhaps recalling happier times and can define the individual in a wider social network.[50] In the case of Ada and Charles this network included a particular culture of East London as the nineteenth century moved relentlessly on through the twentieth. Remembered moments, artefacts, things, might help us assemble 'out of the smallest and most precisely cut components…[a discovery] in the analysis of the total individual moment'.[51] They might provide the basis of a different picture; personal stories and public histories that are not of the abyss, but which emanate from the material of the lives of Ada and Charles Kean.

I do have memories of my grandparents. Ada and Charles's home was, for me, a location for pickles, piccalilli, watercress and shellfish teas and expensive (or so my mum told me) Wonderloaf white bread with blue waxed paper, held over a real fire grate on a toasting fork. For Christmas dinner there were roast *and* boiled potatoes with turkey, boiled ham and stuffing and mustard. Christmas tea meant real and dear ham—not the usual Spam or luncheon meat—and Guernsey tomatoes, extravagant and rare—as it was the wrong time of year to buy them cheaply in East London. Oral historian Alessandro Portelli has suggested, the elaboration of memory and the act of remembering are always individual: it is people, not groups, who remember.[52] But is this simply the stuff of individual memory? Surely there is also a social construction in Ada and Charles's tastes in food, based in time and locality? The late nineteenth century had been a time in which soft food like boiled potatoes was popular: soak vegetables for two hours before cooking; soak cabbage in cold salt water to kill snails, caterpillars and 'other creatures' then boil and fry; boil spinach in water and then stew; boil carrots for one hour, parsnips for 80 minutes, or so the cookbooks recommended.[53] Certainly in the Kean household there were treats, not just those defined as peculiar personal taste, but ones shared by others of that time and place. As Allen has suggested there were distinct regional variations in food tastes. He characterises 'the south' as 'the land of mixtures, of experimental mingling…subtler flavours: saltier bacon, more pungent types of cheese'.[54] In Ada and Charles's home there was homemade seed cake implanted with caraway, the oldest cultivated spice plant of Europe, particularly popular in German and Jewish cookery but also, according to Elizabeth David, a great English favourite.[55] Charles used to enjoy eating skate; apparently in London (in contrast to the north) there was a widespread preference for this particular fish in the early twentieth century.[56] But Ada acted differently. For her this was a 'dirty fish' that 'lived at the bottom of the sea'. I know about this, I realise with hindsight, since it was a story told to me as a child. But there are contemporary stories too: Ada's view is also an idea held by Jews, I have subsequently discovered, for whom skate, a scavenger fish, is not kosher and thus forbidden as part of a strict Jewish diet.[57] I have recently found other contemporary 'skate stories' of female aversion to eating this fish, including the notion that skate have menstrual periods or parts of their bodies resemble human genitalia.[58] Ada's story was a story constructed for a child, but one which, as an adult, I have remembered.

At Christmas I used to be given a sip of Stone's ginger wine, which for decades I had erroneously assumed was non-alcoholic and thus permitted a place in this teetotal household. Shortly after their marriage Ada and Charles had become Primitive Methodists, bringing up their son in its ways.[59] This form of Methodism with its emphasis on strict moral behaviour, preaching and enthusiasm for temperance,[60] had grown quickly in East London with branches established in Whitechapel, Bethnal Green and Old Ford in 1885, growing to eight local branches by 1905.[61] Certainly Charles had preached in Hackney's Chatsworth market, near the marshes, trying to convert the heathen, and playing Sankey hymns on his harmonium. 'Preaching', it has been said, 'was designed to secure a verdict'.[62] And this the Methodists had also attempted in the area of Ada's childhood home. On the industrial estate of Ada's childhood the Primitive Methodists had an outpost; in the nearby Old Ford mission the Sunday school became one of the largest in the area, attended by her young, distant, relative—Victor Sallnow—who would qualify as a Minister by the time he was 24.[63]

As I explore in the next chapter, there may have been particular reasons why the couple vehemently advocated temperance, but traditionally ginger wine was called a sacramental wine—a water infusion of dried raisins, containing just sufficient alcohol to keep the fruit preserved—and was used as religious, communion wine.[64] Stone's too was a Londoner's popular drink, sporting the crest of the city with its motto 'domine dirige nos' on the bottle. It had been considered a protection against cholera and an aid to digestion because of its ginger base; it was also a good free trade drink which would have suited Liberals like the Keans.[65] It was packaged for cooler times, such as Christmas, with a marketing slogan of, 'Sip it, drink it, drain it'; this was a 'warming' drink.[66] It is still being recommended as good for you and still being drunk by descendants of East Londoners (and others, of course) today. As a recent *Guardian* article declared, 'Ginger is a wonder ingredient that has anti-viral and anti-bacterial properties, so you could also drink it to ward off colds and flu.'[67] It was still being promoted—with a special offer—in Whitechapel Sainsbury's in Christmas 2003.

Christmas in Ada and Charles's house also meant pickles. Clearly pickles, watercress and winkles were part of the personal taste of the Keans; they didn't just eat them because their neighbours did. But it was also a taste fashioned outside their home—it came from earlier times and from the locality in which they had been raised. As Dr Wynter declared in 1870, the lower orders loved watercress.[68] Also, vegetables preserved in vinegar had long been a popular London treat. By 1900 the majority of British vinegar breweries were London-based led by the firm of Sarson's located in City Road (the first company to bottle virgin vinegar in 1850, which was sold to greengrocers—rather than grocers—to accompany their sales of vegetables).[69] The chief centre of the English pickle industry was also based in London. As an Edwardian grocers' manual contended:

The penny cabbage must go to the metropolis to be operated upon by the workers from the slums, and return to its native district cut up and divided into some half dozen eightpenny pint bottles before it is fancied.[70]

Piccalilli which Ada and Charles (and their descendants) also enjoyed

23 Ada in her South Hackney garden

had a similar long local history.[71] Traditionally it had been made using Keens and Colman's mustard,[72] which the firm of Keens had sold from their Garlick Hill premises in the City since the 1740s.[73] The yellow, mustardy pickle proved so popular that cauliflowers, the main ingredient, became plentiful in vegetable markets and were bought specifically to make the pickle.[74] It has been suggested that food tastes did not change rapidly over time;[75] but in the Stone's ginger wine and the piccalilli there is a specific meeting of memory, time, taste and place. During the time of my 1950s childhood my grandparents' sterilised milk, caraway seeds and pickles seemed a personal quirk, but they also had another chronological context not in the post-war period but in late nineteenth-century practices that the Keans continued. Other tastes were more modern: the predilection for Wonderloaf and Kitekat for Tinker the cat (and, yes, they did tell me that 'West Indians' mistakenly ate this as human food) were rooted in a particular contemporary time—and place. Such memories of food, domestic practices in a particular context, contrast sharply with stories from domestic manuals designed to teach working-class young women how to fulfil their roles as wives and mothers. A standard textbook for teachers of domestic economy indicated what would be expected of women like Ada Sallnow as the following question (and model answer) indicates:

> *Question*: A labouring man earns 15s per week. a) Describe the kind of supper which, without extravagance, his wife might cook and share with him on his return from work. b) To what points should she attend in order to make his meal a comfortable one?
> *Answer*: a)1) Bacon and new potatoes, 2) cheese toasted in milk

3) Irish stew 4) gullet stew, followed by bread fritters, 5) savoury duck and apple dumplings, will, at a very small cost, provide a nourishing an appetising supper.

b) The food should be 1) well cooked, 2) punctually ready, 3) neatly and cleanly laid, and 4) *the house and wife should be quiet and comforting.*[76] (my emphasis)

Is this a better 'source', this written material than my memory, or the cooking of Ada? Does it tell me she failed, that she wasn't up to scratch? Or might it suggest that the teachers of domestic economy did not have things all their own way? With food you neither change nor mark a landscape in the same way as a brick-maker in Kent or a farmer in Staffordshire, nor do you create beautiful materials like Esther or functional artefacts which endure, like those made by Charles. But those who prepare daily meals (or special treats) may in some sense be 'remembered' very practically in the bodies of the next generation—bones strong with calcium (or teeth decayed by excessive sweets). The memory of piccalilli, Stone's ginger wine and caraway seeds summon up individuals, but also the place and time in which they were popular. They might also provide different traces for stories of women in East London from those of the harridans of 'Outcast London'.

### The woman who gardened in the 'ouses in between

The garden of the rented bottom floors of the Victorian south Hackney house which I knew in the 1950s was full of flowers: roses, bright orange English marigolds grown from seeds, delicate lily of the valley and solomon's seal with its drooping white eyelets, all tended by Ada. Once I picked some flowers thinking she would like them inside the house but about this I was soon corrected, for this was not what flowers were for. These were God's flowers, she explained, and he wanted them kept growing in the garden. The moment of this memory is of the 1950s but this story has poten-tial origins in another time in East London. Photos and personal memory elide into other stories, creating connections with the contemporaries of Esther and William Keen. Both the Huguenots and their indigenous neighbours had liked flowers, cultivated

24 Stanley Kean and Ada's aspidistra

tulips, built summerhouses.[77] This tradition was continued by those in the later nineteenth century living in tenements, dwellings and crowded streets.[78] By the end of the century gardening continued to be well established—and recognised as a local practice.[79] As early as the 1770s there had been a literature celebrating nature in London as 'other' with surprise expressed that green spaces, trees, and gardens existed and flourished.[80] But flourish they did. Concurrently the inhabitants of East London developed a proficiency in horticulture and nurseries thrived locally. From the late eighteenth century fine exotic specimens, including olive and mulberry trees, could be bought locally.[81] Vestiges of this nursery industry still remain today. The Hackney square in which I live was laid out in the 1820s with trees supplied by the famous local Loddiges nursery. Although Loddiges is merely remembered in a street name, many of the trees are still surviving and thriving, despite the rigours of modern Hackney life. Chrysanthemums became defined as a 'London' flower capable of being grown in pots on windowsills or in yards, and a chrysanthemum society was established in Bethnal Green in the 1850s. Gardeners were recommended to use goats' blood, goose dung, sugar-bakers' scum and decayed willow shavings as a good compost for them.[82] While garden 'coffee table' magazines were introduced for the middle class replete with colour prints, specific DIY publications were produced aimed at working-class Londoners for whom gardening was often a hobby of the closes, the places, the 'ouses in between,[83] as Gus Elen would sing in 1894:

Oh it really is a werry pretty garden
And the soapworks from the 'ouse tops could be seen

A specific topography of East London was sketched out in this song:

> wiv a ladder and some glasses
> You could see to 'ackney marshes
> If it wasn't for the 'ouses in between.[84]

I knew this song—it was a favourite of my father's—long before I'd found it again in the British Library and then on a CD of Gus Elen's songs I bought over the internet.[85] In some ways it seems a personal song: it is a narrative about the place where Ada had lived as a young woman by the soap and tallow works on the marshes, and where my father would live as a young man, near the Clapton Orient football ground up by the River Lea. But it is also about another, different world, away from the reality of the congested metropolis. Ostensibly this is a song of a costermonger—the flowers described are unsold turnip tops and cabbages 'wot people doesn't buy'—but it appeals wistfully to a mythical rural pastness which ostensibly the audience could 'remember'.

The song is not mocking the *absence* of gardens or window boxes, rather the butt of the satire is the coster's futile imitation of the horticulturist efforts of his more settled neighbours—and a gentle critique of the desire of another world conjured up by flowers. The manuals issued when Ada was a child had probably been realistic about the state of London soil: 'The garden is the cemetery of mice and kittens. The earth sours and agglutinates under the fogs and bad gases.'[86] 'Night soil' or earth stolen from Epping Forest was recommended as compost; Jewish tenants of Rothschild Buildings made do with earth removed from the churchyard grounds at Christ Church, Spitalfields.[87] Special plants were recommended for sour soil and shady windows; these included the plant I recalled, and my mother also remembered, in Ada's garden, solomon's seal.[88] When Ada grew this in South Hackney was it because it had been one of the few plants that would have grown on the industrial estate of her childhood? Was she simply doing what successive East London women had done—and she liked the plant?[89]

Visual images of plants growing in East London homes certainly exist in public archives as well as family albums; they are not difficult to find. But they are part of a story that seems rather different

25 Flower boxes and people photographed in Providence Place

from the more usual tales of the abyss and outcast London. When I have looked through the early twentieth-century photographs of East London streets kept in the London Metropolitan Archives I have noticed the widespread existence of plants, of 'nature' in this metropolitan, non-rural, place. But I have seldom found this included in modern books about the history of East London. The above image of Providence Place is often reproduced, usually to convey the idea of slums and poverty. The attention of the reader is not drawn to the window boxes stuffed full of growing plants, to the flourishing greenery descending on the left. The shod children surrounded by women (and just a couple of men) might suggest that this is a female, domestic image; but the notion of nurturing children and plants alike is not wanted in a melodramatic tale of destitution. The stance of the women suggests defiance, eyeing the photographer suspiciously, almost suggesting that the protagonists themselves knew how this image would be read—negatively—and how they were becoming objects in a story not of their own construction. As Karen Olsen and Linda Shopes have reminded us, by 'studying down' there is a temptation to exaggerate the exotic, the heroic, or the tragic aspects of the lives of people with little social power.[90] An image of domesticity, implied by floriculture—or carving chairs—sits uneasily with more dramatic stories of familial neglect.

I am able to write stories of Ada and Charles because they left traces of their lives in many forms. Snippets from their daily lives, material culture, memories, are still here and can be used to write a different history of East Londoners. But parts of their life are more difficult to construct from the traces that remain. This was a couple who did not talk about certain things. Like all families they had silences, skimmed over difficult issues, did not talk about aspects of their lives and colluded with each other in keeping it that way. Certain events in the early years of their marriage were not apparently discussed. This was not dissimilar to the practices of Thomas Mankelow, the carrier from Kent and his new wife Ann, who lived in Chelsea. When Ada and Charles's son and Thomas and Ann's grand-daughter married they would both bring to their marriage a strong tradition of silence, the roots of which I will explore in the next chapter.

# 5

# NOT REMEMBERING ANN MANKELOW AND CHARLIE KEAN

## Disruption through silence

There is no memory of Ann Mankelow, my mother's paternal grandmother, within my family. My mother Winifred (and her sister Lily,
the only surviving sibling) knew nothing about her. For many years
Mum had suggested that there might have been a scandal, a marriage
of which the grandparents had disapproved. But she did not *know*,
she said; Winifred had conjectured this because she thought it odd
that she had never been taken to visit her father's mother. Winifred
certainly had no personal memory of her paternal grandmother,
nor, it turned out, could she possibly have had such a memory. Ann
had died in 1895, nineteen years before my mother was born.

Ann Gardener, as she then was, had moved from her native
Wadhurst and married Thomas Mankelow, formerly from Hadlow
in Kent, who ran a carrier business in working-class Chelsea. The
move to London in the 1860s, when Ann was in her thirties, was
probably not solely due to a shift in the fortunes of Tom's carrier
business. For in marrying Ann, Thomas had also abandoned his first
partner who was left to bring up five young children alone. As historian Lawrence Stone put it, divorce was impossible for the poor.
The simplest solution was for a man to abandon his family, 'to walk
out of the house one day and never come back'.[1] Neither Thomas
nor Ann went back but remained in London where Ann gave birth
to her only child, Frederick, my mother's father, who was born a
couple of years after their marriage.

This move to London I had deduced in a fairly straightforward
manner from the census, birth and marriage certificates, electoral
records and post office directories. But in searching the archive
for records of her death Ann was not where she ought to have

been. Logically the location would have been 'ideally' either Chelsea or at least London, or—at a pinch—Sussex or Kent; but there was no such record in these places. She should not have been the Ann Mankelow who, the death register indexes at the Family Records Centre said, died in Epsom, Surrey. She had no reason to be in the countryside. She had left behind her old life outside London when she had married Thomas; what reason would she have to go back? Nevertheless, being thorough and in detective mode I ordered the certificates of the only two Ann Mankelows whose dates fitted.

On Ann's death certificate the nature of her countryside sojourn became clear. I had indeed found the right Ann, 'my' Ann, but she was not where I had been looking. Carrier routes did not go that way across country, circumventing the home counties, but went directly to and from London. This was Surrey, not Kent, nor Sussex, nor Middlesex. I had previously ordered (and paid for) a different certificate, another wrong Ann Mankelow, the wrong husband and wrong place. However, Ann had to be somewhere and here she was, not in a pastoral idyll but in a London County Council institution, the Banstead lunatic asylum. Here she was on the edges of the metropolis, and the margins of 'sane' society. The cause of her death at 67 in October 1895 was given as chronic brain wastage.

Did this mean she had Alzheimer's, I thought? Was it that Thomas, her husband, had dumped her like his first partner? Was it she was too much trouble? Surely fear of the asylum was even greater than that of the workhouse? I thought of the incarceration in 1858 of the novelist Rosina Bulwer Lytton, the daughter of the feminist Anna Wheeler who with William Thompson had written the book, *An appeal of one half the human race, women, against the pretensions of the other half, men, to retain them in political, and thence in civil and domestic, slavery*. Rosina had spoken out against her husband's Conservative politics. The explanation for this could be none other than lunacy and incarceration. But she was released after three weeks due to the publicity she had aroused as the wife of Lord Edward Bulwer Lytton.[2] I also recalled vegetarian Georgina Weldon, who let her children play outside in the street without shoes: her husband tried to declare her insane. She resisted forcefully—and wrote about it in the 1870s in a striking pamphlet, *How I escaped the mad doctors*.[3] But that was different: that was melodrama featuring middle class or aristocratic women who had a voice. They were also women who had resisted.

If Ann had resisted it was insufficiently melodramatic for it to be recorded. And probably it was not Alzheimer's. According to 'KW' who knew about the disease personally and professionally as an Oxford GP, a different phrase was used for this. More likely, he thought, it had signified loss of short-term memory with resulting paranoia and confusion, characteristically, between day and night. Although you could never tell, he went on, because there were no brain scans then, it could well have been athero-sclerotic or multi-infarct dementia in which areas of the brain do not get sufficient oxygen and as the blood supply is progressively reduced the brain ceases to function normally. She could well have been a danger to herself and others especially when paranoid.

What else could Tom have done? There were no daughters; the only son, Frederick, by now a husband and father, was no longer living in the family home, the two rooms that Ann and Thomas had shared in Ashburnham Street on the Chelsea/Fulham borders. Frederick was living and working full-time on the other side of the city in Hackney, a journey of many, many miles even though the 22 bus route then linked the two boroughs. And Fred's wife, Mary, was occupied with their own young children.

Where did the inmates of the public asylums come from? From much the same place, I would discover, as the inmates of residential homes today. Ann was there because she—and her family—could not cope. Certainly there was disgrace and hereditary shame, which was vociferously expressed in the documentation of the asylum. The census returns of the Banstead Lodge lunatic asylum founded in 1877 as the third asylum for the residents of Middlesex, but based in Surrey, and taken over by the newly formed London County Council (LCC) in 1889 said much in few words. According to the 1891 census returns in the Family Records Centre there were over 2,000 inmates, the majority women, mostly older women, the women who still today form the larger part of nursing and residential homes. These were female institutions, staffed by women, inhabited by women, although those who ran the place, the doctors, those who took the decisions, were men.

## Archival deceits

If Ann *had* been committed in 1891 her name would not have appeared in the census returns, only her initials, to save her family from embarrassment. This, said the assistant at the Family Records Centre, was common practice, 'You won't find much information there.' But even the lack of words was eloquent, for the census enumerator did as thorough a job on the asylum as elsewhere. He cited the ages of the inmates, their marital status and former occupation: these were standard entries for 1891. But there was no record of their place of birth: uniformly this was defined as unknown. This was a deceit: inmates gave their full address when admitted. So too was another absence a deceit—the names of the inmates. A life was represented by initials: no longer was there any vestige of a personal identity, the framework of madness obliterating both a personal and family name.

Undeterred I read the microfilm and carefully noted down all the inmates who might possibly have been Ann, since they shared the initials A. M.:

A. M. single female 35 former occupation prostitute
A. M. single female 28 formerly domestic servant
A. M. single female 30 former tailoress

The initials indicated silence but said much about supposed causes of insanity; the jobs suggested a Victorian explanation of sorts for the inmate's condition. It was the women's own disgrace, perhaps caused by their work—the reputed immoral lives of those in the garment trade, the prostitute's actions—which led to their nemesis. The women alone were deemed responsible, not the fathers or husbands, whose names they took with them in their former lives and which were now discarded. But 'my' A.M. was not there. The age wasn't right. She wasn't there in 1891. Because the Banstead lunatic asylum was run by the LCC the records are kept in the London Metropolitan Archives in Clerkenwell so I only needed to search in the admission books from 1891 to 1895 to find 'my' Ann.

## Lunatic stories

When inmates entered the asylum they took with them stories of their insanity which were recorded in the files. But whose stories are these? Is it their own tale or that of their relatives who referred them or the warders in Millbank prison or the workhouse who could not longer cope with them? On the same day that Ann Mankelow was admitted to the asylum, a Mary Herne, a 52-year-old charwoman, was referred to Banstead by the Chelsea workhouse, where she was previously incarcerated. They, like Thomas Mankelow, could not cope. She had hallucinations of hearing, she was childish in her manner, her ideas were 'few and confused'. Many possessed homespun explanations of the supposed cause of insanity. William Hooper, aged 33 from Oswald Street in Clapton Park (near where Ada and Charles Kean would live with their own family) was admitted on the same day as Ann. William had been referred by his local Board of Guardians, the Hackney Union. A former bootfinisher, William was suffering from melancholia and had delusions of persecution. Like Mary Herne he had hallucinations of hearing. The alleged cause of his insanity was 'trouble through want of work'.[4] Banstead also housed those sent by prison commissioners such as Matilda Kelsey, a tailoress from Pollard Street in Bethnal Green. It was the street rather than the name which had drawn my attention for Pollard Street was adjacent to Squirries Street where Esther and William Keen had lived some 40 years before. Even now I was wanting to make connections and create interlinking stories using the material of the archive. Matilda, the records said, was very depressed and suicidal, requiring special care. She had reacted, it was said, to family disagreements; she was not a strong-minded woman.[5] The asylum included women and men who even the prison service could not control, who had tried to kill themselves, whose poor mental health, the administrators said, was often caused by alcoholism or 'self abuse'. Jane Raven, a 40-year-old charwoman, was referred from Millbank prison 'maniacal and restless' in a 'critical period of life' who had been treated badly by her sons. Charlotte Bullard would also have been there with Ann, a 34-year-old former barmaid admitted because of her destructive habits, collecting rubbish off the streets, gone mad, it was said, as she was 'crossed in love'. The asylum was a noisy place of restless, delusional, troubled people.

It was because Ann did not exist in memory that it seemed important to take as much as possible from such meagre documents. Other progeny of the Mankelows of Hadlow, far more productive family researchers in many ways than I, knew nothing of her existence. A Canadian descendant of Thomas's first family, had felt sure he must have died for, unsurprisingly, Thomas's first partner, Sarah, had obliterated both Thomas and Ann from her memory. For Sarah—and thus her children—Thomas and Ann had simply ceased to exist. But Ann certainly had existed and the entries in the asylum record book suggested at least something about her. Ann Mankelow was different from many of her fellow inmates in Banstead lunatic asylum. She was not sent by the Guardians, the workhouse, or the prison. She was quiet, she did not have delusions like others, hers was an absence of noted imaginings, indeed an absence of any imagination. Nothing defined her.

There were traces of her in the records, details of her name; social condition: labourer's wife; bodily condition: fair; mental condition: demented. The log book for 3 September 1894 was specific: 'Dementia. No idea of time or place, memory a blank. Has to have everything done for her.'[6] Neither her past nor present life disturbed her to vocalisation. Her supposed cause of insanity was 'not known'. For others it was illegitimacy, self abuse, trouble at loss of work which sent them to the asylum. But Ann was there because she *had* no story to tell, she was there because of nothing, because of what was *not* there. Her memory was a blank.

Her condition did not improve. A further reception order, keeping Ann in the asylum, was approved nearly a year later in August 1895.[7] On 26 October, some two months after this, she died. Again it was an event circumscribed by the institution and her death was not unique. Two others died the same day; another, like Ann, suffering from chronic brain wasting.[8] On 31 October Ann Mankelow, number 5480 on the register, was buried, the only inmate that day, in the precinct of the Hundred Acres Parish of Banstead.[9]

I wanted to know where she had been buried, to know where her material traces were since nothing else about her existed: no writing, no photographs, no other descendants apart from her silent (and very long dead) son, Frederick, who I had never known, and no stories passed down in the family—absolutely none at all. There was not even the hazy memory of a child (my mother or aunt): because of the constraints of time she would never have been seen by her grandchildren. And she was not talked about.

I did try to check this thoroughly since I found it hard to believe that my mother's eldest sister Sarah, the first child of Frederick Mankelow and Mary Davies, born in January 1891— over three years before Ann's committal—would not have been welcomed by her grandparents; that there would not have been at least a photo. 'D', the daughter of the couple's first baby, is still alive but I have never met her: this is not a sociable family. So I write to her asking whether she has any photos of her late mother's grandparents. 'I wouldn't have thought she would have had any,' said Mum, '"D" was adopted after all. She came from the Salvation Army.' Lily, Mum's last surviving sister and my aunt, had the same view, 'You do know "D" was adopted?' But I reply, she was adopted as a baby wasn't she? Wasn't she brought up as her daughter, her only child? 'Oh yes, but I don't think she'd have any photos.'

Being in their 80s both sisters were no doubt more wary of acknowledging a relative with a disturbing, possibly genetic, trait which was closer to them at this time of their lives than it was to me. Having lived all their lives without such knowledge, what might it mean to them now? Unfortunately, on this occasion, the two normally contradictory sisters were both right in their assessment. 'D', their sister's daughter, coping with deteriorating multiple sclerosis and clumsy social services staff who had dropped her, had more on her mind than the history of her adopted family. She had neither inclination nor capacity to go into her attic to search for photos. She too knew nothing of a lunatic in the family and, like her aunts, did not share my interest. It seemed that even now no one wanted to remember Ann. In her own life something too had changed to make the daily routine forgettable, to remove all traces of the here and now, to send Ann out of London again, to the asylum.

## Prison walls

'I don't expect to find a grave,' I told the helpful Surrey archivist, 'Even an unmarked one.' But I had wanted to find out what the place was now. Since the asylum had existed until the 1980s it would suggest that planning permission had been granted to build on the buried bodies. Normally I would wander—or more accurately drive—around and see what was there but Banstead, the A to Z suggested, is built up and not an area I knew. The archivist wasn't sure but thought it might be a prison; if I wrote in he would check it. But I wanted to know now, being, in a way, thrilled by a family scandal of sorts. I realised that seeing the place now wouldn't tell me what it was like then, what is was like for Ann, how she felt (or how husband Thomas or son Fred felt). But I was inquisitive, nosy. I wanted this story to fit neatly with the story of abandoned children and emigration, a proper nineteenth-century melodrama, a personal version of Wilkie Collins's fictional *Woman in White*, but in this instance the woman did exist and she really was mad. And she was related to me.

The traces of the former Banstead lunatic asylum now lie under High Down prison for category A prisoners. I had never entered a prison before so welcomed the offer to visit the place. Although the cemetery was, a governor advised, no longer within the boundary of the prison estate, it had not been built over and was now part of the farm in nearby Fairlawn Road. Staff would be happy to show me around.

The mantle of the former main building stood preserved between the two prisons surrounded by upright fencing. The perimeter wall also remained: high brick walls still delineating a separation from the everyday world. Some of the old trees planted when the asylum was erected still stood overlooking the visitors' car park, although the nineteenth-century walnut tree avenue had had to be removed on security grounds, I was told. In some ways, High Down prison was a state-of-the-art institution. All was modern: clean walls, toilets in cells, no smell of urine, high tech listening devices in the walls. 'You could have a conversation with them,' an officer joked, 'they can hear what you say.'

Inside the reception area was a brass plaque removed from the former buildings listing the names of the building committee for the asylum who oversaw the development of the site in 1877. It now kept watch over the X-ray machine and security barrier, which I had been more used to seeing at airports. In a governor's office was a copy of Henry Mayhew's writing on nineteenth-century prisons—a book, he said, that prison officers in London used to be recommended to read. 'C' had spent time in his early career in Wandsworth, an old-style prison renowned for its brutal regime. During maintenance work one day he had discovered in the loft a huge tank made of slate with pipes leading all over the prison and to the cells. All cells, he had realised, had been designed to have running water. At some stage this basic sanitation had been withdrawn. 'The Victorians weren't all bad were they?' he asked without expecting a reply.

The staff in the works department were exceptionally helpful and reminded me of similar men I have met throughout my life. I thought of the men I had worked with in local government who'd been previously based at County Hall shaking their heads at the fate of the GLC building, telling me about the strong walls and, with wry pleasure, the immense difficulty the Japanese hoteliers would have physically dismantling this beacon of local democracy. I also recalled those I had met in my childhood when my father used to trail me through the London Electricity Board workshops meeting men who were good with their hands, making things, sorting gadgets and machines, possessing the skills he did not have. Such men have their own stories of buildings and their own sense of the past that they are eager to convey. I don't expect anyone had ever asked the works department staff before about what they knew about the previous building on which the new prison was built. The unusual sense of history that builders and maintenance engineers possess is often ignored because they aren't 'professional historians', but these are the people who know about skill in building, who understand what asylum architects were attempting to do with their careful selection of trees and avenues. They read the landscape in different ways, recognising the extent of the underpinning, the depth of the walls, the extensive sewerage system underground. A different sort of history.

They had got out all the maps and plans they possessed so I could see where the cemetery was, made me a mug of tea, and left me to my own devices. As I suspected, the plans were in no particular order nor condition. I unrolled them trying to make sense of a place I did not know. Working through the maps in the stockroom I was distracted only by the sound of fierce and constant barking. There were, I was later told, 26 dog handlers and two different types of dogs: Alsatians which tore your limbs off and Labradors which passively sniffed you for drugs. If you weren't clean the dog would stand down beside you and didn't move. The same dogs couldn't do both tasks…

The plans did indeed tell me something. The present function of the building, as a site of removal from the everyday, was not new. Stretching away from the site would have been common land and beyond that a long track leading to Belmont station. Up the road was now the Royal Marsden hospital, but on the prison site there had been three hospitals/asylums: Down View, Freedown and Banstead. Since the nineteenth century this part of Surrey had existed as a place of removal. Nowadays it enclosed prisoners; one hundred years ago it had been asylum inmates, but both in their own way removed to the margins of the world and hidden from sight.

The huge grounds had also contained a cemetery on the north-east perimeter abutting its own gas works. There would also have been farm and outlying buildings, the pig keeper's and dairyman's cottages, the governor told me. The asylum had been self-sufficient in life as in death, and as late as the Ordnance Survey map of 1975 it had been functioning as a hospital. This had been a model insti-tution. Symmetry defined it: female wards on the north, male on the south. Ann would have spent her last days with particular women: prostitutes, female prisoners from Millbank, deranged tailoresses and former domestic servants. There would have been scant opportunity for quiet reflection here. Entry through a long drive and lodge ensured that inmates and visitors passed either the church or the mortuary. In front of the wards, built as a series of extensions to the main building, were precise lawns with 45-degree angles and trees. The female inmates, like my great-grandmother, might have seen lawns and flowerbeds; they might also have seen the mortuary.

None of the old buildings nor their layout had been kept by the High Down prison. The plans drawn up in 1988 indicated the foundations of the old asylum and almost deliberately cut across the site at an angle. Now, imitating the former asylum arrangements, there was a chapel. There were also well-kept lawns and well-maintained finicky flower beds with annuals—not easy maintenance shrubs—and a radial system of cells much like Jeremy Bentham had pioneered some 170 years before with his panopticon design. But the cemetery was not there inside the prison grounds.

'Size six?' said 'E' looking at my feet. I nodded with surprise. 'Years of experience,' he said, 'though prison officers tend to be size 12. I'm afraid I've not got small wellies.' I clomped with difficulty through the mud in oversize boots following a governor outside the wall alongside the suburban cottages and back into the former site that was a farmyard with dilapidated buildings. Now it was a stable and riding school, and there were horses stabled where once there had been a dairy for the asylum. The prison service had declared this part of the site surplus to requirements and had sold it to the farmer with the proviso that the cemetery should be maintained. But now most traces of these former good intentions had gone and even the headstones were almost non existent.

Documents had been burned by the current occupant, I was told, and only three or four stones remained visible and horses grazed on the cemetery land. The perimeter was not of fence nor hedging but a tall brick wall, as once was customary enclosing cemeteries in stately homes. One grave was clearly identifiable as a First World War military grave—white and rounded at the top—that of a military man, a young sapper in 1917; the other remains were of toppled early twentieth-century graves, fitting metaphors for the Edwardian fallen. Underneath the rough grass were, I was told, undisturbed graves and bodies. 'Are you sure she was here?' asked the governor. As it started to shower, I showed him the certificate to confirm I was right, 'But I didn't expect to find her, don't worry.'

I had never thought a gravestone with an inscription would have been there though I had wanted it to be. Who would have wanted it to survive? Surely not her husband nor son who had eradicated her existence from family stories. Nor would the authorities have wanted to identify so publicly someone with such an ignominious

end. If the census returns identified inmates merely by letters
why should a permanent stone
monument betray their final
resting place? Institutional
silence had been maintained
through an absence of physical
commemoration. As the
logbook had described Ann's
condition,'No idea of time or
place. Memory a blank.' In life
as in death: no place, no trace,
no memory.

26  Stanley Kean on a windowsill

## Not talking about Charlie

As a child I thought that at least
I knew who were the offspring of Ada and Charles Kean. There
was one son Stanley, my father. I grew up assuming that 'only' children were a feature of the recent Kean family. Whereas Mum had
three sisters and one brother, Dad, I had thought, was like me, an
only child. Stan's stories of his childhood had been solitary stories
of one child and two parents. There was no vocalised memory of
a brother, stories of games played together, larks shared, jokes played.

It wasn't until after Ada and Charles had died and Stan himself
was elderly and in ill health that the existence of a brother was
revealed. But it was clear that decades on from his brother's death
this was a topic that Stan either could not, or would not, discuss.
Indeed it wasn't until several years after my father's death that I even
found a photographic image of the dead brother, that had been kept
by his mother. While moving my mother's effects from her flat into
a residential home (while she lay with a broken leg in hospital) I
came across a piece of golden, if not gold, jewellery in a trinket
box, that had belonged to Ada. On either side of a locket were small
pictures of the faces of two boys.

On one side was an image I had seen in a larger form of a sad
boy in a too large overcoat sitting on a windowsill. I had certainly
found the photograph intriguing. This was a young Stan, my father,

27   Charlie Kean

and certainly the likeness was there: the slightly hesitant look, the long body and awkwardly-placed hands. There seem to be no external rationale for the image. This was neither a day out nor apparently an attempt to play with gadgets, nor different notions of photography as Stan had done with his interior images. Since Stan's birthday—a possible moment in which to freeze the passage of time on film—was in flaming June why was he being photographed in decidedly unflaming weather, pensive and sitting on the windowsill? The plants looked none-too-healthy, but perhaps were placed there to suggest a health and vigour lacking in this pale little boy. Was it that they, like him, were struggling to thrive? Stan had had no serious childhood illnesses, Mum said, so perhaps the pallor was more psychological than physical. Or was it an image of a now solitary child taken as a precaution, a protection against his own possible demise once his brother had died?

Stan's face, taken from this larger photograph, was on one side of the locket. The 'new' boy on the necklace was Charlie, an older brother, someone who had ceased to exist in Stan's stories. He was smiling and sporting a foppish cravat and an Eton-style collar. The jewellery confirmed the existence of two sons, not just the one. While Charlie was surely there in the memory of Stan, the surviving son, he had refrained from passing on stories of his brother or their relationship to his daughter. Mum confirmed that there indeed had been a brother, who, she had been told, had died when he was 16 and who was a 'cripple'. He had been made a cripple, so the story went, by his mother Ada who had unwittingly given him some medicine (mistaking it for another with a similar name) and he had become ill. Because he could not walk, Charlie had had to be wheeled around in 'an old fashioned pram that stuck out in the front'. And that was almost the extent of her knowledge.

## Days out—personal and public stories

I had, though, remembered my father's stories of the cripples parlour which his mother Ada had run from a Methodist Hall in Hackney Wick. Her working-class philanthropy was portrayed as a tale of altruism and practical Christianity. Certainly the Clapton Primitive Methodist Mission in Chatsworth Road, of which she and Charles were members, thrived on activity in the local community. Under the aegis of the local Minister Reverend Ellwood, free meals were provided for hungry and 'neglected' children, dinners for destitute families, distribution of clothing, Christmas parties for poor children and, following the tradition of philanthropists in East London, days out at the seaside or Epping Forest for children who, as an annual report of the Mission declared, 'otherwise would not have had a single day during the year out of London.'[10] The apparently beneficial effects of plants and days out in nearby Epping Forest were well publicised. Thus an image from *The Record of the Tower Hamlets Mission* showed a respectable young woman embodying the apparent benefits of rural Christianity proffering fruit and a decidedly pathetic fern to a sick little boy.[11] The accompanying article praised the work of the mission's forest cottage home in Essex: 'To see these children gambolling like lambs, and playing among the great oaks of the forest, you would never imagine they came from the squalid homes of our East End slums.'[12]

However, this is not just a story compiled from the Methodist reports in the Hackney archives. There was also a particular and individual tale of good works and standing up for 'those less fortunate than ourselves'. This story was repeated by Stan during both my childhood and adulthood enough times for me to recall the essentials of the narrative quite clearly. There was to be a visit to the seaside (or countryside) that Ada was organising for the poor cripple children of East London. All were looking forward to this day out including a severely-ill little boy, who had never seen cows nor the countryside. The other organisers did not want to take him because of his condition but Ada stood firm and said he had to go, and so he did. Two weeks after the little chap died—but for the first (and last) time in his life he had seen the trees (or, in some tellings of the story, the seaside).[13] The running of the cripples parlour, however, was never told as a familial tale, of Ada providing a service for her own older son, as well as others, for this would have necessitated revealing the existence of Charlie and that particular, personal, story could not be told.

The little boy in this story probably wasn't Charlie though in some senses he might have been. Charlie was a boy who, though he probably had seen the sea, or what passed for it at muddy Southend, had not lived long enough to see very much of it. He had not lived long enough to see many trees either for although the Kean family liked outings these were restricted to local venues such as Victoria Park, or the East Enders' favourite, Epping Forest. These few miles were the physical boundaries of their leisure activity and one that would never be breached by the prematurely-dead Charlie. Day trips would continue after Charlie's death but, of course, without the older son.

Another photograph I discovered seemed to illustrate a doleful party at the same cripples parlour. On the left was the local Primitive Methodist Minister Reverend Ellwood, who I recognised from family photos—he always popped round, I was later told, when the family was about to eat. Here he was sitting, holding a little boy with callipers. On the right another worthy, possibly a local alderman to judge by his fur (but lack of mayoral chain) was holding a boy on crutches. Surrounded by children, there in the front row of chairs was Ada looking solemnly ahead while two boys held her arms. This was not a happy event. Christmas seemed to have gone: but there was neither tree nor presents, just the sad remnants of paper chains. The taking of the photo was no cause for smiles but concentration. And if Charlie was indeed in this group photo he looked no happier than the rest.

The event and its commemoration in a staged, professional photograph suggested that being crippled in Hackney was not a unique event. In this image alone children are standing, with their accompaniments of crutches or walking sticks, at the side, providing a framework for the other sedentary children. What is crippling the

*28* The 'Cripples' parlour' (sic)

rest is not immediately visible in this image. But if children so designated could be photographed together and in the company of a
local dignitary, why couldn't one of them, Charlie, be discussed
within his brother's family? Both his life and his death were denied
in conversation: his memory had not merely faded like his physical image on the necklace but his existence had been obliterated
from stories passed from one generation to the next.

In the absence of further material and lack of a death notice in
the local *Hackney Gazette* it seemed that Charlie's death certificate
would need to be obtained to give further information. Using Mum's
clue that she knew he had died when he was 16 and knowing the
date of his parents' marriage it was relatively easy to read through
the registers for 1916 and find his name. But to locate a Charlie in
Hackney or Bethnal Green was elusive. The only dead 16-year-old
Charles Kean in 1916 was registered in Wayland, Norfolk, way
beyond the borders of the Keans' geographical experience. Norfolk
did not fit into their East London world. They were not the children of agricultural labourers, who had worked and then abandoned
the land for the city. Ada and Charles and their parents and grandparents before them had passed their whole lives in Bow, Bethnal
Green or Spitalfields. But this was the only Charles who fitted and
this was indeed 'my' Charlie, son of Charles, a wood carver of Pedro
Street, as the certificate confirmed. He had been certified dead on

25 April 1916 by the medical superintendent of the Guillcross—
or was it Guiltcross?—Institution in Kenninghall, and the cause of
death was simple: epilepsy.

As the twentieth century turned into the twenty-first we weren't
used to going to Norfolk for days out. For bleakness, Suffolk was
better; for neglected faded resorts, Essex was the best. But this time
it was different: we'd been to see Henrietta, a former battery hen
who had been rescued and 'adopted' as my birthday present. If we
didn't go and see her in October, before the winter set in and the
Hillside Animal Sanctuary closed, then we would need to leave it
for another year. So it was we ended up on a late October afternoon driving away from Norwich towards Kenninghall, stopping,
as we often do in our quests, at the church and its graveyard. The
son of Primitive Methodists was unlikely to have been buried here
and our search confirmed this; certainly no Kean appeared on the
headstone. This was an eerie town even for a Sunday at dusk: the
pub was boarded up and there was no one to ask about old schools
or institutions. The village school was new; the only immediate sign
of gainful employment was at the Goldenlay transport depot that
might have transported poor Henrietta's eggs while she was impris-
oned. But there was no sign of an institution, no traces of where
Charlie spent his last days.

The archivist in the Norfolk Record Office was very helpful in
a negative way. No records existed of the institution, but they did
have a smidgen of information from *Kelly's Norfolk Directory*. They
sent me the relevant local page: Guiltcross had not been a model
institution for crippled children. This former workhouse had been
opened in 1904, some twelve years before Charlie died there, as The
Eastern Counties Inebriate Reformatory.

**The effects of demon alcohol?**

Both my parents and paternal grandparents, Ada and Charles, had
been teetotallers, with the exception, as I had mentioned, of Stone's
ginger wine at Christmas. When Charles, my grandfather, the wood
carver and father of Charlie, preached in Hackney's Chatsworth
market for the Primitive Methodists he preached against the
demon drink. One of the few of his books I knowingly possess is

*The Tricks of Trade: Adulterations of Food and Physic with directions for their detection and counteraction.*[14] The section on alcoholic drinks is crossed with pencil markings to emphasise points: gypsum is added to port, lead added to wine. This he would use in his sermons. His *Cruden's Concordance* also carried pencil marks on the frontispiece in capital letters: DRINK. LEV 10–9. This is a reminder of the verse from Leviticus listed in the concordance under drink: 'Do not drink wine nor strong drink, thou, nor thy sons with thee, when ye go into the tabernacle of the congregation, lest ye die.' Charles Kean's abhorrence of drink was both personal and public. Yet this annotated preaching was unlikely to have been a personal railing against his own son, Charlie, a mere child. There might, however, be another explanation for the turn against alcohol. For in the early 1900s an epileptic condition was popularly, and scientifically, regarded as a result of feeble-mindedness, idiocy—or alcoholism.

Feeble-mindedness, as the association specifically established to consider the welfare of those so designated declared, would lead to 'vice, misery, degradation of our race'. If such children, an estimated 42,000 in 1901, were left to their own devices this degradation would grow and lead to increases in crime.[15] Feeble-mindedness and epilepsy went hand in hand. Parliament had determined that if children were intelligent and had fits at less than monthly intervals then they should attend normal schools.[16] However those suffering more frequent attacks were to be educated in semi-rural residential schools around London—but it was not until 1914 that local authorities were obliged to provide such schools.[17]

The London County Council, which was responsible for the education of children in London, was thought to have progressive views on the education of children with disabilities. In 1908, when Charlie would have been eight, a meeting of the special schools sub-committee commended the work of the Lingfield Epileptic Colony run by the Christian Service Union in Surrey, while declaring that 'more than half the children appear to be mentally defective'.[18] It also reviewed the work of the Chalfont Colony, also in Surrey, which catered for epileptic boys from 14 years to train them in useful work. But five years later little progress had been made on increasing the number of places available for London children.

While the government was procrastinating over a bill to require local authorities to provide education for 'mentally defective children' who were 'educable' the LCC was deliberating over the resources needed for the epileptic children currently within its purview.[19] Both the Chalfont and Lingfield colonies had already reached the quota of children agreed by the LCC committee. Only 73 children from across the entire London region would be permitted to attend these schools and in school holidays would be boarded out with foster parents, thereby removing them from the apparently detrimental environment of both the London area and their own parents. Yet on the LCC's own admission, 300 educable epileptic children requiring residential education were out of school since the facilities to educate them did not exist. The cost of a place in a residential school would be a prohibitive £46 per annum per child: the government grant amounted to a mere £4 4s—an unbridgeable gap of over £40.[20] Although children would later be sent to Soss Moss residential school in Cheshire the fact remained that only 73 children out of the 300-plus would receive an education courtesy of the LCC.[21]

None of these institutions were in Norfolk, but Charlie, my epileptic uncle, was and I did not know how. There appeared to be suitable schools in Hackney both near London Fields and later Pedro Street where the Keans subsequently lived, down by the marshes. The 'mentally defective' could have gone to Berger Road or Lamb Lane or Windsor Road off Hackney Wick, and the 'physically defective' to College Lane in Homerton, near where Ada ran her cripples parlour. But, as the council report enumerating these schools also noted, 'Nothing adequate, however can be done to meet the needs of this small but neglected section of the afflicted children until further accommodation has been provided whether by the Council or by voluntary agency.'[22]

Charlie seems to have been one of the children who had not been found a place in a local school. He does not appear in the extant records of the local schools kept centrally in the London Metropolitan Archives. His brother Stan walked up the road to the triple-decker London School Board building, Millfields, as I would also do years later, but Charlie did not. As Mum and the LCC records confirmed, children with disabilities didn't go to school in 'those days' even though the condition which affected Charlie had been recognised some 40 years previously as warranting special provision. The National Hospital for the Relief and Cure of the Paralysed and Epileptic, opened in June 1860 with day rooms, was established to give relief to those 'disqualified for the duties of life' through such conditions, but Charlie had received no such professional medical help at the end of his short life close to his home.[23] Friendly Society or private insurance such as the HSA, to which Ada and Charles certainly subscribed later in life, may well have been a source of support for these Liberal supporters bringing up their son, as the local education authority clearly was not. However, as 'V', an academic specialising in the poor law, suggested to me, Charlie might have been removed to the Norfolk institution under the recommendation of a religious minister; it might have been seen as a way of helping the boy, of giving him a better chance.

In the early 1900s it was uncontroversial to suggest that epilepsy was mainly caused by heredity. Although it could be caught through infectious fevers such as scarlet fever or whooping cough, the main cause it was commonly believed was the influence of alcohol or tuberculosis in earlier generations.[24] Both of Ada's paternal grandparents had certainly died of the poverty disease of TB, or, as their death certificates expressed it, Phthisis.[25] Those who worked in cramped and ill-ventilated workshops inhaling dust or vapours, such as those employed in the wood trade, were amongst the high risk groups.[26] Workers in wood, like Ada's husband, father and grandfather, were particularly vulnerable. In the records of the union of cabinet makers, chair makers and wood carvers, kept in the library of the Bishopsgate Institute, the monthly accounts of payments for death by Phthisis bear testimony to the prevalence of the disease locally in the later nineteenth century.[27] Charlie's great-grandfather on his father's side, William Keen, the hearth rug maker, had also died, according to the death certificate, of a disease of the lungs, bronchitis, which was frequently used as an alternative word for consumption. TB was both a word and a disease to be avoided and one which was widely regarded as hereditary.[28]

Would either Ada or Charles have known the causes of the death of their grandparents who had died even before they were born? Although much closer to their antecedents in time than I, they would not have had the same access to the records which exist today—

even if they had wanted to look for them. Unless these were families in which stories were passed down orally they might have known less about such unsavoury matters than their own grand-daughter. However they would have known about the life experiences of their own parents and, of course, of their own lifestyle. They would have known about the alcohol consumption around them as children and young adults and indeed their own practices. I remember a story that Charles, Charlie's father, had broken from his family because they ran a pub and he would have nothing to do with them. I knew too from the marriage certificate that Ada and Charles did not marry in a Methodist church but in the established church, at St Mark's in Bow. Conversion came after the marriage, and by the time their second child, Stan, was born, in 1906, their home was both a Methodist one and a Primitive one at that. Sharing the general Methodist predilection for good works and a puritanical lifestyle, the Primitive Methodists were distinctive in their total rejection and abhorrence of alcoholic beverages.[29] Although London was no hotbed of religious sentiment, Methodism did grow in the city in the last decades of the 1800s, and the Primitive Methodists increased the most amongst the different branches of Methodism. The London Mission, established in East London, 1885—of which Ada and Charles were members for at least some time in their grew by 1905 to a membership of over 7,000, more than a quarter of the Metropolitan total.[30]

Was the break with a real—or imagined—alcoholic past and the embracing of teetotal Primitive Methodism enacted after Charlie became ill? Certainly Methodists emphasised the value of preaching, and religious conversion, valuing to this end the hymn books of Moody and Sankey rather than simply the Methodist hymn book.[31] Sankey, the American singer, had taken Britain by storm in the late nineteenth century—on his farewell tour in 1900 about 20,000 Londoners had tried to hear him sing in Exeter Hall.[32] The singer's sentiments were those which also gave a framework to the lives of Ada and Charles, and to their surviving son, in their songs of Protestant hard work:

Hark the voice of Jesus crying
'Who will go and work today?

Fields are white and harvest waiting,
Who will bear the sheaves away?'

or:

Work for the night is coming!
Work through the morning hours;
Work while the dew is sparkling,
Work 'mid springing flowers,
Work when the day grows brighter
Work in the glowing sun;
Work for the night is coming
When man's work is done.[33]

As I look through the compilations of the songs Charles performed
that I have now inherited I realise how well I (an atheist) know many
of these hymns. I had previously read some other editions sitting in
the sedate upper reading room of the Bodleian library in Oxford. I
found I had no need to sight-read the scores; unconsciously my scan-
ning unlocked forgotten tunes and I realised I knew the words:

Stand up! Stand up for Jesus!
Ye soldiers of the cross
Life high his royal banner
It must not suffer loss

or:

Jesus loves me! This I know
For the Bible tells me so

I remembered the songs played by Charles on his harmonium
indoors and I remembered them too from church revivalist meetings. In some respects words featured strongly in the household of
Ada and Charles: open air works to the 'churchless masses', outdoor
services even in winter, delivering knowledge of the Bible;[34] but
in other matters—like the shameful illness of their first son—there
was silence.

29 Souvenirs from Southend

Mum, now my only human source, did not know Charlie was epileptic: 'I never heard that', she remarked. All she knew, she now said, was that Charlie couldn't be left alone in a room on his own because of the gas. The idea that a crippled child, who had to be transported around the streets of Hackney in a pram, could rise up out of his bed and switch on the gas light, minus the flame, and thus do himself mortal harm seemed a nicer story than the one I was suggesting. On a subsequent questioning her story changed: the gas was cooker gas which Charlie had smelled—because he was always at home—and had turned off thereby saving the family from disaster and proving that, although he was a cripple, he wasn't daft.

I did at least now have an explanation of sorts of why Charlie was never discussed nor mentioned and why Stan, my father and Charlie's brother, steered himself with equanimity towards the halt and the lame, the 'talking books for the blind', the infirm and dysfunctional (while Mum shied away fastidiously). I now remembered the time in Margate on holiday when seeing sick children in their beds outside the Sea Bathing hospital soaking up the sun he had rushed to the nearest corner shop and bought every child a bag of large pink squidgy sweets. An extravagant act, I remember thinking, for a family I knew to have no money. But Stan had been born into an environment of sickness and to this he had, no doubt, returned seeing the children in their beds in the sun.

**Who is remembered in a souvenir?**

Perhaps I now also had an explanation of sorts for the ornaments which Stan had not thrown away when his own parents had died. When Ada had died in the 1960s, Stan had kept some of her ornaments which were added to an earlier collection. Stan and Winifred had been given some family heirlooms as part of a wedding present, including swirly marbly little pots. Ada had told Winifred that Stan would tell her the stories behind these souvenirs. But, Mum sighed, he never did. Was this because he did not know the stories or the opposite? Did he know very well the circumstances of the acquisitions and declined to discuss them?

And now I have these ornaments, antiques of a sort. There is a little mug of Southend with a robin, made in Germany. There are little china shoes with a faded gold border from Southend, also made in Germany, and a little brown jug with gold lettering, again made in Germany, and bought in Southend. Before the Great War, souvenirs like this, my colleague 'M' tells me, were commonly made in Germany, a particular trade ended by military conflict. By the time the war was over and British souvenirs were being made in Britain, Charlie would have died, and Stan would probably be too old to buy such items for his Mum. These souvenirs, I suspect, date from the time when the Kean family consisted of a mother and father and two boys. All the souvenirs were utterly useless: the mugs were too small for tea—or even flowers. The shoes were too tiny to take indoor plants. These were miniatures which were entirely anti-utilitarian, and were just what they said they were—gifts from Southend bought to remember certain things. With souvenirs, we do not remember who made them, for the maker is unknown, but we remember the 'secondhand' experience of the purchaser and ultimate possessor.[35] Who did the remembering here? If this was a present from Charlie (or Stan?) did Ada remember the child who was no longer with her? Did she remember days out by the Essex mudflats at Southend with the cripples' parlour? Did the child and the parent alike remember the shared experience? Did it then also become a memory for her surviving son, Stan, of both his brother and mother—of times when the whole family was alive? As Susan Pearce has reminded us, souvenirs discredit the present by vaunting the past, but it is an intensely individual past: 'no one is interested in other people's souvenirs'. They have the effect of making public events—possibly group outings in this case or grand themes of war in other examples of ephemera—private.[36]

Thinking about these souvenirs I speculate that Stan was more emotionally involved in aspects of Charlie's death and the relationship with his brother than he vocally indicated.[37] He was not simply the survivor who inherited earlier hoarded pieces through the lack of siblings. Stan commonly referred to ornaments as dust collectors although had scant skills in this since he had no experience of cleaning and had little regard for the idea of cleanliness being next to godliness. These were not kept for decoration but as items valued, at least by him.

Stan could not help being tied into the history of his brother— the Janus-like images on his mother's necklace said as much: his brother on the front (or back); Stan on the windowsill, forlorn, on the back (or front). There were many other pictures of Stan his mother could have chosen to place in her locket: I had seen them in the black plastic bag of jumbled photos. These other images were less wistful, less unhappy, but she did not choose one of these happier photographs to remind her of Stan. There was no balancing image of Charlie similarly posed on a windowsill. But it may have been the case that by the time the photo was taken of Stan he was indeed an 'only' child, the surviving son, who the parents anxiously wished to preserve more extensively on film than they had done with his brother.

Stan would write to Winifred during their courtship:

> I am unfortunately the only son—coupled with this is the fact that owing to my brother—who died when he was 16 years old—a cripple—he never walked a single step—when he passed over—the affection and care and (how can I put it) minute attention that had been at his beck and call was transferred to me in such a manner as to be almost an obsession.[38]

At one time Stan could write of this to his future wife as a partial explanation of his parents' relationship with him. But of the child who could not go to school, who died early, who died of epilepsy, he could not speak to the next generation of the Keans in his own words. Even though Charlie, my father's brother, was of a generation to be remembered, there was no memory perpetuated by my father to his own child because it was too difficult, too painful to remember. A couple of photos, a possible souvenir, a statement on a death certificate are the mere vestiges of Charles's existence.

Ann Mankelow and Charlie Kean did not know each other: it would not have been possible. They lived in different places, different parts of the metropolis. Even their dates of birth and death were incongruous: Ann had died well before Charlie's birth. But a connection of sorts was made through their respective, successive families, the Keans and the Mankelows, brought together through the marriage of my parents. The silence surrounding their very existence was similar: the lives of both Charlie and Ann were eradicated from spoken family stories. And such silence would govern much of the lives of the descendants of Ann and Thomas Mankelow and Ada and Charles Kean.

# 6

# ARCHIVAL STORIES AND SILENCE

## FREDERICK MANKELOW AND MARY DAVIES

The silence surrounding Ann Mankelow who had ended her days in the lunatic asylum was transmitted in different ways to her son Fred, my maternal grandfather. Within his marriage to Mary Davies he was, I've been told, 'the quiet one'. His father's own carrier business in Chelsea had only lasted a few years: by 1886 the premises in Beaufort Street were being used by the Hyde Park cab company. Fred would speak to his children of his own childhood experience driving around London in his father's cart delivering parcels as an explanation for his good knowledge of the metropolis in which he lived.[1] Fred had also told his children that his father had come from Hadlow in Kent, but not much else of his early life, or perhaps more accurately no details that his surviving children have remembered or have wanted to pass on.

Although he only died in the 1930s this death seemed, in certain senses, to have taken place much earlier. Both Fred and Mary died years before I was born. There are scant material traces of this man and his wife in the homes of his descendants—my mother did not even possess a photograph of her own parents to show me as a child. It is true that I live near to Homerton the area of Hackney in which Fred and Mary lived most of their married lives. I know the streets I have read about in the archive; I pass their former 'tied cottage' driving to the Blackwell tunnel slip road. However, the absence of *personal* material, or even a wealth of anecdote and reminiscence that crosses the gap of a mere 70 years, makes this seem like writing about people who are very distant, very old, very other.

They appear to me almost as inhabiting the same distant past as their ancestors William and Mary Mankelow in early nineteenth-century Hadlow or Edward Eicke in early nineteenth-century Shropshire. When my Aunt Lily, their youngest child, says her parents

'were always old' and that even her older sister Ivy thought that
their parents lived in the nineteenth century it seems to reflect the
absence of extant contemporary material in their descendants' lives.
Reflecting upon this, I realise that as a child I was told virtually
nothing about these dead grandparents. I knew they had both died
before my parents had married; I recalled clearly the story of Mary
being obliged to comb her father Tom's hair. But that was about it.
Silence seemed to characterise much of Mary and Fred's relationship—at least according to their children.

## Maritime stories

My aunt Lily, however, has recently told me about Fred's job before
his marriage as 'fifth marine engineer for P&O' since she remembered the trunk with his name and the company written on it.
Perhaps 'about' is too strong; for all she knew was what she remembered seeing on the trunk—and that he gave up the job, she said,
through seasickness. As a lifelong sufferer I was not entirely
convinced by this explanation. If you have this malady it is certainly
both debilitating and something you do not necessarily overcome
despite years of travel; even days out on Italian pleasure boats or
boating trips to Scottish islands, as I have experienced, are to be
avoided. To embark upon such a career sounded foolish, if he was
indeed a sufferer.

At first I could not see the attractions of such a job although 'J',
a maritime historian, tried to convince me otherwise. But she writes
about stewardesses on 1930s liners, gay sailors and women pirates;
her tales of ships as adventure and the height of modernity failed
to persuade me about sailing in the 1890s, although I conscientiously
followed up her suggestions of archives and libraries to visit. Reading
for the first time books on ships, engineers' records and P&O history
in the National Maritime Museum I remembered the story of 'B',
the Mankelow descendant from another branch of the family with
whom I had discussed possible identities in Chelsea photographs
and a mutual interest in Benjamin Britten operas.[2] I had wanted
to make her photos fit my story of the carrier business in Chelsea
and 'B' had been hoping I would solve for her the mystery of Lucy
Jones the woman who visited her family in Hadlow arriving by

motor cycle from Portsmouth. And Lucy was, 'B' recalled, either married to, or the daughter of, a ship's engineer. Somewhere this must have lodged in my mind.

I had never visited the National Maritime Museum Archive in Greenwich before and on this January day, when snow was falling fast and the streets would soon be clogged with traffic, it seemed like a bad idea, especially since I had no expectation of finding anything to corroborate my aunt's snippet. But the first volume of the engineers' register I dipped into confirmed that F. J. Mankelow had indeed entered the workshops of P&O as a junior engineer on 21 May 1890 and had subsequently been placed on the vessel *Kaisar i Hind* (Empress of India).[3]

This was no ordinary vessel as a large cuttings file from the contemporary press established. Built in Greenock in 1878 it had been the P&O's 'largest, longest and fastest' ship to date.[4] As the *London and China Express* enthused, it was 'a veritable floating castle of enormous dimensions, but yet…riding the waters as gracefully as a yacht'.[5] It would make the fastest passage then on record from Bombay to Suez,[6] and, the P&O pocket book claimed, would provide the perfect 'ocean cure' for passengers suffering from ill health or nervous exhaustion brought about by 'over brain work'.[7] For passengers there were luxurious decorations: swinging oil lamps (rather than candles), coloured tiles, electric bells in the cabins to summon the staff, a smoking room with settees and the benefits of refrigeration—the first P&O ship to possess this.[8]

Below decks there was much need for skilled engineers. The 4,000-ton ship boasted two engines each of 700 hp, eight boilers and 24 furnaces which required a number of men to ensure they operated efficiently.[9] On the trip that Fred took on 25 July 1890 there had been five engineers and Fred was the most junior. There was even a specialist refrigerator mechanic, a winchman, boilerman and electrician—all experienced men who had worked on other ships. Fred was both the only newcomer—and the only Londoner. (There would have also been engine-room ratings recruited from East Africa or Bombay who acted as firemen and coal trimmers.)[10] There were, however, no Joneses nor men from Portsmouth in the *Kaisar i Hind* crew list with which I might make a direct familial connection to another part of the family—although, I confess, I couldn't but help look for them, still emotionally eager to tie up ends and complete stories, despite my intellectual cynicism. But the contemporary eulogies to this floating luxury did suggest a rationale for such employment. Being a marine engineer—even a junior one—on a luxury boat really was, I was starting to realise, a cut above being a boilerman. As Campbell McMurray has suggested, the status was comparatively elevated 'somewhat above that of the common sailors but not quite on a par with the navigating officers'.[11] Photographs in a book celebrating P&O's history contained not only images of the officers who considered themselves the elite of the merchant service but also separate images of engineers being photographed because of their work—and revelling in the high status it enjoyed.[12]

I had known from my study of labour history that engineers were seen as the 'locus classicus of labour aristocracy', that the Amalgamated Society of Engineers, or ASE, was considered 'the largest and wealthiest trade union in the world'.[13] I had known such men were defined as representatives of a new industrial—and political—age: 'the men of metal took the stage as the old craftsmen left it'.[14] Famous amongst their ranks were Tom Mann, the revolutionary socialist and organiser of new unionism and syndicalism, and John Burns, 'the man with the red flag' and first working-class man in the cabinet.[15] I had taught about the ASE, the politics of such men, but never quite seen it as a tangible, paid job—nor one which had any personal connection.

Apprenticeships and short courses provided the necessary training for marine engineers.[16] As a nineteenth-century textbook outlined, skills were needed in arithmetic, algebra, weights, pressure, volume and temperature to pass marine engineer exams. Quick thinking was also a prerequisite as the specimen exam papers suggested: 'Suppose your furnace crown came down, what would you do?' (Answer: put girders and staybolts on top to prevent further collapse.)[17] Practical skills combined with work experience were key to promotion.[18] Engineers worked on four-hour watches day and night to regulate and maintain the efficient sailing of ships in the P&O fleet.[19] The skills of this new age of power and energy were epitomised by the progress of the *Kaisar i Hind* cutting its speedy way through the Mediterranean. On his first journey Fred was away for two-and-a-half months sailing to Antwerp and back and thence to Gibraltar, Malta, Suez and Aden. By the time he left the ship on 16 October with his £7 wages for the trip he had seen more of the world than he would ever see again in his future life. By the age of 22 his travelling days were over.

## Dahn the plug 'ole

It could, of course, have been seasickness, vomiting the stipulated crew provisions with 'no spirits allowed', exacerbated by enclosure in the boiler room. But other factors might also have stopped Fred's adventure into the modern world. Less than two weeks after he had finished his first voyage, Fred was married to Mary Ellen Davies, then just 17 years old, in the Chelsea Register Office. Three months later on 23 January 1891 their first child, Sarah, was born. Baby Sarah would have been conceived before he signed up at the P&O workshops in May 1890. She was probably not named after the first abandoned partner of Frederick's father but after Mary's mother, the woman whose kiss had tasted of raspberries. Before Fred embarked on his first voyage in July, Mary would surely have known she was pregnant. But Fred did not stay away, jump ship or abandon her as his father had his first partner: he came back to Chelsea and to married life. This heroic, romantic 'explanation' is one possible story.

As 'J' reminds me there can be other, more mundane and less benign, stories which have little to do with loyalty or commitment. For at this time unemployment in engineering, shipbuilding, iron and steel ran at 26 per cent above the average for all industries.[20] The particulars on the crew list included details of the wages collected for the voyage and an explanation that the entire engineering complement were discharged.[21] For the only Londoner in this Scottish milieu it may have been even more difficult to get placed on another ship. Mary's pregnancy or not, the return to Chelsea then may not have been envisaged as permanent: there may have been the hope of further adventures, with the story of seasickness masking the failure to obtain employment.

And what stories are there of Sarah, the first unplanned child of the marriage? I remember Sarah as an elderly but sturdy woman—

we used to go to her house sometimes in the early 60s on a Saturday and—as she had a television and we did not—we'd watch the *Beverly Hillbillies* together. She had become a clippy during the 1914–18 war and had married her bus driver, Alf. She lived until she was nearly 80,[22] having worked as a dressmaker, and to augment her pension took in washing for the Leyton (amateur) football club in the Leabridge Road (which always seemed less prestigious somehow than if she had washed strips for the professional Leyton Orient...). When Sarah was three years old her maternal grandmother Ann was incarcerated in the lunatic asylum: this fact about his mother Fred kept quiet. And if Fred had known about the circumstances of his own parents' marriage he was also silent about this to his children.

Jointly with Mary another silence would be created about the circumstances of their own marriage. Both Mum and my aunt have said, 'You didn't ask things in those days,' frustrated that they didn't know more about their parents' former lives. But then, as now, children know that there are things they must not ask. Neither sister was particularly surprised when in their 80s they realised through checking the parental marriage certificate and ascertaining their dead sister Sarah's birthday that their parents 'had had to get married', as they explained it. Neither sister knew when their parents' wedding was—their anniversary was never celebrated when they were children. Was it because the date revealed circumstances their parents wanted hidden or was the very act of marriage something they would have preferred to forget? There was, though, a story, a subterfuge it would seem, about Sarah as a baby.

My mother born some 23 years later would obviously have not known her eldest sister as a baby, yet in this family not given to oral stories she did know a story about Sarah's very earliest days. Reputedly Sarah had been so tiny as an infant, that she had been washed in a jug. Here was a story to suggest a premature baby, a story to explain a sort of birth that probably never was, to suggest that a child was frail and ailing. But this sounds almost like the fictitious baby of music hall comedy, 'Your baby has gone dawn the plug 'hole... The poor likle fing was so skinny and fin he should ave bin washed in a jug...'[23] rather than an actually existing baby who physically thrived as an adult.

In the second chapter I first mentioned Mary, the daughter of Tom Davies and Sarah Eicke, who was obliged to comb her father's hair if she was in late. If the patriarchal act was designed to prevent morally transgressive behaviour it clearly had not worked—or was it, in fact, a punishment for her pregnancy? Had that been a story that was not just about her father but her distaste at the situation in which she had found *herself*, a connection between the combing of the hair, the shameful pregnancy, the early marriage? As a recent commentator has suggested, children who are sexually abused have a need to find someone close whom they can trust, which sometimes leads to a hasty marriage, often undertaken mainly to escape from the abusive home.[24] This was not a story, of course, about hair as I had thought as a child, but shame and disgust, a story which both was and wasn't told.[25] Neither the story of the jug washing nor the hair combing were *about* the ostensible narratives they told; but that they were told at all and were remembered by a daughter who says she knew little about her parents suggests a significance which belies the words themselves. As recent writers on trauma have suggested, 'speakers about trauma on some level prefer silence so as to protect themselves from the fear of being listened to, and of listening, to themselves'.[26]

The first few months of the marriage were passed in the same house, if not household, of Tom and Sarah, Mary's parents, in Chelsea.[27] Escape of sorts came in the Spring of 1891 when Fred, Mary and baby Sarah moved, not to one of the exotic places visited on Fred's travels but to Homerton in Hackney where Fred took up employment as an engineer and where he stayed for the rest of his working life.

## In and out of the workhouse

Some might call the attached image of elderly women a 'family photo' since the original had been amongst an album belonging to Fred. But this photo from Frederick's family album is not a comfortable image. Some of the elderly woman are smiling, engaging with the photographer, doing what is customary when confronted with a camera on a day out—smiling. But it disturbs me, this image of elderly women, in which some turn their faces away, and one places her head in her hands averting her gaze. Certainly it's sunny, so sunny there's a need for a parasol—but only to protect one woman who is dressed slightly differently from the rest[28]—and for the door to be covered with a curtain to protect it from the heat of the sun, but it's not a conventional family summer snap. For these women are not part of my family but inmates of the Hackney workhouse where Fred worked as deputy engineer from the spring of 1891 until his retirement in the 1930s. Photos of people in institutions, even the Hackney

30 Workhouse residents in the family album

workhouse of which there are examples in the Hackney archive, are rarely taken by those who are inmates.[29] Often the photographers are those keen to show the efficacy of the administration of bureaucratic arrangements and the people become mere adjuncts to such intentions.

This, however, wasn't an image of the quotidian; after all, photographs of everyday routine life do not usually find their way into a family album.[30] It probably is what it looks like—a day out. Owning a camera meant the ability to record events which were different, out of the ordinary, to later remember time away from the routine. The steps, Mum thought, knowing the workhouse as a child who had lived with her parents in the adjacent tied cottage, were not there in the Hackney workhouse. And she may have been right. For on 23 September 1921, 130 inmates of the workhouse were taken in motor charabancs for a half day outing to the beach.[31] This I surmise is a record of that—or a similar—day. It seems that Fred, the photographer, had wanted to conscientiously note down who was in the picture as he had recorded the names of the women, or rather their individual surnames only—all shared the prefix of 'granny'. Next to them he had appended dates, apparently their dates of birth indicating the alleged value of longevity, and had ensured that the right names would be read with the correct person:

> 'Granny Seney 1837
> Stockton 1837
> King 1830
> Sparks 1832
> Eldridge 1833
> In order from top left hand corner.'

In her study of Norfolk workhouses Anne Digby has suggested that generally the Norfolk guardians maintained a benign administration of indoor relief to old people; she illustrates her study with an image of four elderly women with bonnets taken in 1930 at Freebridge; but this is a different sort of image from that taken by Fred. In the Norfolk image the women are not named and they are not smiling.[32] I am not suggesting that the routine in twentieth-century Hackney was more benign because many of the women were smiling.[33] However, an image of an institution's inmates which names them is unusual. Perhaps Fred felt he needed to do this because the names were not well known to him: how often does one record the names of family or friends on the back of snaps since there is the assumption that these friends of one time will be remembered in another? This is probably not a photo taken for the women but of them and for himself. Perhaps it is to remember these women after their pending deaths, or is it the obsession with recording and noting which comes from being an engineer? This was both part of his daily, working life and separate from it.

Fred, this 'quiet man', who did not say much, can have a narrative written about him because of the documentation of employment, and a particular sort of employment. He was the first of my ancestors to be employed by the local state (and for most of his life) so there are materials about both his work and his provided housing that are relatively easy to access in the minute books of the Board of Guardians in the London Metropolitan Archives. From here it is possible to draw on material to create a blurring between personal beliefs and practices and broader histories of the politics of this particular workhouse. On 6 May 1891, a month after James Spink had resigned his position, Fred replaced him as an assistant engineer earning 25s. a week plus daily breakfast and dinner. He also received an annual allowance of £2 in lieu of beer, suggesting a temperance ethos within the Board of Guardians commensurate with their Liberal persuasions.[34] It also suggests, of course, that Fred himself was not a drinker. Had this marked him out as different from the Scottish engineers on the *Kaisar i Hind* with their reputation as hard drinkers? Within a year his wages had increased by 2s. a week[35] and by 1901 to a yearly salary of £85 16s.[36] But temperance was not the only feature of Radical Liberalism manifest in the Hackney Board of Guardians.

One of the Board of Guardians' members for the area around Chatsworth Road market,[37] where Frederick would bring up his young family (and Charles Kean would preach), was William Beurle, a leading national campaigner in the National Anti Vaccination League (another local activist was a resident of the house in Hackney I now occupy). Beurle, like other activists, objected to state interference in everyday life, legislation which was opposed as 'class legislation'.[38] Enacted under the aegis of the Poor Law the inoculation of children against smallpox had been made compulsory in 1853.[39] While working people's opposition to the Poor Law ensured hostility towards vaccination it was not until the 1870s that this perceived state intervention into people's lives—'we are becoming an over-legislated-for people'[40]—became the focus of considerable campaigning particularly by political radicals.[41]

William Beurle had been prosecuted several times in the 1880s for refusing to have his child vaccinated against smallpox. As he had told the court, this was 'from a natural fear of a probably evil result'. Magistrates, he argued, had heckled and bullied poor people not sufficiently educated to be able to plead their cause.[42] By 1889 the Hackney Board of Guardians had passed a motion to take no action against those not complying with the Vaccination Acts. William Beurle was amongst those voting for the motion.[43] In 1896 the Royal Commission had recommended abolition of the hated compulsion and the introduction of the category of conscientious objector. Within two years over 200,000 conscientious objectors nationally had registered, and although vaccination was still required

**Hackney Union.**

_No._**111**

VACCINATION OFFICER'S RECEIPT FOR STATUTORY
DECLARATION OF CONSCIENTIOUS OBJECTION UNDER THE
VACCINATION ACT, 1907.

**J acknowledge,** _that a Statutory Declaration purporting
to be witnessed by a Commissioner for Oaths, Justice of the Peace,
or other Officer authorised to receive a Statutory Declaration, that
the parent or other person having the custody of the Child,_

_Winifred Phœbe Mankelow_

_born on the_ _15_ _day of_ _Jany_

_has a conscientious belief that Vaccination would be prejudicial to the
health of the Child, has this day been delivered to me in accordance
with the Vaccination Act, 1907._

_Dated this_ _21_ _day of_ _2_ _19 14_

_H Jossaid_

_Vaccination Officer for the_

_South_ _District of the Hackney Union._

31   Certificate of exemption from compulsory vaccination

for a number of jobs, including teaching, and certain forms of housing and insurance, much of the argument had been won. Over a
quarter of children in the London area went unvaccinated, with no
recorded rise in the number of smallpox cases.[44]

This story seems not to be 'about' Fred, who was simply
employed by the Guardians, one of whom was William Beurle. (Fred
was also one of his constituents.) But a piece of paper possessed by
one of his daughters suggests a potentially different story, an elision
of the public and the personal. This is the 'Vaccination Officer's

receipt for statutory declaration of conscientious objection under the Vaccination Act 1907'. It declares that a month after his daughter Winifred's birth in January 1914 Fred had stated to the local vaccination officer his 'conscientious belief that vaccination would be prejudicial to the health of the child'. According to his daughter, my mother, in response to my interested questions, she had heard of no distant relatives or friends who had died of the vaccination, nor did he share the concerns of some vaccination opponents about experimentation on animals, which led to the vaccine's development and implementation.[45] However, although Winifred insisted that her father 'wasn't political' she knew nevertheless that 'he voted Liberal'. Certainly such a stance had not been unusual in later nineteenth-century London. As Susan Pennybacker has reminded us, within the first years of the London County Council when the Liberals held 71 seats, temperance advocates and Non-Conformist zealots far outweighed those espousing 'labour politics'.[46] The Liberal government of 1906 had made it easy to voice objection and Fred's stance would have been supported at work.[47] Yet it was also a personal decision: a small measure, perhaps, of taking control and resisting state interference. His youngest daughters bore no marks of the vaccine on their arms—and retained their exemption certificates throughout their lives as important pieces of documentation alongside state certificates of birth and old school reports.[48] Certainly his youngest daughter, Lily, refused to be vaccinated when serving in the WAAF (Women's Auxiliary Air Force) during the war, because she never had been, and out of some sort of loyalty to her dead father.

## A different photograph

I had not even seen a photo of this grandfather, Frederick Mankelow, until I was over 40 and in the house of a much older cousin, himself an amateur photographer who found it difficult to believe that I did not recognise the man that he had known well as a grandfather. Unlike the amateur image Fred had taken of the workhouse women, the photo I was shown was a composed studio picture. Fred was not wearing military uniform—both his age and employment in the workhouse gave him exemption from active service. This was Fred in his firefighter's uniform; it was also the

*32* Fred in firefighter's uniform

photo I would take with me to show to 'A' in Kent, the photo which linked me to a Mankelow history. Volunteer firemen, such as Fred, were needed in the Great War when the London brigade was under strength.[49] Fred was attached to the Homerton fire station; indeed the station itself was linked by alarm to the casual ward of the workhouse.[50] Forewarned about approaching zeppelins by phone (and apparently the acute hearing of the family dog) Fred was active at least in this aspect of the war. The Fire Brigade too may have reminded Fred of his earlier career at sea: many young men were sent into the merchant navy to enhance their chances of subsequent acceptance into the Brigade.[51] And certainly firefighters needed to study the nature of gas and electricity to do their job effectively.[52]

When the Metropolitan Hospital in Dalston held its annual carnivals, there would be Fred, his youngest daughter recalled, sitting with the local firemen on the fire engine. For this her memory must suffice for no images exist in the hospital archives now held at St Bartholomew's hospital in the City. Here I could read of donations acknowledged from the Hackney Board of Guardians, minutes of the whist drive and auction committee, details of the garden party committee, correspondence with the Chamber of Commerce and debates over insurance against inclement weather, but neither records of the carnival nor any photos.[53] Still, the photographic image he had chosen to have taken and the visual memory his youngest child had held for some 80 years helped suggest the importance Fred gave to his role outside his main employment.

## Another job of the new age

By the time of his retirement and death Fred had developed his expertise and had specialised as an electrical engineer, another job of the new post-war age, albeit undertaken in an institution the era of which was drawing to a close.[54] I had found Physics unfathomable at school so to sit in the Bodleian Science library reading the writings of electrical engineers was not a task I welcomed. Yet even to me, enthusiasm and vitality leapt off the page, the newness of things, adventure, discovery.[55] Science alongside self-education characterised publications such as the collection *Electrical Educator*, compiled by electrical engineer J. A. Fleming, both about technical data but also the history of electricity and accounts of famous engineers. Descriptions of house wiring and theories of alternating currents vyed for space with 'what we owe to the arc lighting period'. Certainly the impression projected was that electrical engineering was prestigious, educational and forward moving. As Fleming wrote after the general strike of 1926:[56]

> No general strike on the very largest scale could inflict a tithe of the damage which would result if the work of the electrical engineer during the last century were withdrawn or undone. The electric current is now our potent and obedient master...[57]

Nationally, university-educated electrical engineers had formed their own professional association and by the 1920s had around 12,000 members and their own distinctive premises on the Victoria Embankment.[58] Such a claim to authority and status was reflected locally in the debates of the Hackney Board of Guardians. When the chief engineer Frederick Bethell raised his concerns about parity with the master of the workhouse, the General Purposes Committee endorsed his proposals. As Mr Bethell had explained, 'the extent of his responsibility and the importance of the duties he has to perform are such that status should be advanced from that which has been previously recognised, when the Principal Engineer was little more than a working mechanic.' But by 1917 things had changed.[59] Drawing on arguments from the Departmental Committee on Engineering the workhouse General Purposes Committee agreed to give the engineer 'all the authority necessary for him to manage his important department', including personally presenting reports to the committee and interviewing his own staff.[60] Unsurprisingly requests for pay increases followed from both the chief engineer and his deputy Fred Mankelow. The chief engineer received pay parity with the master of the workhouse.[61] In lieu of a pay rise Fred Mankelow was permitted to move his family into the tied house recently vacated by the chief engineer due to the latter's 'domestic difficulties'.[62]

## Less than a week away from the workhouse

Thus in the spring of 1918 the Mankelow family moved into 62 Sidney Road,[63] adjacent to the railway line and alongside the 'cottage homes'—as the workhouse orphanage was known. Although Fred Mankelow's salary of £2 6s remained constant there would be free coals, gas and water, and electric lighting and even an internal telephone to connect the house to the workhouse.[64] The workhouse itself by then had been fitted with electric lighting—cheaper and more efficient than gas—and the electrical workers were employed in the workhouse at trade union rates.[65] An image of the sophisticated electrical installations in the power-house of the hospital that existed in the same site is held in the Hackney archives—donated to the collection by an engineer.[66] This was where Fred ended his employed days as the workhouse regime came to a close—and someone thought the machinery worth depicting visually, and certainly an engineer thought it deserved preserving.

In this way Mary and Fred Mankelow and their children came to live not in, but next to, the workhouse. In the pre-war years one is told that 'the poor were never more than a week away from the workhouse'. But what if the realisation of where one might 'fall' was closer than a week away, over the fence at the bottom of the garden? How would the physical presence of the workhouse affect Mary who did not work there (or indeed do any paid work) or the children? There is a story of Ivy, an older sister bathing—in the bathroom with hot running water—screaming at a man who espies her through the window as he escapes from the workhouse over the fence. There are stories too of parties, concerts and entertainments in the workhouse which the family attended, and of the girls eating 'big petit beurre biscuits not the small ones that you get nowadays'. These I had interpreted simply as personal stories of distinction from the inmates, of outsiders, separate and a tad superior to the rest. But this is not just a Mankelow tale. A similar story was recounted by the grand-daughter of the master of Erpingham workhouse in Norfolk: 'I remember Christmas days in the workhouse, some of the happiest of my life…sweets for the children, tobacco for the men and tea and a cap and apron for the old ladies. To me everyone seemed happy.'[67] Anne Digby has analysed this as a nostalgic account commenting on 'the naiveté of a child's perception'.[68] They are stories of the workhouse as a location of childhood leisure, that might be enjoyed by those who were not constrained within its walls and a knowingness, albeit on a child's subconscious level, that they were not like the residents.

Living next to the workhouse, Mary in her house with running hot water, internal phone and electricity—far superior accommodation to most of Homerton—seemed to develop a particular sense of propriety and distinction from her neighbours. And from this home she instilled into her four daughters[69]—as I suppose all women do—what it meant to be a woman. This, her youngest daughters remembered, included wearing gloves at all times out of the house even when going on errands to the corner shop; only eating chips in wrappers from the chip shop walking around the back garden where the vulgarity of it could not be seen, and no walking to the marshes down the street opposite where the rough children played who reputedly wore no knickers. But the transmission of such memories through Mary's children make it difficult to distinguish the different generations. In this snippet is it the mother or a daughter speaking, remembering a childhood story: 'you didn't go down Mabley Street because there was a red path at the end where they were always finding bodies'? On a summer evening Mary and Fred would stand by the front gate keeping an eye on their youngest daughters who would walk up and down the street from the post office to the corner 'sometimes as much as six times', my aunt recalls, in their pinafores—and gloves. There were no other children around—apart from those in the cottage homes, who were not allowed out in the evening. Such was Mary's own fastidiousness—

or was it by then that of her daughters?—that in due course she would daily peel oranges for her then adult girls who commuted into the City. She first removed the white pith and then replaced the segments neatly in the outer peel.

I do not know whether the workhouse move changed Mary's perceptions or merely reinforced earlier held opinions. For a woman who did not work outside the home, who did not engage in the good works of Ada in her nearby Cripples Parlour or Primitive Methodist Mission, there are no records in council archives. When Mary died a widow in her 70s she was living in Hackney with her two youngest and unmarried daughters. Her other three older, married offspring—Sarah, Fred and Ivy—also lived nearby. I do not know who of the five adult children cleared her belongings or her personal effects. But no ornaments or jewellery or treasured items seemed to remain with her surviving children except for a few coins of Maundy money. Lily has described her as an unaffectionate woman, and perhaps such a woman had been treated reciprocally by her children after her death. Certainly it is difficult to write of *her* life, as opposed to its influence on her daughters. The traces that exist of her married life—or before—exist only in the snippets her offspring recount and those which they have remembered—and chosen—to pass on.

## Speaking and not being heard?

I realise that I am also using what has stuck in my mind: the only story I remember being told about Mary when I was a child, of Mary apparently combing her father's hair. And it is this earlier know-ing, this childhood memory, which has provided a framework for other stories that I have only been told in recent years, when I have encouraged the recounting of my mother's own memories of her childhood. Here, as told by her daughter Winifred, was a new and strange story of Mary's own childhood in the nineteenth century:

Mary went blind as a child because boys at her school had put spiders down her neck. Then one day her mother Sarah dropped a needle on the floor while she was doing needlework and Mary said, 'Oh there it is'. And her mother said, 'Oh you can see again,' but

*33* Mary Mankelow at the seaside with three daughters and first grandson

Mary then went blind again and her mother said, 'I should never have said that. If it happens again I'll keep my mouth shut'.

Medically, a GP informs me, this narrative is possible. Hysterical blindness can exist. It's a form of hysterical conversion (more usually found in cases of young people becoming mute) resulting from a traumatic experience. And yes, theoretically it could be brought on by spiders, especially if you had a particular aversion to them. But in practice it is likely to be linked with sexual abuse: it indicates a withdrawal, an avoidance of the trauma, in this instance by the back of the brain effectively going on strike and refusing to see.

In the case of mother Sarah, though, it suggests a taking on of the blame, a personal responsibility for the blindness. If the daughter is deprived of sight, then the mother is deprived of language to express her feelings about this. Shoshana Felman and Dori Laub have argued that as traumatic events take place outside the parameters of normal reality, trauma as an event has no beginning, no ending, no before, no during and no after. Thus, trauma survivors cannot live with memories of the past but with an event which could not and did not proceed through to its completion. The trauma continues into the present and the survivor remains trapped. The only way of undoing such entrapment is to construct a narrative, a history which externalises the event.[70]

Mary told this story to her own child, to whom she had also told the story of the combing of the hair, and despite the brevity of the tales they had achieved an impact in the very act of trans-generational remembering. Mary's childhood experiences seemed to remain with her in her present—even with the telling of a story. Yet there is also a silence around her past, perhaps a silence to protect herself from the fear of being listened to and of listening to herself. For survivors of trauma, to not return from such silence is the rule rather than the exception.[71] In a recent broad-brush study of sexual abuse Louise Jackson has argued that to consider the topic before the 1920s is difficult as there are few people to ask and 'sources are at best random, at worst non-existent'.[72] She too is unable to listen to and hear the silences.[73] In contrast, as Sally Alexander, a careful feminist historian, has reminded us, by listening to the gaps and the silences we might construct a history which begins somewhere else.[74]

In the course of Fred's final illness I am told that Mary could not bring herself to cut her husband's toenails. Fred, her husband of more than 40 years, lay seriously ill in bed in their retirement bungalow in Rayleigh, where the couple had moved with their youngest daughters. He had suffered a stroke and could do little for himself. The toe-cutting task had to be performed by daughter Ivy, then a married woman with children of her own (the unmarried daughters were not asked to do this). I know of this detail neither from Mum nor Lily but from the daughter-in-law of the now dead toe-cutter; it was a sufficiently significant event to be recounted many years later to some-one who had married into the family. The context of the story was not the act itself, but the refusal which gave rise to it: the refusal of the wife to tend to her dying husband's feet. 'An odd woman', comments the cousin by marriage who passes on the tale.

Near the end of Mary's widowed life she had moved back to Hackney with her youngest daughters, who were reluctant to return to the city from Essex. Of this time back in London there are recently told stories of transgressive behaviour: household budgets were mismanaged and money was spent when it should not have been. Winifred's behaviour was sharply criticised and she was threatened with a carving knife, 'Although,' she told me of her mother 'I suppose, she only did this once'. During the Second World War Winifred, then in her late twenties, and Stan, a courting couple, took refuge from an air raid in a shelter on Hackney Downs, and Win therefore came back very late. Her mother did not greet her with relief that she was alive. 'Don't you dare wake your sister, she's been asleep for hours,' Mary had raged. That Winifred remembered this apparently minor event of some 60 years ago suggests its importance—at least to one of them. This is a story of the 1940s but it also relates back in time to the injunctions against transgression, the punishment for 'being in late', that Mary herself had learned, in different ways, as a young woman in the 1880s. And I, some 60 years on from this moment, know this as well; this is now a family story I have heard time and time again of the war, courtship and maternal anger.

Daughter Lily, the only child to stay unmarried, is now in her 80s living in a bright modern flat. In the middle of the living room is an anachronistic clock. This, she tells me, is not a grandfather clock but a rather smaller grand-daughter clock. On it there is a presentation plaque thanking her father Frederick Mankelow for his services to the Hackney Board of Guardians. She treasures the clock and has seriously considered which of her nephews should inherit it once she is dead.[75] For Lily it recalls happy times when her sister Ivy came to Raleigh for the first holiday she could afford with her husband and two little boys who had sat entranced listening to the clock chiming the hours. The timepiece both marks the time and crosses from one time to the next. It comes from earlier circumstances and places, and it is also a tangible artefact that needs dealing with, sorting out, passing on. This object exists because of the nature and locality of the work of Fred, Lily's father; but it also exists because he was a man who was seen as a good father, whose presence deserved to be remembered. Perhaps of the mother, Mary, however, the traces are different: there were those who heard her stories but did not listen to or could not comprehend what she was—and was not—telling them.

But it is too simplistic to say Mary's stories were not listened to since it is me who has chosen to listen (and chosen to disregard for the purposes of narrative continuity and word length all the snippets I know). So who are the tellers of these stories? The stories of workhouse parties, biscuits, orange peeling, wearing gloves, eating chips in the garden, standing on the street and avoiding rough children emanate from both Winifred and Lily; the stories of hair and blindness come exclusively from my mother, Winifred. Who else knew and spoke about Mary? There is Mary's description by a daughter-in-law, 'an odd woman'; there are the observations of a son-in-law (my father)—first as a sympathetic boyfriend who advised Winifred in his letters not to be too concerned about her mother's tirades, 'Your mother is now feeling the loss of her life-long companion and she naturally wonders about the future. On more than one occasion your Mum has said to me "I am not wanted here"—she's lonely.'[76] I remember, too, comments made later, less sympathetically. As my father Stan sometimes said, Lily, the youngest daughter, had 'got off lightly' when she went into the WAAF, leaving Win to stay and look after Mary: 'she could be a difficult person your mother' he had said to his wife Win. For Stan, of course, who first met Mary at the end of her life, this was an old woman and not someone he had known from birth—a different chronological knowing from Winifred, Mary's daughter. To me, Mary is neither old nor young since I do not (and did not) know her. She is a subject of this writing, not a person with whom I had to engage personally; I did not have to deal with a woman with problems.

I realise that there are other stories both of Fred and Mary: his comments on his children's school reports thanking the teachers for their hard work, the man who encouraged his youngest to take the scholarship exam to a prestigious secondary school, while taking his other daughter to the Tower of London—a treat resented some 70 years on by the exam-taker. There is also the story of Mary as an asthmatic (on which both sisters agreed) noting that she was encouraged to go to Southend and other 'resorts' in the Thames tidal estuary—to walk back with the tide. Both speculated about their own births to this (by then) middle-aged couple after a gap of over a decade. For one this was explained by a probable improvement in physical health (the Southend mud must have helped) or it was simply a mistake. For the other it was a story about public events and Lloyd George: a story of the father being pleased with Lloyd George's creation of national insurance—which history books tell us was in 1911—who allegedly said in response, 'we'll have some of that'. As an 'explanation', however, for the birth of a child some three years after the event this is unconvincing. It suggests, at least to me, both a family in which Liberal politics were acknowledged and supported and also one in which children were not encouraged to ask questions. This story both seems to answer the questions of, 'Where did I come from?' 'Why was I born?' and simultaneously effectively creates silence.

I acknowledge that I could have written a narrative of some kind about Fred without recourse to transgenerational memory—the material traces of a working life within the framework of the central and local state (and the merchant navy) were sufficient to have enabled this—but this narrative of Mary could not have been written without the input of at least two of her children. This written story of Mary is mine, but it is also a story built upon the narrative memories of women who knew her as children and as young adult daughters. I am writing as a historian but also as a daughter of a daughter. In this writing, but also in my life, I have been influenced by the stories Mary told to her daughter, Winifred, who told them in turn to me, her daughter and only child.

# 7

# PERSONAL AND PUBLIC ARCHIVES

## WINIFRED MANKELOW AND STAN KEAN

### Landscapes of religion

Winfred, my mother, the daughter of Fred Mankelow the work-house engineer, had not personally sorted her things in preparation for moving to a residential home. However, she had given me, as I noted in the introduction, precise instructions from her hospital bed of what should go and what should stay with her, including some of her utility furniture from 1946, the year of her marriage to Stan Kean. There were also framed prints given to her as wedding presents (as the date on the back testified), photos I had taken of Bobby the late cat, and her own embroidered achievements: carefully constructed pictures, crocheted runners, appliquéd mats—works of skill that I duly applied to the furniture surfaces and walls in her institutional room, which began to resemble the topography of the flat she had left. These artefacts were also, of course, statements about herself, her past—and continuing—life. A recent study based in French-speaking Canada has suggested that the move from a house to a residential home, with accompanying divesting of goods, is a particular ritual (with a particular name 'casser maison').[1] People try to place goods, and to donate them according to their own wishes. In Winifred's case the donations were not to any member of her family (except to me her only child) but rather to handi-craft organisations and the church.

From her childhood it had been organised Christian religion that had provided a framework for her religious, social and cultural life. Fred and Mary Mankelow had not been regular church-goers, but, as she told me when I interviewed her on tape about the reli-gious world of her childhood, a school teacher had joined her up to the local Sunday school. This had been run in the nearby Glyn

Road mission, a satellite of the larger church, the Clapton Park Congregational Church, usually known as the Round Chapel. The temperance Band of Hope, the church youth club, and then the girl guides had followed. She recalled lining up the guides at the end of the Chatsworth market—where Charles Kean preached against the demon drink—near her parents' tied house next to the workhouse. She would then march them through the streets between the market and the main road, Lower Clapton Road, to anniversary events at the Round Chapel. Religious Non-Conformism was part of both her (and Stan's) personal topography and one that had dominated the Hackney area physically for some 200 years. Famously Richard Price, the supporter of the French Revolution who had so incensed Edmund Burke with his writing, had lived and preached locally.[2] Here radical scientist and Unitarian Joseph Priestley had been given sanctuary when persecuted by Royalists in Birmingham who had burned down his home.[3] In eighteenth-century Homerton, opposite the future workhouse, Dissenters had established their own college training young men for the ministry,[4] and from the late nineteenth century the Salvation Army had almost appropriated the Lower Clapton Road as its own domain: their 'citadel' headquarters was in the former orphans' asylum; their hospital, The Mothers', was on the other side of the road; and various homes nearby were taken over for 'fallen' women or orphans.

Winifred's childhood and much of her young adult life was spent in an area physically dominated by the chapels, missions and institutions of a peculiarly English form of Protestantism. Adherence to Congregationalism was not simply a matter of personal preference, or a conscious intellectual choice over rival religious sects: it was also part of the past physical landscape of Hackney. The main road, Lower Clapton Road, still exists and in some ways is much more widely known now than in the past. Although The Mothers' hospital was shut down and the Salvation Army has transferred its remaining local operations to less grand buildings, the Round Chapel is still standing, now as a heritage piece, a putative arts centre in the grade II★ listed building; opposite the church is a small plaque to commemorate the sojourn of Joseph Priestley, though I doubt that many notice it, it's so small and difficult to decipher. I live nearby—

34  The Round Chapel, Murder Mile, April 2004

off the opposite side of the Lower Clapton Road to my parents' early sojourn—but although many of the buildings are there, their character has changed.[5] This is no longer a Non-Conformist enclave but murder mile. And, for once, the tabloids are accurate. The road that was formerly marked out by religion is now refigured through violent death: the murder of the owner of the sub-post office, arson above the laundrette, the killing of the owner of the Asian supermarket next to the former Mothers' hospital, and numerous drug related shootings near Clapton Pond. The streets that were there in my parents' early and mid-twentieth century Hackney life are still here, and so am I.

I do not share their religious beliefs. Congregationalism and then Methodism, an eighteenth-century breakaway from the Anglican church, dominated my mother's (and father's) entire life. Congregationalists, now part of the United Reform Church, were descendants of the earlier Independents to whom Oliver Cromwell had belonged; they had been the most important of the Puritan sects in the religious conflicts and civil war of the seventeenth century. They were strong on autonomy: there was to be a direct relationship between an individual and God, and an insistence on the independence and autonomy of each local congregation.[6] The hierarchy of the established Anglican church, with its bishops acting in a mediating role, was rejected. They were also evangelical in their approach: it was not enough to believe in order to be saved, there was the obligation to do good works, to testify to the work of God, and to bear witness to this within the wider world.[7]

It says much about the changing culture of this country that I feel the need to include a brief summary of such religious beliefs, for these sects are neither part of twenty-first-century cultural life— nor part of the background that most readers born in the twentieth century would know about from their personal experience. In earlier chapters I have speculated how a hot man mowing a Kentish grave- yard or men maintaining prison buildings have a different historical knowledge gained from experience: I had forgotten that I too have distinctive experiences and thus knowledges, not simply from a polit- ically active adulthood, but from a childhood steeped in religious practices of another time. I had not realised that in some ways such knowledge is now a personal knowledge. I had made assumptions that an understanding of Protestantism was still widely known: a friend reading a draft of this chapter put me right. Perhaps things I knew historically as a child still count for less in my internalised intellectual world of the present.

Even if Winifred had not told me about her past religious life, if I had not known her throughout my life, I could still have found traces of these early activities in photographs of guide camps, and Sunday school book prizes, which still remained with her after the activities themselves were no longer possible. Religion would also provide a location for friendships, romance and, finally, residential care. After Winifred's marriage to another Congregationalist, Stan, the relationships within her family were less encompassing: engage- ment with her siblings or their children usually consisted of only occasional meetings for the ritual exchanges of Christmas presents.

**Making an archive—Winifred Mankelow**

According to Jean-Sebastien Marcoux the emptying of a home and the purging of a former place is an attempt to reconstruct the self in other people's homes and memory. It is an attempt to survive one's own physical presence, accede to a form of transcendence and to renegotiate one's status.[8] In Winifred's case she had chosen to keep embroidered decorative pictures and runners, mats, small images of framed flowers, and singing birds in bright colours. These were still a strong part of Winifred's life: embroidery had been a lifelong passion. In hospital for months in her 85th year she had carefully crafted an image of a vase of blue cascading flowers. Defying the

35 Winifred Mankelow as a girl guide

nurses who dumped her belongings in a locker she could not reach, she managed to keep the tension of the stitches correct despite the lack of an embroidery frame in her hospital bed. During her retirement Winifred had joined the local branch of the Essex Handicrafts' Association, sported their badge on her outdoor coat, and from the group had adopted the practice of embroidering Christmas and birthday cards for those deemed worthy recipients of this time-consuming work. She had also entered competitions for her colourful tapestries, winning prizes and commendations (and keeping the examiners' comments about the work) and having the exhibits framed and hung on the walls of her flat.

Although frequently intolerant of the imperfections of human beings Winifred brought patience, meticulous attention to detail and steadfastness in her engagement with the inanimate objects of her own creation. Where others might be content with a printed template on canvas her preference was for transferring the image by eye and memory, counting the tiny strands of canvas, measuring and remembering the length of stitches, weaving the threads surreptitiously and neatly behind the canvas's facade. Such control and precision—often conducted over a period of months changing into years—resulted in impressive images: the imagined domes of Russian Orthodox churches depicted in gold and silver thread had been admired by many in the course of its long completion and framed by the woodwork teacher in the school where she had been a secretary for years. Such frivolous and impractical artefacts were part of the substance reflecting her life,[9] alongside the more serious collection of Bibles, religious homilies and oratorios.

Embroidered images of flowers, birds, seascapes, York Minster and country cottages were a contrast to a life lived mostly within the metropolis. When I was a child she used to create desert islands from carrot tops placed in a saucer of water in the kitchen, listening to the sounds of waves in a tropical paradise created every week on the wireless by Roy Plomley in his *Desert Islands Discs*. I used to think these tropical isles were created for me; I now surmise that they were for her own pleasure, for her own dreams of other worlds. But the dreamer of other imagined places had no desire to actually go abroad, and never even had a passport since there was so much to see in 'our own country'.

The material culture she had accumulated, the archive she had constructed of her life, stayed with her. Important objects remained on display—the 'useful' books, the 'useless' embroidery—and documents, photos, letters, testimonials, stayed hidden away in the drawers of the utility furniture. She was proud of her achievements and pleased to see her craft displayed even though the audience was predominantly herself. Suffice to say some of the staff in the residential home who wandered in and out of her room everyday barely noticed her, let alone her things. Cleaners moved around the embroidered flowers in frames simply to show they had been and almost wilfully replaced them upside down, turning the runners that she had made for her bottom drawer inside out, and shoving framed photographs horizontally on top of others, obliterating the images and thus exemplifying their utter contempt for an elderly woman in their so-called care. But her sharp sense of the predicaments posed by her contemporary life, and her particular sense of herself, was reinforced by the presence of artefacts and ephemera that spanned her entire life starting with the certificate that had exempted her from smallpox vaccination in 1914, that her father, Frederick Mankelow, had obtained within weeks of his daughter's birth.

### Making an archive—Stanley Kean

For Stan Kean, the son of Ada Sallnow and Charles Kean, the wood carver and chair maker, it had been different. He had not sorted his stuff for a residential home—or death—but only for the move in 1978 from the chaotic, rented house in Dalston in another part of Hackney to the tiny one-bedroom flat on the Debden estate in Loughton that he had shared with Winifred until his death in 1989. If he had cleared out the flat's cubby hole, with its accumulated ephemera, it would have been an acknowledgement of the inevitability of his future death.[10] But the relics he had placed there had also been chosen by him for keeping, some 11 years before he had died, as part of the move from the city. He had never listened to me when I told him his pristine collection of newly fashionable 1950s *Eagle* comics (that he had ostensibly purchased to help in his Sunday school teaching but enjoyed reading himself) would be valuable and that he would make money if he sold them. Instead he left behind in Hackney several of his collections: photography journals, DIY magazines, bulky Victorian furniture inherited from his parents and piles and piles of stuff which just could not fit into the cramped council flat. The house they had occupied for nearly twenty years had been a slum, a Victorian privately-rented house of some ten rooms latterly occupied by just Winifred and Stan. The house with its with crumbling walls and floors, a home for cobwebs and mice, despite the late addition of Bobby the cat, had been packed with things which were kept rather than used: furniture, books, utensils, ornaments, musical instruments (cello, double bass and violin, which Dad no longer played) and two pianos acquired over their—and their predecessors'—lifetimes.

Before their move I had taken some things for the house I was then squatting in Stepney and which, as I discussed earlier, I have kept in subsequent house moves: a utility kitchen table, my grandfather's dining room chairs, a Windsor chair, a piano stool—but I had turned down as too hideous the offer of the heavy Victorian wardrobes, chests and a Victorian clock that no longer worked. The council—Stan had told me—had said they would clear the house. He assumed that they would find a good home for what remained. I knew this would not happen. This repository of the abandoned material of lives was left to rot, gutted by weather and marauders, the windows smashed, the fabric attacked until the house was pulled down together with the trees and garden in the back to make a housing estate on what was then the Dalston drugs front line, at the time an isolated phenomenon but now so widely spread throughout Hackney that the term front line, suggesting areas of abstinence, is no longer applicable.

There was, however, a rationale for what Stan had kept and taken to Essex. These were often things that he would continue to use until his health prevented it: his careful notes for talks—homilies on Christianity, and outlines for his slide lectures on the buildings of London and where they were given, including the Cosy Corner pensioners' group at the Leysian Mission, and a class at the Orsman Mission in Hoxton. He had also kept notes from the training he had undertaken in retirement years as a voluntary educational welfare officer, and alongside this a summary of a talk on the same work, the same sort of homilies as the Christian ones: drunken father, neglected child, redemption. There were other notes too for stories about his voluntary work at Moorfields hospital denoted by reference to 'foreign man' or 'child.' At Mum's suggestion, I had taken from the Debden flat all the boxes of slides, which he had kept in the move, though I had never looked at them properly until I drafted this chapter. He had vaguely organised them—on a few he had even placed a number and a title. For others the address label from Agfa provided a dating. These were kept neither for me nor posterity; many were intended to be shown contemporaneously to those in the images: the Sunday school on their outings to Maldon, or the Thursday class outings to Southend. There were also the snaps of the post-retirement holidays, coach tours to Scotland and Wales, that he would also show in talks to different church clubs. I borrowed a projector from college to ensure that I looked at all of them carefully, noting the dates and places, and in many cases analysing why he had taken them, while 'T' looked on puzzled at both the photographer's rationale and my interpretation. These were not images of a couple on holiday having a good time but places they had visited, sights that had amused or interested him: the London black taxi outside the Edinburgh tattoo, a floral clock with moving floral hands to celebrate the investiture of the Prince of Wales, a large jar of Marmite in an antiques shop in Scotland, a road sign saying do not enter the box unless your exit is clear, the box measuring the length of one car only on a straight, two-track road. There was a penchant for what he would have thought quirky, or 'witty', as well as landscapes, sheep and horses.

Winifred was in some of these, although never on her own, merely included when there was a group photo of a coach party, or the Sunday school teachers were organising the children. There Winifred would be in a corner, head down checking lists, or sitting on a park bench with the members of the church class she ran. I looked at the slides recognising some of the people from decades ago, from my own childhood in the church, and thinking about the gaps, those who were no longer there in his photographic images. The slides—he had moved on from black and white printing—were of an external time when this visual form was popular in the 60s and 70s. This was also the personal time when Stan's parents, former frequent subjects of his posed images, were dead or I, then his teenage daughter, had either left home or refused to go on holiday with them any more. Neither his parents nor his daughter were there. There were no slides of his numerous cousins. His mother Ada had been the one who organised the Sallnow ties created through her five sisters and their children, the cousins of Stan, and on her death he had simply lost touch. However, reading these images for gaps and omissions may be the wrong way in which to analyse them. Stan was surely photographing what *was* there, the people who were there, and who, in their own way, were important to him. Places too had always been important in his photography: the images of a changing London captured at evening classes, places visited away from Hackney. The images from this period were not conventional family photographs but they did depict his other 'family', that of the church.

Stan's voracious interest in all things London had led him to attend classes for training as a blue badge guide but he had refused to do the exams—recalling childhood failure. And he had been conscious that such a job would offer no financial security, no pension for himself nor a future widow. He loved London, a particular London—the city, its alleys, its livery companies, its physical land-scape rather than the city of finance—as his books, photos and evening class notes indicated. He collected books, pamphlets and guides about London and knew London stories, which flowed off his tongue as easily as his biblical tales and religious homilies. He told stories of the Roman garrison, the grasshopper on top of the Royal Exchange, the statue of the horse without stirrups. He knew

36 Stan in a photography class, Waterloo Bridge, 1950s

where to change tube lines without looking at the maps, what buses to get, the short cuts round the back, and how to give directions to taxi drivers. Most of the stories he told were not histories of his own family of whom he spoke little but of 'real' history, the London he loved.

Some of his books were old as he had owned them for many years; others he had acquired in secondhand bookshops or church bazaars or had passed on to him as someone interested in reading (and London). 'Mr Kean would be interested in this', the members of the church congregation would say. I now own them, using some of them for writing the sections of this book about London, but also wishing that they might tell me something, something different about the man I knew only as a father for nearly 40 years. Certainly his scribblings in the Gollancz book issued at the end of the war *Vote Labour? Why?* interested me for he possessed few books explicitly on politics.[11] The sections that seemed to engage this Liberal were those headed 'I am a Christian' and 'I am a practical man', but whether the marginal dashes and circles indicated agreement, fierce opposition, or merely a noting for use in talks is not clear from the text. Did he vote Labour in 1945 when the Liberal vote collapsed? Was he associated, albeit as a single voter, with the

37 Stan posting a letter, Glyn Road, Hackney, 1930s

demand for (and implementation of) a welfare state? Was this anachronistic religious man really ever part of a contemporary political moment? Did his personal and broader histories ever neatly elide? Possibly, but a moment recalled by Winifred suggested otherwise. She could have benefited as one of the first women to be covered by maternity provision under the new National Insurance Act when I was born, but Stan decided otherwise. 'The hospital's treated you very well,' he apparently told my mother, 'so I don't think we (sic) should claim any maternity benefit.' So mother and (presumably) baby went without as part of this vestigial nineteenth-century Liberal stand against state intervention.

This man who would be a supporter of the Bible Society and missionary work had shown an interest from an early age in Africa and 'foreign climes' as several books indicate: a book on Livingstone in Africa, *Native Life in South Africa*, *The Clash of Colour* and an autobiography of the medical missionary Albert Schweitzer. There was also a stamp album inscribed to Stanley from his parents, full of traces of empire, countries which no longer existed, their names and boundaries blurred through political change in the later twentieth century. As a young man he had wanted different things from his parents. Trained in a Hackney central school, a cut above an elementary school, but which never acquired the status of the fee-paying secondary schools, he had wanted to apply to be a clerk in Hackney council, but father Charles declined to sign the consent form. 'That sort of work is not for the likes of us', Charles had told his son and Stan would recall this remark with bitterness. He had also applied to work 'abroad', although I had forgotten he had told me this. However, an unusual photograph he had kept prompted me to speculate and make connections. This is different from his early black and white photos I was used to seeing—posed portraits of his parents, often indoors—for it is taken outdoors and its subject matter is of an apparently ordinary event, posting a letter outside a post office in Glyn Road, near where he lived with his parents. In the fascinating film, *Smoke*, a shop keeper, played by Harvey Keitel, takes a photograph every day at the same time of the street outside his shop. To the customer and writer who frequents his shop this act of capturing the quotidian seems bizarre until he realises that this practice has ensured an image captured of his own wife moments before her accidental death. Even the ordinary can become extraordinary if we make it so. The act of posting is a hopeful one, poised in a moment of time; and if Stanley had set up the image that might have been the intention to capture this instant. But is he the photographer here? Is he the one who wanted this moment frozen? And is this an image that Stanley himself had kept? There may be another who wanted the moment recorded and who would be available during the daylight hours to perform this act of commemoration. Was this an image taken by his mother Ada witnessing an act which she did (and did not) want recorded of a moment when her surviving son might move away? Although the image was within Stan's possessions, by the last years of his life his own things and those of his father Charles and mother Ada had been mixed together—at least in the jumble of photographs and ephemera. Stan did obtain a job abroad but his hopes for a life away from Hackney were dashed; the firm went bust before he could leave the country. But this, of course, is my imagining of connections; this creation of an instant of hope may have had a different substance, known perhaps only to him and the anonymous photographer. He had, however, kept the photograph, allowing another person to create meaning from these traces long after his death.

So Stan lived for over 70 years in Hackney; for much of that time he worked here too as a clerk in the now defunct LEB. The Clapton offices have been sold off, packaged as a 1930s Art deco building, The Strand, with a junk furniture shop underneath; the Shacklewell Lane premises have also been transformed into expensive gated properties. I pass both premises regularly, since I live almost opposite the old Clapton LEB and Shacklewell Lane is on the route to the Euston Road (and Oxford). But although the buildings are here, I notice them merely as buildings with a connection to my father; they are not part of the landscape of my own paid employment, but buildings passed on the way to other places. They will never be as

38 Certificate of long service, from
London Electricity Board, 1963

materially important to me as they might have been to him when he worked there. Stan would have never been able to afford such converted property: throughout his life he had lived in rented accommodation. His parents, Ada and Charles, had been offered a house by a relative in Highams Park, a suburb to which some East Londoners aspired, but as this would have entailed a mortgage, a form of hire purchase, independent and Primitive Methodist Charles had turned this down as a type of imprudent gambling.[12] When married, Stan had also wanted to move away to the suburbs. Ponders' End—the butt of 1980s jokes in Steve Bell's *Guardian* cartoons as the birthplace of Norman Tebbitt— became an object of such desire in the 1950s, but the money had never been available to fulfil even this meagre aspiration. So he never moved, staying in Hackney until a Compulsory Purchase Order on their rented slum dwelling gave them some leverage in the rented council market. In the moment before the Greater London Council, under the pre-Ken Livingstone Conservatives, disposed of all its considerable property in the suburbs and beyond, Stan and Win managed to be in a favourable position with which to negotiate with Hackney council. The desire to be 'out of London' and 'with a garden' meant they obtained a flat they were happy with, albeit one without the desired 'spare' bedroom by which they might entice their daughter to stay—or, perhaps more realistically, use to store their still considerable hoardings and life collections.[13]

## Personal story: public history

If the 1945 Labour government had not been a moment in which personal and wider histories elided for Stan then perhaps the 1939-

45 war was, though not in conventional ways. Stan did not volunteer to fight in the Second World War, nor had his father Charles Kean fought in the First World War, although neither of them were pacifists nor conscientious objectors. Through the exigencies of employment Stan remained far away from European or Far Eastern warfare—in Hackney. His clerical work from the late 1930s for the London Electricity Board in Lower Clapton Road—his length of service testified by the long service award he kept—provided him with the status of a reserved occupation during the war, in much the same way as Frederick Mankelow had gained such exemption in the First World War through his workhouse employment.[14] The Home Guard gave him opportunities for useful work and he seemed to value what he did. Stan had had a professional photo taken of him in his Home Guard uniform to give to his fiancée, Winifred— replicating the act of her father in earlier times choosing to be photographed in his fire brigade uniform. The idea of the Home Guard, then called Local Defence Volunteers, had been agreed before the end of May 1940: the 35th City of London Battalion was established in the City and East London to defend specifically factories and public utility companies, including those in Hackney, using the men who were employed in them.[15] A recent history of the Home Guard has concluded, 'It was rarely glamorous, was often uncomfortable, and its significance in freeing regulars to go overseas was sometimes exaggerated in order to boost Home Guard morale and deceive the enemy.'[16] A 1940s commemorative booklet describing the Home Guard company in which Stan volunteered was more complementary, suggesting that by 1943 the company was 'worthy to rank with the victors of North Africa and Sicily as members of the great British Army'.[17]

When I was a child my father used to tell me about difficult manoeuvres on Wanstead Flats, lying in the mud or playing the role of a courting couple with Winifred, overhearing the opposition's discussions to outwit another group's tactics in war games. I remembered too what I had thought was simply a personal belief that 'action' in the Home Guard (and as an air raid warden and on fire duty) had been more difficult than that undertaken by many men in the army, who had gone to Africa and who were, 'sat idling in the desert smoking cigarettes and drinking beer'. As a child I had

39 Stan in Home Guard uniform

believed this; as an adult I was rather more sceptical, interpreting the tale as a Non-Conformist temperance story—but I probably thought both as a child and adult daughter that this was simply Dad's own story. However, 'war stories', I know intellectually, are often public stories, narratives of wider resonances.[18] Thus in his moving account of imprisonment and torture on the Burma–Siam Railway, Eric Lomax recounted similar tales, also set against religious Non Conformity. Eric had attempted to tell his young wife of his experiences in South East Asia but she had brushed them away suggesting she had had a hard time too: the difficulty of getting eggs, the air raid warnings and waiting in queues. In the local chapel Eric noticed that 'most of the veterans had done very little in the war, their complaints about how awful firewatching duties had been did not, under the circumstances, engage my full sympathy.'[19] Here were indeed war stories but ones imbued with the rhetoric of a particular sort of Puritanical endurance.

I am conscious that I am drafting this chapter at a time when war again, in the Middle East, is a present reality; when my thoughts, like many of my friends—and the readers of this book—have been directed towards the American-British invasion. Unsurprisingly I am conscious of features of Stan and Win's life that occurred during the Second World War: they fit with current preoccupations. However I don't think this is simply a new concern for me as a writer. For Stan the war was personally important: here indeed was a particular correspondence between his personal life and broader events. The elision between a time of personal change, particularly the start of a relationship with his future wife, and the external chronology of warfare served to ensure that in his spoken stories and hoarded ephemera the Home Guard and air raid duties featured prominently. He had kept the records of local Home Guard attendance (which reflected a predilection, amongst many of the men, for absence and taking holidays). He—or was it his future wife?—had kept the epaulettes cut from the uniform and his certificate 'from King George' thanking him for his Home Guard service from 30 July 1940 to 31 December 1944.

40  Home Guard epaulettes

Winifred had kept it safely in her new residential home: she had recently come across the certificate and passed it to me as 'I was interested in History'. It conformed both to her idea of history as big events and my interest in ephemera—and the smaller moments.

## The moment of the marriage of Winifred Mankelow and Stanley Kean

The Second World War—a public moment in time—structured their personal chronologies and brought them together.[20] And for me, growing up in the 1950s and 60s the war was also a narrative presence in the weekly visits to the cinema, in the bomb sites in the City, and in the stories they both told me. In 1940 Stan was 34 and Winifred 26: their courtship was conducted through the Round Chapel and against the backdrop of war. Certain records of life in wartime Hackney are publicly available: the bomb damage map in the London Metropolitan Archives confirms what I had known through a family story. A V1 bomb had landed near the home of Ada and Charles and their son Stan in Pedro Street (near the marshes and the electricity sub station and a ten minute walk from my current home) and the houses were damaged beyond repair.[21] Such a map could not, of course, convey the same stories my father had told me—of his father Charles sleeping through an air raid with broken glass on top of his bed in the morning as the sole evidence of the night's bombing, or of Stan rescuing someone nearby who had been in the toilet at the time of an air raid and who allegedly said, 'Blimey

I only pulled the chain, I didn't think it'd bring the house down.'
I remember too the story of the singing of the Harvest hymn at
the Round Chapel, 'We plough the fields and scatter'; the lines 'All
good gifts around us are sent from heaven above…' being accompanied by the sound of bombs falling outside. Others have written
of their lives in Hackney at this time including former residents of
Thistlewaite Road near the pond further up Lower Clapton Road.
It was here that Winifred, her younger sister Lily and widowed
mother Mary, had first lived on their return from Rayleigh in 1938,
after their father had died. Winifred and Lily had wanted to stay in
Essex; Winifred was already active in the guides—her photo albums
and testimonials portray her as a camp quartermaster and tawny
owl—and had transferred her Congregational membership from the
Round Chapel to Rayleigh. The sisters had even got round to choosing wallpaper for a new home, Winifred remembers, but their mother
was homesick and so they dutifully returned with her, both continuing in the same clerical jobs in the same office of the same stationery
firm near St Paul's cathedral to which they had daily commuted
from Rayleigh, until Lily volunteered for the WAAF. [22]

I read the published accounts of the Thistlewaite Road experiences of writer John Gross and Harold Pinter knowing that
simultaneously they were, and were not, the tales of my mother and
aunt in wartime. Gross described returning to this road of childhood memories, 'the street where [his] grandmother…had lived,
along with an uncle and aunt and their children. Harold [Pinter]
had lived opposite.' [23] Harold Pinter, who had lived with his parents
at number 19 Thistlewaite Road during the war, experienced,
'Sporadic but pretty intense bombardment. Air-raid warnings all the
time. A real sense of an extreme and perilous life. The blackout also
left a sharp memory. You lived in a world in which in winter after
five o'clock it was totally black.' [24] Wartime was also a defining
moment for the Mankelows at number three. Lily, then, was a warden
checking that residents had adhered to the blackout. Living in the
upper part of a house she could recall looking out the windows
towards the docks fascinated, seeing the bombs drop almost like a
firework display over East London. You sometimes went to the shelter in the garden, sometimes you didn't, you just 'carried on', she
recalled. She too remembered the Jewish people who lived in the

street as they were then, (rather than who they might become). For Lily, Jews in Thistlewaite Road were frightened and cowered in the shelters as soon as there was an air raid warning. I was both embarrassed and, in some ways, pleased by these remarks: an example of the inter-action of personal and broader histories, a realisation that they are not necessarily the same histories though one is structured by the other. For a cousin who lived the other side of Leabridge Road, the memory was different. Her father had worked with Harold Pinter's—both were ARP (air-raid precaution) wardens. The Pinters at least hadn't seemed to cower in a basement.[25]

A relationship between Stan and another churchgoer (which was not spoken about) had ended and Win and Stan started courting against the backdrop of bombs and Congregationalism. The relationship continued for six years before they finally married—a full year after the end of war—coinciding with Stan's 40th birthday. Where other couples had rushed into marriage he had waited despite Winifred's suggestions. He didn't want to get married in case, she says, he was called up and then, in the course of war, was injured. He did not want Winifred to have to look after him. (He didn't want this some 40 years later either when suffering with Parkinson's and from her disdain: perhaps he knew she would be like this, a woman without his experience of a disabled sibling, who had known a traumatised mother and who hated incapacity and weakness of health including, in later years, her own physical disabilities.)

Stan and Winifred had found their different ways to the Round Chapel in Lower Clapton Road, which, like all Congregational churches, was run by a group of deacons (diaconate), elected annually by the church members. Stan Kean was one such deacon at the Round Chapel, regularly re-elected to this post of responsibility, as the minutes in the Hackney archive confirm. He also worked in the Sunday school, organised support for overseas missions, helped backstage at scouts' concerts, sung in the choir and participated in reviews and plays. The tin containing elderly Leichner greasepaint which he transferred to Loughton dated back to these dramatic occasions. Certainly I remember watching a concert in which tall male members of the congregation, including I'm sure Dad, were dressed as cygnets (but wearing boots) and were awakened by an alarm clock to dance the cygnets routine from *Swan Lake*. Modern cultural historians are divided on the interpretation of such cross-dressing shows, if this is how such entertainment might be defined. Post-war commercial reviews like 'Soldiers in Skirts' were understood, some suggest, by audiences to be played by ex-servicemen who, deprived of women whilst serving abroad, were obliged to drag up to entertain each other.[26] But cross-dressing, others argue, whether intermittent, public or private is neither equivalent to nor entirely separate from sexual object choice.[27] Certainly despite the austerity of aspects of church life, the all-encompassing nature of church membership ensured that social needs also had to be catered for. As a young man, instead of attending a Primitive Methodist mission like his parents, Stan had gone to the Grove Mission, an offshoot of the Round chapel, where the tennis club had proved one of the attractions.

It was here, in the Round Chapel, that Winifred and Stanley had met. In one story he had noticed that she had a hymn book with music and could read it so invited Winifred to join the choir; in another Stan first noticed her moving chairs, clearing up after a church social event. The imagination of such a moment seems of a much earlier time, another century, like so much of this sect, reminiscent of an encounter created by Thomas Hardy in 'A Church Romance':

'She turned in the high pew, until her sight
Swept the west gallery, and caught its row
Of music-men with viol, book, and bow
Against the sinking sad tower-window light.'

By the time Stan and Win met at the Round Chapel, Non Conformism had indeed passed its zenith. In his well received book, *Classes and Cultures England 1918–51*, Ross McKibbin suggests that the concerns of Non-Conformist churches were seen as out of date by the 1920s.[28] The ideas of independent thought and action, moral excellence, temperance, the valuing of the Sabbath day, hostility to the established church and promotion of secular education to which they adhered as Congregationalists had indeed declined in England.[29] Even as a child I realised that most people were permitted to spend money on a Sunday, to buy tickets to travel on a bus or purchase ice cream if it was hot. Although sweets and ice cream were forthcoming on six days of the week, on the Sabbath I had to go without. I also sensed they were different in other ways: on holidays, I realised, most people didn't make a beeline for the local church (while being relieved that we only needed to attend once on a Sunday as we were away). While Ross McKibbin is undoubtedly correct in describing the decline of Non Conformism several decades before I was born, individuals do not solely conduct their lives within the norms of external time. Win and Stan continued to adhere to their anachronistic religious precepts; if they had not done so they would never have met and then continued their lives together as a married couple.

## A stranger's stories: Hackney tales

As an only child I have never had any siblings with which to share reminiscences of family life or life in the church. This childhood isolation (and adult atheism) meant that I never expected to meet anyone socially in the present with memories of the Round Chapel. And I never have in Hackney. Far away, on the co-operative farm in France where he worked, I'd met 'J' in voluntary exile from his place of birth. I'd not thought about 'J's' common surname or made connections with stories of my childhood until 'J' challenged what he deemed to be my political naiveté in complaining about local council services, 'What do you expect? How long have you lived in Hackney?' Unlike him, of course, I was still here so in a competition for Hackney longevity I had won. He talked of his grandfather, a deacon at the Round Chapel, a self-educated man who had made it to grammar school (the same one as Harold Pinter from Thistlewaite Road) and, as 'J' spoke, I realised that I 'knew' his now dead grandfather, not from personal memory, but parental stories. Memories which are embedded are not forgotten, and tales which have been told are remembered although we often need triggers to bring them back to the conscious mind. When Stan and Winifred were recently married and without any money they had house-sat Mr 'J's' house (and garden) in Highams Park, the suburban site of Stan's early thwarted ambitions for self advancement. Mr 'J' was the man, I remember they said, who on return from holiday had to water his garden before even having a cup of tea, a characteristic my parents clearly thought odd.

I only knew I knew this when confronted by the memory of another person far away from Hackney in the south of France. The absence of the context of the actually existing place had given rise to shared recollections unfettered by different agendas of our own daily lives; the broader timescale of generations in another place had allowed for a meeting point in the present. And yes, 'J' confirmed, his grandfather had been prominent in the chapel. But 'J's' parents had not had such a benign relationship with the Round Chapel— as conscientious objectors in the war their views had not found favour; they had been ostracised and had left the church in disgust, subsequently turning aside from religion. When I recounted this story to Mum she had been pleased that her memories had been externally confirmed—although failing to recall the people who had left the chapel—and it reawakened further stories of Mr 'J.' Whenever he preached, she could now recall, he talked about 'the green grass', and when she had been in the Mothers' hospital on Lower Clapton Road giving birth he had brought her gladiolis from his garden. And it made her wonder, yet again, why she and Stan had been cast asunder from the same church.

## Public archive, public and personal stories

I thought it unlikely I would find personal documents about events that have happened within my own lifetime in a public archive (conventionally documents such as hospital or school records are closed for at least 70 years). I had known, however, that the Congregationalists and Methodists favoured the written word, that they were organisers, minute takers, note takers, doers full of their own sense of identity and witness in the world. I was not particularly surprised to find that their records had been deposited in the local archives. I had previously looked in the Hackney archive at the records of the Primitive Methodist mission that Ada and Charles Kean had frequented. There I had read of the days out organised by the mission. I had absorbed too the charitable work with widows to prevent the women ending their days in the workhouse, where Winifred's father worked (and had photographed the female inmates) and I had used this material in an earlier chapter. Although Charles Kean was not mentioned as an official preacher I speculated on whether he was one of those referred to as preaching the gospel to 'the churchless masses in Lower Clapton Park'.[30] Also here in these public Methodist depositions I had noted the appointment of the Reverend Ellwood I had seen in Stan's photos, captured on one of the dining-room chairs I now possess.[31]

My return to read the Congregational minutes was more from a sense of researcher's duty, thoroughness and attention to detail, however irrelevant, simply because they were there and had been revealed as such in an internet archive search.[32] I had been trying to make other connections between memory and external time through a close reading of the *Hackney Gazette* for the 1950s in the newspaper library at Colindale; I had been searching for an external corroboration of a childhood memory but had been frustrated in my attempts. I thus did not expect anything different in the Hackney archives, and did not expect to find an account of the apparent moment that had turned Winifred and Stan from stalwarts of the Round Chapel into outcasts—and then Methodists.[33] This was a narrative I'd known snippets about for most of my life. The story had gnawed at the back of my mother's mind; in recent years she had often returned to the event of some 50 years before, frustrated that she could not remember what had led to them walking out of the church. This was not a case of senility but of amnesia about what had been a difficult time, and perceived by Stan and Win alike as an important turning point in both their lives. What had they been accused of—and that they had not done—she insisted? In her 80s she had often retold the story of subsequently bumping into the minister whilst crossing Lower Clapton Road. Alluding to their chronic housing problems, the man had asked whether they they had found a house yet. To this she retorted, 'We've always had a house, what we wanted was a home.' The domestic metaphor of home was also a signifier of the importance she gave to her sense of religious community, her search for a spiritual home in the church. The meeting at which the minister had said, 'You will be suspect wherever you go,' had remained in different ways in her and Stan's memory and also in my memory of their story and my knowingness as a small child not to ask questions about what had happened.

My mother sometimes stated in her re-telling of the story how 'good' I had been. 'You never said anything, you never asked, "why don't we go to that church any more Mummy"'. As a child I had learnt my lessons well, of silence and of who we were. 'Don't look in that shop window Mummy, we don't have any money,' she reminds me I said; and on another occasion apologising to her, saying sorry, rushing into the kitchen, a child of no more than six, bleeding profusely when I had slit my tongue open on a neighbouring child's scooter bars. Silence I had already learnt at a young age, a silence I had perhaps inherited from the silences and omissions in the Mankelow and Kean family practices of many decades before, but they had also been reforged anew in my own childhood. Stan like Winifred did not speak—at all, and sometimes for months—when they had 'arguments'. Often it was over seemingly trivial things—sometimes she would move some papers and he became enraged and turn to silence for weeks or even longer. And sometimes if I had done something out of turn I too would be subjected to paternal silence and ostracism for months. But my banishment was of a different kind to their estrangement from the congregation of the Round Chapel.

Teaching *Silas Marner* in the 1970s I too had thought back to this moment of exile, and made connections, empathising with Silas in a way I suspect most of my colleagues, who did not have Non-Conformist backgrounds, could not. In George Eliot's narrative the dissenting religious sect expelled Silas from their community: his treacherous friend had accused him wrongly of theft and planted money in Silas's home. It didn't seem unrealistic to me that in the novel Silas, some 20 years later, returned to the site of his earlier trauma to see if evidence of his own innocence had emerged in the intervening years. The fictional chapel, it transpired, had long gone and the congregation with it. Silas realised, 'I shall never know whether they got at the truth o' the robbery'. As a friend in the village consoled, 'You were hard done by that once, Master Marner, and it seems as you'll never know the rights of it; not that doesn't hinder there being a rights, Master Marner, for all it's dark to you and me'.[34] I too had thought the Hackney incident would remain totally 'dark'. But the minutes of the deacons' meetings preserved in the Hackney archive were thorough. They helped provide a detailed insight into the twentieth-century workings of a religious sect, the character of which seemed rooted in much earlier times. Even *Silas Marner* written in 1860 was set in the past time, of the previous, eighteenth, century.

Sitting in the cramped Hackney archive[35] in the spring of 2003 I started to read the minutes from 1949 noting any references to Stan or Winifred. Stan a deacon is re-elected; Winifred is one of the scrutineers. Stan in his Sunday school capacity visits scholars at home to increase attendance, visits backsliding members who are not maintaining their duties of attendance. He organises outings to Littlehampton and London airport; under his leadership the Sunday school children perform a pageant about London's river and several are entered successfully for scripture exams. The details of daily Congregational life are minuted energetically. Stan reports on problems that have been caused by the introduction of organ accompaniments before the singing of the hymn that had created uncertainty. The Congregation had not known the length of the accompaniment to be played and often it was too short a time in which they might find the hymn in their books. In this instance the deacons agree that there should be at least four lines of accompaniment to be played or that the amount would remain the same but the congregation were to rise immediately the organist began to play. In the case of unfamiliar tunes these would be played right through. All the agreed recommendations are then passed to the choir committee for consideration. There are also recorded disputes: evidence that church members had boycotted the Players' production of 'Babes in the Wood' as ticket sales were below those of previous years and there 'had been interference with the cast' leading to the establishment of a committee of inquiry, on which Stan had sat.[36] Subsequently it is decided that there should be no pantomime in 1950 due to low attendances and that instead the Players should perform a play and the youth club a review. I find these minutes amusing in a way, the seriousness, the intensity projected onto such trivial events. Here was an alternative community to that of the surrounding materialistic and irreligious world. And I feel able to smile since I see in them my own experience, not of religious communities but of certain far left sects in the 1970s. Disputes over plays and pantos remind me of another time, another place, when I had voted against the 'line' in public on how often campaign meetings against internment in Ireland should be held. I had thought the issue more important than the comrades: I resigned—but was still duly expelled at the same meeting. I could perhaps relate to the intensity of the Round Chapel world, without empathising with the content.

It's strange sitting in the archive basement reading about events in my parents' lives, many of which I would have known nothing about, but others which bring back hazy memories of my own childhood. Certainly the minutes confirm my memories were not mistaken of concerts, plays and parties with coconut pyramids, and trays of cakes from a baker's in Chatsworth Road. There are names I vaguely remember—the British and Foreign Bible Society and Miss Formby, the local secretary, who I recall we visited when I was older and she had retired to Broadstairs. I also can recall trips to the BFBS shop in Holborn and the old coppers box for ship halfpennies for missionary work which we had at home. And I find out too about the moment when we temporarily occupied the church manse, near the Round Chapel, which had previously been just a memory.

Reverend Schofield, the minutes say, was taking up another post as a Royal Air Force chaplain, which he felt obliged to do as he could not ignore 'this call of God'.[37] In January 1953 'Mr Kean' enquires whether a Mr and Mrs Dolby might occupy manse in the interim until a new minister is found (which is agreed); by September 1953 it's reported that Mr and Mrs Kean are now occupying the manse and paying 'at their suggestion' a rental of 25s. a week.[38] When they leave in the summer of 1955, nearly two years later, on the arrival of Mr Franklin the new minister, they are thanked for their occupancy.[39]

This is not a personal narrative, it is a record kept in a public archive. Thus it acquires a different status, it is accorded a particular respect I don't apply in necessarily the same way to my own memories or parents' stories. So I make notes not just on the content (and my emotional response) but on the nature of the document and how it has been produced. Not only is this account 'about' Stan and Winifred, my parents, but the minute taker from July 1954 is my father. This is my own knowledge. The archive doesn't record this—and the minutes are signed by the chair, the minister—but I recognise the handwriting, the neat and elegant hand, the clear legible and consistent handwriting. In different ways the minute book has become a personal record, one which I will read differently from others because of what I choose to see as a personal connection, a meeting point of memory, material and imagination. The last entry in his hand is 30 January 1956. He records that the teachers of the junior church had requested that Sunday school finance be controlled by the teaching staff. But it was minuted that as the church was responsible for the Sunday school and since the request did not come from a formal teachers' meeting, but only a meeting of a section of the school, this request was therefore not official and thus not agreed.

I look very carefully at the handwriting. I try to make connections between the personal story, the memory of my mother and the written archival word. I make the assumption, I realise, and have always realised, that she is indeed telling the story 'truthfully'. If this had indeed been the offending moment, 'the' occasion when Stan would walk out of the meeting and say to Winifred, 'Come on we're going', would the writing have continued in the same paced, elegant way? Would he have continued taking the minutes at all if he'd walked out? Simultaneously this was—and was not—the occasion. These were, however, the last minutes in Stan's handwriting. The next month's minutes are taken in a different hand and Stan is not in attendance. A report is given by the minister, Mr Franklin. The minister read a letter from 'Mr Kean' tending his resignation from the office of deacon and all other offices and requesting that his name be removed from the church roll. Mrs Kean had also written, resigning her membership. It was agreed to postpone action, to endeavour to persuade them to return: a letter from Mr Ingham would be followed up by a visit from Mr Waite. The pastor would inform the church meeting that resignations had been received but that efforts were being made to get them withdrawn. For his part, 'Mr Franklin sought "enlightenment" on certain statements he had heard from teachers on the subject of deacons' co-operation on Sunday school matters and on the subject of finance and it was felt that an early opportunity should be taken to let the teachers know the truth of these matters'. A subsequent letter is received from Mr Kean in which he refuses to withdraw his resignation. The deacons therefore agree to recommend that his resignation from the diaconate, representative to the Bible Society and to the Free Church Federal Council, be accepted. His office in the Sunday school would be dealt with by the teachers' meeting, and his secretaryship of missionary work by the missionary committee. Three months later at the annual church meeting new deacons are elected, including two new members from the Sunday school.

Throughout the minute book letters are appended that relate to the substance of meetings, often on the most trivial matters. But neither in the pages of entries for Spring 1956 nor anywhere else in the full volume are the letters from Stan and Winifred. Someone had chosen not to keep them, or forward them into the public domain of the archive. Also excluded are the minutes of the meeting Mr Franklin had had with Sunday school members, the meeting it seems at which he accused the Keans of 'being suspect'. Minutes of sub-committees do not find their way into the deacons' minutes, they are insufficiently important, and thus are omitted from the status of preservation in an archive.

Stan, although honest, was never good with money. I read this account in the archive, this revisiting of a story, as not about theft, although ostensibly a financial matter. I use my experience of local government finance (and political sects of a more secular kind) to read this differently. This moment seems to be about audit practices, or the control of the direction of the chapel, and the autonomy of a section of the church. It also seems to be about the new minister attempting to assert his authority on his new congregation. As Winifred recalls, several Sunday school teachers said later that they should have said something, and stood up to the minister (they should have been like the prophet in the lion's den, following the sentiments in the hymn, 'Dare to be a Daniel') but they did not and the moment had passed.

I realise I have told the story of leaving the Round Chapel in the present tense—not in the tense of the archive minute. Archives record and organise past events, they are never themselves of the present. But this past moment has come again into the present and now has another written future. In order to prove the minister wrong in his allegations of 'being suspect', and to affirm the moral high ground, Stan and Winifred chose to go outside the borough of

Hackney to worship, to start again from scratch building a new church life in the Methodism of the Leysian Mission in City Road on the Hackney/Islington borders. Founded by old boys of the Leys, the Methodist public school in Cambridge, to bring God's word to the nineteenth-century slums, the huge building still stands, saved through a heritage listing before conversion into apartments for city workers. The Sutton estate,

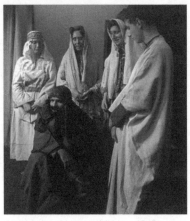

41 'Amdram' Leysian Mission, 1960s

the nineteenth-century dwellings for the poor, who were intended to benefit from the mission, still remains on the other side of the road, defying attempts at gentrification. Although doctrinally separate from the Puritan traditions of the Congregationalists, in reality Methodism shared many practices: teetotalism, an emphasis on conversion, preaching and choral singing and the value of personal religious experience.[40] According to the influential historian Halévy, in Methodism ' a moderately conservative Protestantism was substituted for the revolutionary Protestantism' of the seventeenth century.[41] The more radical strand of Methodism, Primitive Methodism, which Charles and Ada had joined, had also been atrophied when the different strands of Methodism united in 1932.[42] Like Congregationalism, Methodism has struggled to survive with a current membership of less than 250,000 and, yet again, is discussing reunification with the Anglican church. Despite its fading popularity, for Stan and Win the Leysian Mission (and later the Loughton Methodist church) became a focus for their daily lives in much the same way as the Round Chapel had been before. As the photo indicates Stan turned to directing Easter plays in which Winifred acted; they both ran Sunday school and weekly class meetings, with the photographed outings to the country and sea; they joined the choir singing in performances of Stainer's *Crucifixion*, keeping the scores, adding them to their earlier collections of oratorios.

A theologian has suggested that the highest duty of a Christian is to be a 'happy person'.[43] If that is the case then Stan interpreted it in his own particular way. Trying out a new tape recorder (the passion for gadgets did not diminish with the years) he interviewed and kept recordings of conversations with those who attended the annual Christmas day meals and parties at the church they both helped organise. I am listening to a voice of a dead man on the tape asking rhetorically, 'Are you enjoying yourself? If you're not you've only yourself to blame.' His own happiness, such as it was, was bound up with notions of service. He had written (and kept) what seemed to be a short speech for his LEB retirement party, scribbled on a plastic calendar for 1971: 'Service is the rent we pay for our room on earth. I've tried to work with that in mind. Thank you all for helping me'. The 'service' had taken different forms: buying cups of tea in Liverpool Street station for 'down and outs', inviting unknown old ladies for Boxing day lunch, visiting the sick in Moorfields eye hospital, taking books for the blind around Loughton, 'helping', 'being useful'. In Loughton they had both run TocH and the day care centre on their housing estate, established by local churches; Winifred continued this into her 84th year, taking the minutes, doing the accounts, being of service. As Winifred, then Stan's widow, had written for the church magazine, his favourite expression was, 'If you can't help someone in need you might as well clear off the face of the earth'. And this he seemed to do. In the late 1980s Parkinson's disease, diverticulitis and blindness—the latter disability that had also prevented his father from continuing in his lifetime's work—meant Stan could no longer do things for others, nor, in some ways, for himself. He had hated this sense of uselessness, as he might have seen it, which his death in June 1989 ended. When Winifred was asked to write about her own life in the church in the same Loughton Methodist newsletter she too could write about her many activities; but she also chose to write about the leaving of the earlier church, 'never to enter that church again...looking back to my life I feel I was led to leave Clapton Park Congregational Church [the Round Chapel] and to pursue the way I have since, because never once have either of us wished to go back there and Hilda has never queried why we stopped going there'.[44]

As a child I had not asked but as an adult I too had become fascinated, though in different ways I suspect from my mother, with this earlier moment. The importance my mother attached to it was not of my making and certainly it seemed to grow in stature after Stan's death. But finding material in the public archive about this moment my mother had seen as personally defining seemed significant. I came home excited from my visit to the Hackney archives in March 2003. 'T' knew the story well by now, for Winifred had even told him several times. He was worried about what her response would be when I rang to tell her what I had read; he cautioned me against informing her of a story that had implications of wrong doing and misappropriation. His was a different reading of the substance of the archive, for what was it that I *could* tell her? The answer to her concerns was not really there; she had always known that she and Stan had been in the right. The public sentiment of the famous Methodist hymn, 'And can it be?' was also a personal characteristic:

Bold I approach the eternal throne,
And claim the crown, through Christ, my own.[45]

As I surmised, Winifred felt vindicated by my phone call for she had always had the confidence of rectitude, of the sure and certain hope implicit in Wesley's hymn. In some ways, of course, it had never been the incident as such, the nature of the disagreement in a meeting that had been significant. Despite her inability to remember the substance of the dispute, she had always known that she and Stan were not in the wrong. Had she not told people in other churches? Had she not written this down? What the Minister had said, however, had stuck in her mind. She dismissed him thus in our phone conversation, 'He'd not been there long and wasn't very popular I think. He went off to Australia and he's died since'. I haven't, of course, told Mum 'what really happened'. I have no more power to do that than she had. But since the minutes of the church were in the archive the event has acquired some public status; it is no longer just a personal tale, and thus the archived information seems to vindicate her stance. She suggests, 'It's history then, isn't it?' and concludes the conversation with, 'Thanks for the information. It's been most interesting.'

I too have 'found out something': the dates when we lived at the manse, and that I was both right and wrong about losing a place to live. In my own memory staying in a nearby Salvation Army hostel off the Lower Clapton Road, forced to leave a room we had been using in a council flat for the owner's fear of his own eviction, sleeping on a floor in my grandparents' house had been jumbled up with leaving the Round Chapel. And indeed the archival events seemed to suggest this. It was not the contents of the archive that had silenced me as a child and it was not the records I had read as an adult historian that had moved me to write about this. Winifred, the daughter of the 'quiet man', Fred, whose ageing mother could no longer remember, and of the 'difficult woman' Mary, whose stories were remembered but not necessarily heard, had passed onto me her own concerns, moments by which she had traced her life. Her personal story had been transferred to me and it was this familial knowledge that had encouraged me to go into the archive, the books, the cuttings, the photos. In his work on the power of the archive, Derrida analysed that if we want to know what the archive will have meant, 'we will only know in times to come. Perhaps'.[46] In the weeks that followed this archival visit the ambiguous external validation of an internal moment also took on other interpretations and contexts, for both set and uncontested meanings are not cast in stone.

In less than a month Winifred was dead, suggesting perhaps, to some readers, a simultaneous context of closure, some sort of personal resolution enabling a peaceful death. I doubt whether she would have seen it that way. But the way in which we read the past, refigure it anew in the present, changes. I had often suggested to Winifred that she contact the only couple alive (and still on the Christmas card list) from the Round Chapel to whom she might talk about those days, but she never did. Her death meant that I could do what I had urged my mother to do in life, but felt I could not initiate myself while she lived. I scribbled a hasty note to 'E' on the general word-processed letter, advising my mother's past friends of her death and funeral arrangements, asking if I might contact 'E' for her perspective. 'E' had never realised that this event had been so important in my parents' life—the Keans had continued their Christian life elsewhere, built up reputations in the Methodist church, not mentioned it in the annual Christmas cards, and had not spoken about it on the rare occasions when they met. 'E' believed the incident wasn't about dishonesty, rather that Stan had been accused of inefficiency and there was some personal animosity. 'E' thought it was also about the speed with which they had had to vacate the manse with no home to go to, their distress at their homelessness, the temporary lodgings, the moving on, sleeping on floors, the uncertainty. This had been my own personal childhood memory but, I realise, it was also becoming a different sort of history, an interpretation of the past shared by others outside the family. It was also a story which I could only talk about, write about, now in the present.

Clearing out her room in the residential home I re-found the obituary Winifred had written about her dead husband many years before and created another meaning and context for this moment. Describing Stan's character, she had written that he was:

> A man of the highest principles. Stan was sacked from his first job with Thackers, a publishing company in Ludgate Hill, because he had informed on an employee who kept 'putting his hand in the till'. This was not believed and later found out to be true.[47]

This incident had happened decades before the occasion when the minister had said that Stan would be suspect but it provided, I conjecture, a context for their reactions to his allegation, that they might not have consciously articulated. It was only after Winifred's death that I too could find different material and think in other ways about creating explicit, different connections.

# A CONCLUSION

No snags. The Nile rises in April. Blue and White.
The humming-bird's song is made by its wings, which beat
so fast they blur in flight. I knew the capitals,
the Kings and Queens, the dates...
I want it back. The captain. The one with all the answers...[1]

In some ways I identify with the protagonist in this poem, 'The captain of the 1964 Top of the Form Team', even though he's a reactionary sort. I too knew answers. If I had written this book 25 years ago I would have had lots of them, but the questions would have been very different. But I was never interested in histories of family in those politically heady days of the 70s and early 80s. My historical interest then was in past struggles of 'the' oppressed. I'd guessed my ancestors weren't syndicalists, militant feminists, revolutionary socialists—and, as far as my recent research has suggested, they were not. I would have wanted them to have been Chartist agitators, dockers in the strike waves of 1889, defiant match workers in the Bryant & May factory in Bow. But they were not: my family had let me down, disappointed me in a way. I had embraced the 'enormous condescension of posterity' in a particular, personal form. I would never have considered taking time away from campaigns to research or write about chair makers, workers on the land or female silk weavers. In those years there was still a world yet to win. But times, both personal circumstances and political contexts change, and mostly not for the better.

I used to think life was straightforward—you did things, you changed the world, you went forward, you didn't look back, you moved on. In later years I realise it's no longer as simple as this. In a time of public and personal defeat there is an overwhelming collective (and individual) need to look back, to tell ourselves the stories of what was—and might have been—to contact former friends through Friends Reunited, to waste time in endless Google searches to track down people we once knew to confirm that perhaps not everything, not everyone, has changed for the worst. There may indeed be an emotional need for certainty about the past, still there with the passing of personal and public time; but this contrasts with an intellectual knowledge of this impossibility of certainty. Earlier I quoted Raphael Samuel's view that history could be a means of questioning ourselves and offering more disturbing accounts of who we are and where we came from. This statement could be applied baldly to the exploration of family ancestors; but what Samuel is also suggesting is that the process of writing history is itself, 'a form of inquiry…a journey into the unknown.'[2]

Like him I too have had uncertainties journeying into the unknown process of exploring ways of writing this book. I have been wary of the illusion that the story is simply in the archive, materials, things, while recognising that this is a powerful discourse for those attempting to make connections between the past and the present in the writing of history. Certainly, I admit it, I have enjoyed moments of discovery beloved by historians of the 'detective school'—the mad great-grandmother in the lunatic asylum, the deserted family from Kent emigrating to Canada, the abused daughter in Chelsea, the epileptic child whose existence was not mentioned. The enjoyment is of an intellectual buzz, a 'getting it right' like knowing the answers on University Challenge, the Round Britain Quiz or, one of the few treats of Christmas, the King William School quiz.[3] Enjoyable though such activity is, we can never understand what it was really like to live in earlier times.

A contributor to the Rootsweb website run by the East London Family History Society asks, 'Can someone tell me what East London was like in the 1880s?' The questioner receives several responses people more confident in their knowledge than I. In a way I admire the faith of the questioner, the belief that there can indeed be a definitive response. However, there can never be *the* conclusion, the end, the narrative which is complete. There will always be material which could have been included, ideas followed, enthusiasms pursued. Personal and public concerns will change over time: there will be different books to be written and there will be those that go unwritten. The particular moment passes both for the writer and the potential readership.

## Public histories

Unlike my ancestors I have a professional, as well as a personal, relationship with written and read words. Their spoken words formulated into stories were only occasionally remembered—the raspberry kiss, the combing of hair, the boy on the cripples outing. Instead they mostly created identities and histories in different ways: through weaving silk, tending animals, sawing wood, planting gardens, embroidering pictures, using greasepaint and promoting philanthropy and good works. I no longer make things with my hands: the time for the intricate Patricia Roberts jumpers with fiddly fruit and bobbles which I used to fashion has passed, together with the meetings where I knitted them. To be remembered in another time, written words may need to substitute for land worked, bricks dried, parcels delivered, boilers serviced, chairs carved and children raised. Unlike the ancestors whose stories I have told in these pages I will have no direct descendants; unlike the Mankelows residing in the Kentish graveyards I doubt I will have a gravestone. I am more likely to be burnt in a crematorium incinerator, turned into shards of bones resembling the texture of the litter I use for my cats. There will be books and written words— but neither sibling nor child to leave them to. Who then will clear the house, my chaotic archive, my cabinet of curiosities and cling to the traces with the sentiment of a relative of another generation? The stuff, the ephemera of this lifelong hoarder and accumulator will disappear, unless it is fashioned into someone else's story.

Brecht's once famous poem 'Questions from a worker who reads' can be understood in different ways but partly it is a poem about the way in which ideas of the past and present are constructed:

Who built Thebes of the Seven Gates?
In the books stand the names of Kings.
Did they then drag up the rock—slabs?
And Babylon so often destroyed,
Who kept rebuilding it?

...
So many reports
So many questions[4]

In Brecht's poem socially constructed public events provide a framework for questioning the nature of conventional history. Answers are provided, but they are revealed through a silence, by what is not said, at least in words. However, the experiences of those without a voice have been marked in the landscape, in the material culture of the past and present enabling a different history to be suggested. The source of the 'answers' in this Brechtian extract— the rock slabs, the cities, the military campaigns—of themselves are not sufficient to provide different historical perspectives; it is the questions that the reader asks which create new histories.

**Personal lives**

As I discussed in the introduction, clearing my widowed mother's flat had been a starting point for writing *London Stories*. Thinking about the contents of her flat as traces of different lives over several generations led me to decide to write the book in this particular way. Her death some four years later had occurred while I was drafting the previous chapter. I would need, again, to sort her possessions, only this time without her explicit instructions. However, I adhered, I think, to her silent requests: the furniture ended up with someone who needed it via the National Children's Home; clothes went to a Mind charity shop, the aims of which she had previously approved during a recent clearout; most of the religious books were taken by her latest Methodist church for a jumble sale; needlework books and materials were given to a new acquaintance, a handicraft enthusiast who had become a regular visitor and one who had reintroduced her to the pleasures of knitting. But I did, inevitably, keep things.

Two days after my mother died I should have been running a conference I had spent months organising on personal and public histories. It was about the ways in which we can create meaning from the substance of individual lives; although material might in one sense be personal, by sharing ideas and approaches we could be exploring the creation of new and accessible forms of history, a history that starts outside a higher education lecture or seminar room, a form of public history. I didn't attend. Sometimes there is an unsettling relationship between the lived experience of personal lives and the way we can write about them. In the days that followed, as the only child and executor of my mother's paltry will, I would inherit things, troubled by the different roles of a daughter and historian. The ephemera that remained and that I kept included:

> Two horseshoes made of silver paper, formerly used with flowers on wedding bouquet held by bride at wedding on 1 June 1946, with album of telegrams, best wishes, seating plans, formal cards, photos of aforesaid wedding June 1946

> Wooden chest, painted brown, of type used by skilled craftsman say for tools, containing embroidery threads, embroidery material, paper bags with shops' logos containing aforesaid items dating from purchase in Rayleigh 1930s and Hackney 1940s–1950s

> Memorial card, Mary Mankelow, 1943

> Two shoulder flashes cut from Home Guard uniform, COL 35 (City of London company)

> Two late nineteenth century (?) male fob watches: one (still) working

> Joey the amazing dancing clown, baby's cardboard toy. 'Joey can be made to dance anywhere.' Mint condition (although used) 1950s.

Am I merely keeping this in some sort of custodial role for a dead mother, or is this now part of my own life? Has this now become an integral part of my historical archive? Is this new stuff simply personal material or material capable of broader resonances? I am not sure. But because these traces of previous lives continue to exist, I can continue to ask questions and suggest if not certain, then possible, answers.

> So many things
> So many questions,
> Whose archive is this now?
> Whose story?

# APPENDIX

## FAMILY NAMES, DATES AND PLACES

### Paternal ancestors

**Esther née Mountford** (*c.*1819–80), a silk weaver, and **William Keen** (*c.*1820–1869), a hearth rug weaver, were both born in East London. She was the daughter of Edmund Mountford, a silk weaver, and he was the son of John Keen, a bricklayer. Esther and William had six children, William, John, George, Edward, Charles and Lydia. Their son Charles (b. 1852), a wood carver, now called Kean and his partner Elizabeth Carr (1857–?) had two sons, John and **Charles** (1878–1964).

    **Rebecca née Mansfield** (1834–1900), a dressmaker, and **John Charles Sallnow** (*c.*1836–99), a carpenter, were both born in East London. She was the daughter of Mary and James Mansfield, (*c.*1798–1870), an instrument maker. He was the son of Harriott Anne née Martin (*c.*1808–72) and **John Charles Sallnow** (1813–69) a cabinet maker, who had several children: William, George, Sarah, Harriet, Jane, Henry and **John**. John and Rebecca had six girls, Annie, Minnie, Eliza, Florence, Eleanor and **Ada** (and one son, who died as an infant). Their daughter **Ada** married **Charles Kean**.

    **Ada née Sallnow** (1878–1961) and **Charles Kean** (1878–1964) lived in Bethnal Green and Hackney. He worked as a chair maker and wood carver. They had two sons, Charlie (1900–16) and Stanley. Their youngest son, **Stanley Kean** (1906–89), a clerical worker, married **Winifred Mankelow**, a clerical worker and secretary, in 1946. They lived in Hackney, moving during their retirement to Loughton in Essex.

## Maternal ancestors

**Edward Eicke** (*c.*1770–1853), a farm worker, and **Mary Peploe**, who he married in 1800 in Tettenhall, Staffordshire, were both born, and lived and died in the Shropshire/Staffordshire borders. Their children included Ann, Richard, William and **John Eicke** (1808–*c.*1880s), who became a farmer, and who married Hannah (*c.*1801–*c.*1870s). In turn they had at least two children, Ann and Sarah. **Sarah Eicke** (1837–1914) married **Tom Davies** (*c.*1838–1919?) a joiner, in 1860, in Wolverhampton. They subsequently moved to Chelsea, and had two daughters, one of whom was **Mary Davies**.

**William Mankelow** (*c.*1796-1869) was a descendant of: William Mackello (1658–1748), the husband of Martha Joy (*c.*1680–1740), and his son William Mackello (1701–78) of Pembury. After William Mackello's marriage to Mary Hills in Pembury he moved to East Malling where he died in 1778. **William Mankelow** was the grandson of James Mancktelow (1745–1819, a son of William Mackello) who had married Ann Richards (1743–1830) from Yalding in 1767; and son of John and Ann Manktelow. **William Mankelow**, a farmer, brickmaker and carrier was born and lived in Kent in the environs of Hadlow near Tonbridge. He married **Mary Hayward** (1799–1859) in Hadlow in 1820 and they had eight children. Only one child, John, died in infancy. Those surviving to adulthood were William, Sarah Ann, George, Henry, Jonathan, **Thomas** and Eliza Jane. Thomas and **Sarah Page** had five children, Elizabeth, Sarah Ann, Harry, William and Florence. **Thomas Mankelow** (*c.*1835–1907) subsequently married **Ann Gardener** (*c.*1828–1895) from Sussex, in 1866, and lived in Chelsea where he worked as a carrier. The couple had one child **Frederick** who, in 1890, married Mary Davies.

**Frederick Mankelow** (1868–1935) an engineer and **Mary Davies** (1873–1943) moved to Hackney in East London in 1891. The couple had five children: Sarah, Fred, Ivy, Winifred, and Lily. Their daughter **Winifred** 1914–2003, married **Stanley Kean**. They had one child, Hilda Kean.

Please note that there are irregularities in the spelling of surnames in documents consulted including the census, International Genealogical Index (IGI), and birth and death certificates. I would be most happy to hear from descendants of the ancestors cited above, particularly those descended from East London Mountfords and Keens.

People referred to in the text by an initial are those with whom I have shared information or explored ideas in the present. Their contribution has been invaluable and has been noted in the acknowledgements.

# NOTES

## Introduction

1. Elizabeth Hallam and Jenny Hockey, *Death, Memory and Material Culture*, Oxford, 2001, p.119.
2. Sally J. Morgan, 'My father's photographs: the visual as public history', in Hilda Kean, Paul Martin and Sally J. Morgan (eds.), *Seeing History. Public History in Britain Now*, London, 2000, pp.33–4.
3. Ludmilla Jordanova, *History in Practice*, London, 2000, p.102.
4. The Trefoil Guild is the organisation of retired girl guides. Toc H was an ecumenical movement founded in the First World War to provide social activities for servicemen; it continues as a social, philanthropic organisation.
5. A contemporary review had described the thousands who thronged the Ideal Home Exhibition: 'many are still looking eagerly for a home, not so much an ideal home, but any sort of home'. Deborah S. Ryan, *The Ideal Home through the 20th century*, 1997, p.92.
6. Tim Brennan, 'History, family, history,' in Kean, Martin, Morgan, *Seeing History*, 2000, p.48.
7. Classically Sheila Rowbotham, *Hidden from History*, Pluto 1973, and the early issues of *History Workshop Journal*, 1976 ff.
8. See pamphlets issued by Ruskin History Workshop, for example, Bob Gilding, *The Journeyman Coopers of East London*, Oxford, n.d.; Raphael Samuel (ed.), *History Workshop. A Collectanea 1967–1991*, Oxford, 1991; David Englander (ed.), *The Diary of Fred Knee*, Society for Labour History, 1977; John Burnett (ed.) *Useful Toil*, 1971, reissued Harmondsworth, 1984.
9. Notable examples are Paul Thompson, *The Edwardians. The Re-making of British Society*, St Alban's, 1977; the work of the London History Workshop as discussed in Samuel, *History Workshop. A Collectanea*, 1991; Raphael Samuel, *East End Underworld. Chapters in the Life of Arthur Harding*, London, 1981.
10. It must be acknowledged that such views have been challenged in the more recent past and Paul Thompson, for example, has re-evaluated his earlier approach.
11. Michael Young and Peter Willmott, *Family and Kinship in East London*,

Harmondsworth, revised ed., 1962, p.114.

12. E. P. Thompson, *The Making of the English Working Class*, Harmondsworth, 1963; Sheila Rowbotham, *Hidden from History: 300 Years of Women's Oppression and the Fight Against It*, London, 1973; Paul Thompson, *The Voice of the Past: Oral History*, first edition, London, 1978.

13. Thompson, *The Making of the English Working Class*, p.12.

14. Raphael Samuel, Preface p.xvii in Raphael Samuel, Barbara Bloomfield, Guy Boanas (eds.), *The Enemy Within. Pit villages and the Miners' Strike of 1984–5*, London, 1986.

15. Raphael Samuel, Preface, *The Enemy Within*, p.ix.

16. Stuart Hall as discussed in Ken Jones, 'Against Conformity: Raphael Samuel', *Changing English*, vol.5:1, 1998, pp.22–3.

17. Raphael Samuel, *Theatres of Memory*, London, 1994.

18. Unpublished draft letter 'Memory Keepers' in author's possession drafted in response to Patrick Wright, 'Heritage clubs slug it out', *Guardian*, Saturday 4 February 1995, p.29. See Hilda Kean, 'Public History and Raphael Samuel: A forgotten radical pedagogy?' *Public History Review*, forthcoming, 2004, Sydney, Australia.

19. Keith Jenkins, *Refiguring History. New Thoughts on an Old Discipline*, London, 2003, p.29.

20. Described as such by, inter alia Verso books, the publisher of Richard Evans's book, *Telling Lies about Hitler: The Holocaust, History and the David Irving Trial*, London, 2002.

21. Evans, *Telling Lies about Hitler*, 2002, p.257.

22. He rightly accuses Irving of doing this in *Telling Lies about Hitler*.

23. Walter Benjamin (translated by Howard Eiland and Kevin McLaughlin), *The Arcades Project*, Harvard, 2002, p.206.

24. As quoted in Hilary Lees, *English Churchyard Memorials*, Stroud, 2000 p.11.

25. Raphael Samuel, *Island Stories*, London, 1998, pp.222–3.

26. Brennan, 'History, family, history,' in Kean, Martin, Morgan, *Seeing History*, 2000, p.49.

27. Joanna Bornat, 'Oral history as a social movement', in Robert Parkes and Alastair Thomson, *Oral History Reader*, London, p.191.

28. Hugh David, *On Queer Street: A Social history of British Homosexuality 1895–1995*, London, 1997, p.ix.

29. Gilda O'Neill, *My East End Memories of Life in Cockney London. The Golden Age*, London, 2000, p.80.

30. Paul Martin, *Popular Collecting and the Everyday Self. The Reinvention of Museums?*, Leicester, 1999; Susan Pearce, *Collecting in Contemporary Practice*, London, 1998.

31. Adrienne Rich, 'Natural Resources', *The Dream of a Common Language*, 1974–7.

32. Introduction, Kean, Martin, Morgan, (eds.), *Seeing History*, p.13.

**I In the archive, in the streets**

1. 'Compendium of press and cartoons' in James Lingwood (ed.), *Rachel Whiteread House*, London, 1995, pp.132–9.
2. Doreen Massey, 'Space-time and the politics of location' in Lingwood (ed.), *Rachel Whiteread House,* pp.34–49.
3. Death certificate of Esther Keen registered in Mile End Old Town, 28 October 1880. Cause of death 'Apoplexy 24 hours certified by Rogerson PRCP'. 'Keen' was the original spelling of the surname. It seems to have become changed into Kean through illiteracy when registering a birth.
4. In 1891 Edward and his wife and children, daughters Ruth, Lydia and three-week old twins, Mary and Elizabeth, lived at 9 Medway Road. RG 12/269 f.92 (Family Records Centre). In 1891 at number 9 lived Chas Phillips, a box maker, and his wife, Lydia, 34 (née Keen), and son, William RG 11/417 ff.110–12 (Family Records Centre).
5. Carolyn Steedman, *Dust*, Manchester, 2001, p.81.
6. The core of the London Metropolitan Archives photograph collection is formed from the former LCC/GLC archive.
7. David F. Mitch, *The Rise of Popular Literacy in Victorian England. The Influence of Private Choice and Public Policy*, Philadelphia, 1992, p.1.
8. Mitch, *The Rise of Popular Literacy in Victorian England*, p.31. Also see Thomas Kelly, *A History of Adult Education in Great Britain*, Liverpool, 1962, pp.147–9.
9. H0 107/1541. ff 447. Return for 6 Squirries Street. Esther is recorded here as a 'silk weaveress'.
10. Raphael Samuel and John Shaw, *A Farewell to Spitalfields. An exhibition at the Bishopsgate Institute arranged by Raphael Samuel and John Shaw of Ruskin College, Oxford*, London, 1988, p.2.
11. William H. Manchee, *Memories of Spitalfields*, London, 1914, p.7; Alfred Plummer, *The London Weavers' Company 1600–1970*, London, 1972.
12. Frank Warner, *The Silk Industry of the United Kingdom. Its Origin and Development*, London, 1921, p.36; Natalie Rothstein, 'The eighteenth-century English silk industry' in Natalie Rothstein (ed.), *Eighteenth-Century Silks: the Industries of England and Northern Europe*, Riggisberg, 2000, p.16; Robin Gwynn, *The Huguenots of London*, Brighton, 1998; Peter Thornton and Natalie Rothstein, 'The importance of the Huguenots in the London Silk Industry', *Huguenot Society's Proceedings*, vol.xx1, 1959, pp.60–8.
13. Samuel Smiles, *The Huguenots; Their Settlements, Churches, Industries in England and Ireland*, London, 1869, pp.251, 263.
14. Charles F. A. Marmoy, *The French Protestant Hospital. Extracts from the archives of 'La Providence' relating to inmates and applications for admission, 1718–1957*,

*and to recipients of and applicants for the Coqueau charity, 1745–1901*, London, 1977; William Chapman Waller, *Early Huguenot Friendly Societies* reprinted from *Proceedings of the Huguenot Society of London*, printed for private circulation, 1901. The journal, *Proceedings of the Huguenot Society of London*, dates from the late nineteenth century.

15. J.L. Hammond and Barbara Hammond, *The Skilled Labourer 1760–1832*, London 1919, p.205.

16. Barbara Drake, *Women in Trade Unions 1920*, reissued London, 1985, pp.134–5.

17. Women were included under the amended Spitalfields Acts after 1811. Plummer, *London Weavers' Company*, p.339.

18. Plummer, *London Weavers' Company*, p.336.

19. Anna Clark, *The Struggle for the Breeches. Gender and the Making of the British Working Class*, London, 1995, p.127.

20. Report from Committees, Silk Ribbon Weavers, *Parliamentary Papers*, vol.IX, 1818; Reports from the Assistant Hand-Loom Weavers Commissioners *Parliamentary Papers*, vol.23, part 2, 1840.

21. John Burnett, *Idle Hands. The Experience of Unemployment 1790–1990*, London, 1994, pp.42–77.

22. Reports from the Assistant Hand-Loom Weavers' Commissioners, *Parliamentary Papers*, vol.23, part 2, 1840.

23. Eileen Janes Yeo, *The Contest for Social Science*, London, 1996; Angela John, *By the Sweat of their Brow: Women Workers at Victorian Coal Mines*, London 1984; Ellen Jordan, *The Women's Movement and Women's Employment in Nineteenth-Century Britain*, London, 1999, p.63.

24. Reports from the Assistant Hand-loom Weavers' Commissioners, *Parliamentary Papers*, vol.23, part two, 1840, p.224.

25. George Dodd, *The Textile Manufactures of Great Britain*, series 1 and 2, London, 1844, p.200. At this period the weaving of plain silk dominated the trade with far fewer weaving velvets or Jacquard or figured silk (for furniture fabrics). Plummer, *London Weavers' Company*, p.366.

26. Steedman, *Dust*, p.68.

27. *Parliamentary Reports*, vol.23, part 2, 1840, p.224.

28. Leonard Cohen 'Dress Rehearsal Rag', *Songs of Love and Hate*, Columbia/CBS, 1971. Lyrics available at www.azlyrics.us/06635 (site visited 26 November 2003).

29. *Parliamentary Papers*, vol.23, part 2, 1840, pp.247–8.

30. Parish records of St John the Baptist church, Shoreditch, 23 December 1841 X31/9, p.218, LMA.

31. While it is likely that they were man and wife rather than brother and sister, the 1841 census does not record the familial relationships, merely giving their respective ages of 20. Thomas Mountford is not Esther's brother since they have different fathers. Thomas is the son of Charles Mountford and Esther of

Edmund. This suggests that Thomas and Esther may have been cousins.

32. Ed. C.R.J. Currie, *A History of the County of Middlesex: Early Stepney with Bethnal Green, Victoria County History*, vol.X1, Oxford, 1998, p.115; documents on the lease of 34 Squirries Street, 1868, Tower Hamlets 2346 (1867), Tower Hamlets Archive; *Dictionary of National Biography*, vol.59, London, 1899, p.348, *Who was Who*, vol.1, 1897–1915.

33. Hilda Kean, 'Save "our" Red Squirrel: Kill the American Grey Tree Rat. An exploration of the role of the red and grey squirrel in constructing ideas of Englishness', in Hilda Kean, Paul Martin, Sally Morgan (eds.), *Seeing History. Public History in Britain Now*, London, 2000, pp.51–64.

34. www.touruk.co.uk/houses/housekent_squerr.htm (site consulted 31 October 2001), *Dictionary of National Biography*, vol.59, 1899, *Who was Who*, vol.1, 1897–1915; *Squerreys Court Official guide*, Westerham, n.d. (2002?).

35. *Early Stepney with Bethnal Green, Victoria County History*, p.124; Rate assessment books, vol.268, St Matthew's, Bethnal Green, 1878, Tower Hamlets Archive.

36. Hector Gavin, *Sanitary Ramblings being sketches and illustrations of Bethnal Green*, London, 1848, p.11.

37. Thompson's *London Commercial Directory*, London, 1844.

38. Gavin, *Sanitary Ramblings*, pp.28, 33.

39 Gavin, *Sanitary Ramblings*, p.115.

40. Gavin, *Sanitary Ramblings*, p.19.

41. *City Mission Magazine*, London City Mission, October 1849, p.211; Norman Longmate, *King Cholera*, London, 1966 p.178.

42. *City Mission Magazine*, October 1849, p.207.

43. *Parliamentary Papers*, vol.23, part 2, 1840, p.240.

44. *Graphic*, 1 July 1893, Cutting in London Metropolitan Archives, SC/PZ/BG/092/001.

45. *Parliamentary Papers*, vol.23, no.2, 1840, p.241.

46. Bartholomew & Sons, Hackney Road Crescent, Collings & Johnston, Hoxton Old Town, D & B Gladding, Hoxton Fields, *Post Office Directory*, 1842.

47. Henry Mayhew, 'Home is home, be it never so homely', pp.258–90, in *Ingestre or better times to come*, London, 1852, pp.264, 268; Walter Besant, *East London*, new ed., London, 1903, pp.119–20.

48. George Dodd, *Days at the Factories*, series 1, London, 1843, p.7.

49. William G. Crory, *East London Industries*, London, 1876, pp.141–2. Mace Bros in North Bow also made similar floor coverings.

50. Only 330,000 women were listed as having paid occupations in London at this time and 9000 were working in the silk industry. Sally Alexander, 'Women's Work in Nineteenth-Century London. A Study of the Years 1820–60', *Becoming a Woman*, London, 1994, p.15.

51. Hilda Kean and Bruce Wheeler, 'Making history in Bethnal Green: Different stories of nineteenth-century silk weavers', *History Workshop Journal*, vol.56,

2003, pp.219–32.

52. John Matthias Weylland, *Our Veterans or Life Stories of the London City Mission*, London, 1881.

53. 'The State of Bethnal Green', *The Builder*, 3 October 1863, pp.709–10. Many cow keepers were Welsh. Morgan Evans, 'Keeping cows in the East End', *Cockney Ancestor*, East London Family History Society, no.8, Autumn 1980, pp.3–8.

54. W. H. Manchee, *Memories of Spitalfields*, 1914; J.F. Flanagan, *Spitalfields Silks of the Eighteenth and Nineteenth Centuries*, London, 1954; J. H. Clapham, 'The Spitalfields Acts 1773–1824', *The Economic Journal,* vol.26, 1916, pp.459–71; The Rector J.H. Scott, *Spitalfields. A Short History of Spitalfields 1197–1894*, London, 1895–6.

55. *The Queen*, 21 September 1861, p.37.

56. Kelly, *A History of Adult Education*, p.105.

57. Hilda Kean, 'East End Stories: The chairs and the photographs', *International Journal of Heritage Studies*, vol.6: 2, 2000.

58. Thanks to my Seeing History group Spring 2003 for this particular observation.

59. *The Builder*, 16 April, 1853.

60. Photograph by Revd. J.H. Scott in Manchee, *Memories of Spitalfields*, 1914, p.40; Weavers' photographs cuttings file, Bishopsgate Institute.

61. G. Holden Pike, 'The last of the weavers: a walk through Spitalfields', *The Quiver*, December 1892, pp.173–4.

62. *The Pall Mall Magazine*, vol.35, April 1905 supplement 12, cuttings file, Bishopsgate Institute.

63. Peter Burke, *Eyewitnessing. The Uses of Images as Historical Evidence*, London, 2001; Lisa Tickner, *Modern Life and Modern Subjects. British Art in the Early Twentieth Century*, Yale, 2000; Griselda Pollock, *Differencing the Canon. Feminism and the Histories of Art*, London, 1999.

64. L.D. Schwarz judges that 'essentially the Spitalfields silk industry was limping from 1826', Schwarz, *London in the age of industrialisation. Entrepreneurs, Labour Force and Living Conditions, Cambridge*, 1992; David Green, *From Artisans to Paupers. Economic Change and Poverty in London 1790–1870*, Aldershot, 1995, p.158.

65. The first records date from 1839–40 and some are missing. The following volumes were consulted in the London Metropolitan Archives: BeBG 267 /1 1839–40, Be/BG/267/2 1840, BeBG 267/3 1843, BeBG267/7 1850, BeBG267/8 1851, BeBG267/17 1860–1, BeBG267/26 1869–70, BeBG207/27 1870–1, Be/BG 267/32 1880–2, BeBG2677/43. They are also absent as applicants for Huguenot support, according to a consultation of Marmoy, *The French Protestant Hospital*.

66. Statement of Eliza Lewis, Settlement records, Rough Examination Book, 1869–70, St Matthew's Bethnal Green, p.275.

67. Peter Wood, *Poverty and the Workhouse*, Stroud, 1991, p.101.

68. E.P. Thompson, *The Making of the English Working Class*, London, 1965, p.12.

69. *The Builder*, 1 June 1861, pp.365–7.

70. Walter Sickert was married to Ellen Melicent Cobden. Wendy Baron and Richard Shone, *Sickert Paintings*, New Haven, 1992, p.34. Novelist Patricia Cornwall has mounted a campaign to demonise Sickert as Jack the Ripper.

71. Warner, *The Silk Industry of the United Kingdom*, p.84, Plummer, *London Weavers' Company*, p.369.

72. *The Times* editorial, 11 February 1860, as quoted in Plummer, *London Weavers' Company*, p.368; *Hansard* Third series CLVI, 1 March 1860, columns 2100–25.

73. Barbara Drake, *Women in Trade Unions*, 1920, reissued London, 1984, pp.27–8; and Clementina Black, *Married Women's Work*, 1915, reissued London, 1983, pp.16–25.

74. Using similar iconography to that of Booth in his (in)famous map of London poverty, colouring streets of Jewish migrants in dark blue and those with less than 5 per cent in red, we find that Pollard Row, Robert and Squirries Street, Orange and Duke Street, Princes Court and Satchwell Rents (amongst others) all are coloured red as the nineteenth century turns into the twentieth, marking an absence of migrants. C. Russell and H.S. Lewis, *The Jew in London. A Study of Racial Character and Present Day Conditions*, London, 1900.

75. Christopher Husbands, 'East End Racism 1900–1980: geographical continuities in vigilantist and extreme right-wing political behaviour', *The London Journal*, 8 (1), Summer 1982, as printed in ed. Colin Holmes, *Migration in European History*, vol.1, Cheltenham, 1996, p.6.

76. 'Leaves from the Greville diary 17 February 1832' as quoted in Wolf Wayne, 'The Spitalfields Silk Weavers: their Place in the London Radical Movement and the Decline of the Community 1820–59', unpublished BA dissertation, University of Sussex, 1975, p.20.

77. Lynda Nead, *Victorian Babylon. People, Streets and Images in Nineteenth-Century London*, New Haven, 2000 p.29.

78. Register of electors, Bethnal Green South West, Autumn 1924 (London Metropolitan Archives).

79. Thomas Linehan, *East London for Mosley: The British Union of Fascists in East London and South-West Essex 1933–40*, London, 1996, p.62.

80. Waller, *Early Huguenot Friendly Societies*, reprinted from *Proceedings of the Huguenot Society of London*, printed for private circulation, 1901; Samuel Sholl, *A Short Historical Account of Silk Manufacture in England*, London, 1811.

81. Census return Princes Court, 1861.

82. Rate Assessment Books, St Matthew's, Bethnal Green, vol.268, 1878 (Tower Hamlets archive).

83. There were also two younger children: George six, and Edward one.

84. Raphael Samuel, 'The workshop of the world', *History Workshop Journal*, 3, Spring

1977, pp.34–9.

85. Mary Sharp, *A Traveller's Guide to Saints in Europe*, London, 1964, p.129.
86. Thomas Dormandy, *The White Death. A History of Tuberculosis*, London, 1999, pp.57, 77–8. When John C. Sallnow, a great-great-grandfather also in my father's family, died in 1869 of the same illness it was called phthisis.
87. Lynda Nead, *Victorian Babylon,* p.29.
88. Hayden White, 'The historical text as literary artifact' in (ed.) Geoffrey Roberts, *The History and Narrative Reader*, London, 2001, p.227.
89. Joseph Hatton, 'On a grain of mustard seed', *English Illustrated Magazine*, November 1892. Thanks to Alice Mackay for drawing my attention to this article.
90. Achim Borchardt-Hume, 'Rachel Whiteread: an introduction' in *Rachel Whiteread* (Catalogue of Serpentine Gallery Exhibition), London, 2001 (pages unnumbered).

## 2 Outside the archive and inside a memory

1. Sarah Eicke was christened 9 April 1837, in Tettenhall Regis. Baptismal records 1364/1/6, Lichfield Record Office. Her father is recorded as John a laborer (sic) resident in Pirton (a small village between Oaken and the Shropshire borders).
2. Samuel, *Theatres of Memory*, p.17.
3. *Guardian Media*, 2 January 2002; *Guardian*, 9 January 2002.
4. Jones, 'Against conformity', *Changing English*, vol.5:1, 1998, pp.17, 23.
5. William Pitt, *General View of the Agriculture of the county of Stafford*, London, 1794, p.163.
6. www.blackcountrysociety.co.uk visited 8 March 2002 as quoted in Dave Reeves, 'An Engagement with History: The Wooing of Wednesbury and a search for a relationship with the past.' Unpublished MA in Public History dissertation, Ruskin College, Oxford, July 2002.
7. Arthur Young, *Annals of Agriculture and Other Useful Arts*, 1785, vol.4, pp.166–8, as quoted in Francis D. Klingender, *Art and the Industrial Revolution*, rev. ed., London, 1968, p.77. See also Stephen Daniels, *Fields of Vision. Landscape Imagery and National Identity in England and the United States*, Chichester, 1993, pp.66–73.
8. Malcolm Andrews, *The Search for the Picturesque. Landscape Aesthetics and Tourism in Britain 1760–1800*, Stanford, 1990.
9. Daniels, *Fields of Vision*, 1993, p.48.
10. Daniels, *Fields of Vision*, pp.68–73; Francis D. Klingender, *Art and the Industrial Revolution*, pp.75–81; Clifford Lines, *Companion to the Industrial Revolution*, London, 1990.
11. Humphrey Jennings, *Pandaemonium 1660–1886. The Coming of the Machine As Seen by Contemporary Observers*, eds. Mary-Lou Jennings and Charles Madge,

New York, 1985.

12. John Fletcher, *Works,* London, 1836, vol.1, pp.20, 31, 99 as quoted in Daniels, *Fields of Vision*, 1993, p.70.

13. James Nasmyth, engineer, *An Autobiography*, 1830, ed. Samuel Smiles, 1883, as printed. in Humphrey Jennings, *Pandaemonium*, 1985, p.171.

14. Klingender, *Art and the Industrial Revolution*, 1968, p.76.

15. Apportionment of Sherriffhales, 1848, Shrewsbury Record Office.

16. Sutherland estate map, 1834, D593/H/3/409, Staffordshire Record Office, Stafford; Reverend Frederick W. Kittermaster, *Shropshire Arms and Lineages*, Birmingham, 1869.

17. Rowland Bowen, *Cricket. A History of its Growth and Development throughout the World*, London, 1970, pp.143, 321; C.L.R. James, *Cricket* (ed.), Anna Grimshaw, London, 1986, p.47. Thanks to Ken Jones for these references.

18. Ron Gibson, *Toppling the Duke—Outrage on Ben Bhraggie*, Highland Heritage Books, 1996; G. Gaelic Arts Agency, *MacTotem: Reviewing the Duke of Sutherland Monument. 30 Artists, Amendments, Interferences, Interventions, Ideas.* An Lanntair, Stornaway, 1998; David Craig, *On the Crofters' Trail. In search of the Clearance Highlanders*, London, 1990.

19. W.H. Auden 'Musee des Beaux Arts', December 1938 (lineation reproduced here follows Auden's original).

20. *A Plain and Earnest Address to Britons, especially Farmers,* by a farmer, Ipswich, 1792.

21. W. Pitt, *General View of the Agriculture of the County of Stafford*, extracted from the 'Animals of Agriculture of Arthur Young', 1794, pp.46–9, 65, 75.

22. Tithe map of Oaken in the parish of Codsall 1838 Staffordshire Record Office, Stafford; John H.F. Brabner, *The Comprehensive Gazetteer of England and Wales*, six vols, London, 1894, 1895; John Alfred Langford, *Staffordshire and Warwickshire Past and Present*, vol.1, London, 1884, p.355; James P. Jones, *A History of the Parish of Tettenhall*, 1894; *Kelly's Directory*, 1892, entry for Codsall; N.J. Tringham, D.A. Johnson and Ann J. Kettle Codsall in *A History of Codsall, Patshull and Pattingham*, extract from ed. M.W. Greenslade, *Victoria County History Staffordshire*, vol.XX, reprinted 1989, p.82.

23. Pitt, *General View of the Agriculture of the County of Stafford*, 1794, p.114; eds. C.R.J.Currie and C.P. Lewis, *A Guide to English County Histories*, Stroud, 1997, p.361.

24. N.J. Tringham, et al. in ed. M.W. Greenslade, *A History of Codsall, Patshull and Pattingham*, reprinted 1989, p.84; Plan of Oaken in Codsall and key, 1850, in Staffordshire Archives D743/17/16.

25. Census returns: 1871, RG10/2927, f.164, p.5, f.163 p.4; 1881 RG 11/2789 f.79 p.15; 'No professional occupation' refers to Honourable Charles Wrottesley, unmarried son of Dowager Baroness Wrottesley.

26. David Hey, *The Oxford Guide to Family History*, 2nd ed., Oxford, 1996 p.105;

David Hey, 'The distinctive surnames of Staffordshire', *Staffordshire Studies*, vol.10, 1998, p.20; E.A. Wrigley, 'Small-scale but not parochial: the work of the Cambridge group for the history of population and social structure'. *Family and Community History*, vol.1, November 1998, pp.27–36; Arthur Redford, *Labour migration in England 1800–1850*, 2nd ed. revised William H. Chaloner, Manchester, 1964.

27. N.J. Tringham, *A History of Codsall, Patshull and Pattingham*, reprinted 1989, p.80.

28. Marriage in presence of John Williams and Benjamin Dalton. Edward was illiterate but Mary signed her own name. Marriage register, Tettenhall, 30 September 1800, 1364/1/11, Staffordshire Record Office, Stafford; Tettenhall Regis baptisms 25 December 1808, 1364/1/12/2, Staffordshire Record Office.

29. HO 107/2017, f.40 p.10.

30. Census 1881, RG 11/2789, f.79, p.15.

31. *PO directory, Codsall, Staffordshire*, 1863, p.462.

32. Codsall wakes, with bull and bear baiting, were held in 1821 and 1823, N.J. Tringham, *A History of Codsall, Patshull and Pattingham*, 1989, p.80. It was not finally outlawed until 1835, E.S. Turner, *All Heaven in a Rage*, first published 1964, reissued Fontwell, Sussex, 1992, pp.114–15, 137.

33. Hilda Kean, *Animal Rights. Political and Social Change in Britain since 1800,* London 1998/2000; 'Imagining Rabbits and Squirrels in the mythical English countryside', *Society and Animals Journal of Human-Animal Studies*, vol.9:2, pp.163–75, 2000; 'Save "Our" Red Squirrel: Kill the American Grey Tree Rat. An Exploration of the Role of the Red and Grey Squirrel in Constructing Ideas of Englishness' in eds. Kean, Martin, Morgan, *Seeing History*, pp.51–64, 2003; 'Commemorating the Animal or Celebrating the Human? An Exploration of the Statues of Greyfriars Bobby in Edinburgh and the Old Brown Dog in Battersea', *Society and Animals Journal of Human-Animal Studies*, vol.11:2, 1995; 'The Smooth Cool Men of Science: The Feminist and Socialist Response to Vivisection', *History Workshop Journal*, 40, Autumn 1995, pp.16–38.

34. Admission and Discharge records of Seisdon workhouse/Indoor relief list 1837–9, 1839–44, 1845–8, 1852–6, 1864–7; Indoor relief lists, 1837–40, 1845–8, 1854–7, 1861–3 Staffordshire Record Office.

35. Currie and Lewis (eds.), *A Guide to English County Histories*, pp.337–47, 355–65.

36. William Pitt, *A Topographical History of Staffordshire*, 1817, p.185–6.

37. James P. Jones, *A History of the Parish of Tettenhall*, 1894, p.3.

38. Revd Frederick W. Kittermast, *Shropshire Arms and Lineages*, 1869.

39. Currie and Lewis (eds.), *A Guide to English County Histories*, p.346.

40. Currie and Lewis (eds.), *A Guide to English County Histories*, p.363–4.

41. Hey, 'The distinctive surnames of Staffordshire', *Staffordshire Studies*, vol.10, 1998, p.20.

42. John Bignell, *Chelsea Seen from its Earliest Days*, revised ed., London, 1987 p.153.

See also E. J. Willson, *James Lee and the Vineyard nursery*, Hammersmith, 1961.

43. Bignell, *Chelsea Seen from its Earliest Days*, 1987, p.153.

44. C. W. Shaw, *The London Market Gardens*, London, 1879, p.137.

45. William Cobbett, *The English Gardener*, London, 1833, pp.199–203.

46. *Illustrated London News*, 27 June 1846, p.421. See also Angela V. John, *By the Sweat of their Brow: Women Workers at Victorian Coal Mines*, London, 1980.

47. Barrie Trinder, *The Industrial Revolution in Shropshire*, second ed., London, 1981, p.214.

48. *Illustrated London News*, 27 June, 1846, p.421.

49. Thomas Davies 24, bachelor and joiner of Art Street, and Sarah Eicke, of Tettenhall Road, 23. Thomas's father is named as Thomas Davies a labourer. Witnesses are Richard Rowsoml? and Mary Ann Foster. Marriage certificate from St Mark's, Wolverhampton, 10 December 1860; Census, 1861 RG 9/1984 f.140 p.7.

50. RG9/1984 f.140 p.7.

51. Writing about other parts of women's bodies was also included, for example, legs, as a form of consciousness-raising about the social processes involved in gender identity.

52. Frigga Haug (ed.), *Female Sexualization*, London, 1987, pp.103–5.

53. Haug (ed.), *Female Sexualization*, 1987. p.43.

54. Steedman, *Dust*, p.81.

55. Steedman, *Dust*, p.17.

56. Sally Alexander, 'Memory, generation and history. Two women's lives in the inter-war years', *Becoming a Woman*, London, 1994, p.231.

57. Alexander, 'Memory, generation and history', *Becoming a Woman*, p.240.

58. Alexander, 'Memory, generation and history', *Becoming a Woman*, p.233.

## 3 Graveyards and Bricks in Kent

1. Sir Samuel Morton Peto 1809–89. Baptist, Liberal MP for Norwich 1847–54, Finsbury 1859–65, Bristol 1865–8. He was partly responsible for building the Houses of Parliament and for constructing a large part of the south eastern railway between Folkestone and Hythe, *Dictionary of National Biography*. See also Deborah Wiggins, 'The Burial Act of 1880', *Parliamentary History* 15:2, 1996.

2. Arthur Hussey, *Notes on the churches in the counties of Kent, Sussex and Surrey*, London, 1852, p.169.

3. As quoted in Lees, *English Churchyard Memorials*, p.11.

4. Hayden White, *The Content of the Form: Narrative Discourse and Historical Representation*, Baltimore, 1990, p.24.

5. The landscape of the nineteenth century remains at least visible to this day in traces. Walter Benjamin, *The Arcades Project* (translated Howard Eiland and Kevin

McLaughlin), London, 2002, p.478.

6. Mark Taylor and Dietrich Christian Lammerts, *Grave Matters*, London, 2002, p.40.

7. Steedman, *Dust*, p.145.

8. Doreen Massey, 'Places and their Pasts', *History Workshop Journal*, 39, 1995 p.183ff.

9. www.rootsweb.com.

10. Lees, *English Churchyard Memorials*.

11. Victor Jeleniewski Seidler, *Shadows of the Shoah. Jewish Identity and Belonging*, Oxford, 2000, pp.32–3.

12. Michael P. Steinberg, *Walter Benjamin and the Demands of History*, New York, 1996, p.66.

13. Lees, *English Churchyard Memorials*, pp.12, 21.

14. Only one child had died in infancy, namely, John, born 12 June 1825, who had died 1 July 1828. Those surviving to adulthood were William, Sarah Ann, George, Henry, Jonathan, Thomas and Eliza Jane. Information from Arthur Mankelow and also Hadlow parish registers, Kent County Council archives, Maidstone.

15. William Hastings Kelke, *The Churchyard Manual Chiefly Intended for Rural Districts*, London, 1851, pp.59–60, 63, 103.

16. William Mankelow signed his name; Mary Hayward gave her mark. Marriage record, Hadlow parish, 29 February 1820, in Kent County Council archives, Maidstone.

17. Jacques Ranciere, 'The Archaeomodern Turn', in Steinberg, *Walter Benjamin and the Demands of History*, p.29.

18. Taylor and Lammerts, *Grave Matters*, p.23.

19. Jetter Sandahl, 'Proper objects among other things', *Nordisk Museologi*, 1995:2, pp.97–106 as translated into English on website (visited 26 February 2002): www.umu.se/nordic.museology/NM952/Sandahl.html. Thanks to Paul Martin for this reference.

20. They were also often the indigent inhabitants of the casual wards of workhouses. Raphael Samuel, 'Comers and Goers', in eds. H. J. Dyos and Michael Wolff, *The Victorian City. Images and Realities*, vol.1, *Past and Present/Numbers of People*, London, 1976, pp.138–9; Taylor and Lammerts, *Grave Matters*, p.20.

21. Michael J. Winstanley, *Life in Kent at the Turn of the Century*, Folkestone, 1978, pp.79, 82, 85.

22. Ann Hughes, *Hop Pickers' Memorial*, Hadlow n.d.

23. Raphael Samuel, 'Comers and Goers', pp.138–9.

24. Ibid.

25. A similar example concerning Pegswood colliery, Northumbria, is discussed in Jack Halliday, 'The Land of Lost Content. The Life and Death of a Mining Village', Certhe dissertation, Ruskin College, Oxford, 1999.

26. Hughes, *Hop Pickers' Memorial*, Hadlow n.d.

27. T. Collings, *A New and Complete History of the County of Kent*, London, 1834, p.134.

28. In the case of Ann Richards through marriage. Most of the inscriptions are difficult to read, however it is clear that one is of Ann, who died 27 November 1830 aged 87(?) years. This would appear to be the grave of Ann Mancktelow née Richards who was married to James Mancktelow grandson of William Mackello (b. 1658) and grandfather of William Mankelow born in Hadlow in 1795. The dates correspond with the dates of 1743–November 1830 on documents transcribed by Arthur Mankelow.

29. The west tower dates from the thirteenth century, though much restoration took place in the nineteenth century. John Newman, *West Kent and the Weald*, Buildings of England series, Harmondsworth, 1969, p.299–300.

30. Edward Dobson, *A Rudimentary Treatise on the Manufacture of Bricks and Tiles*, London, part 1, 1850, p.21.

31. Ronald W. Brunskill, *Brick Building in Britain*, new ed., 1997, p.18.

32. Molly Beswick, *Brickmaking in Sussex. A History and Gazetteer*, West Sussex, 1993, p.76.

33. William Mankelow/Mackello born 1701 in Pembury. After his marriage to Mary Hills in Pembury he moved to East Malling/Pembury where he died in 1778. Thanks to Arthur Mankelow for this information.

34. By the early eighteenth century there were only three furnaces and one forge in Kent producing ordnance. Michael Zell, *Industry in the Countryside. Wealden Society in the Sixteenth Century*, Cambridge, 1994, pp.126–7, 242.

35. Robert Furley, *A History of the Weald of Kent*, vol.2, part 2, Ashford, 1871 p.607; Zell, *Industry in the Countryside*, p.132.

36. Faggots of wood had been plentiful in Kent and these had long been used in burning bricks and lime. John Boys, *General View of the Agriculture of the County of Kent*, 2nd ed., London, 1813, p.198.

37. Giuseppe di Lampedusa, *The Leopard*, 1958 (English translation, 1960).

38. Entry for Sir William Nevill Montgomery Geary, barrister and inhabitant of Hadlow, Kent. He had contested both Durham and later Gravesend for the Liberals. *Who was Who*, vol.4, 1941–50.

39. Alec Clifton-Taylor, *The Pattern of English Building*, London, 1962, p.217.

40. Clifton-Taylor, *The Pattern of English Building*, p.229; Kenneth Gravett, *Timber and Brick Building in Kent. A Selection from the J. Fremlyn Streatfield Collection*, London, 1971, p.22–3.

41. Christopher Powell, *The British Building Industry since 1800*, 2nd ed., London, 1996, p.43.

42. Extract from *The Digest and Index of the Report of the Commission of Excise Inquiry*, 1836, as published as appendix to part 2 of Dobson, *A Rudimentary Treatise on the Manufacture of Bricks and Tiles*, 1850, p.81.

43. C. W. Chalklin, *Early Victorian Tonbridge*, Maidstone, 1975, p.14. Many new houses

were built in Tonbridge—not necessarily of high standards. Houses were often constructed directly over sewers and few possessed piped water; the brick-makers also benefited by 'recycling' the waste from the privies and cesspools to make further bricks. M. Barber-Read, 'The public health question in the 19th century. Public health and sanitation in a Kentish market town, Tonbridge 1850–75'. *Southern History*, 4, 1982, pp.174–9.

44. Nathaniel Lloyd, *A History of English Brickwork*, London, 1925, p.52.
45. Dobson, *Rudimentary Treatise*, part 1; 340,000 bricks were sufficient for paving a mile of road nine feet wide. Boys, *General View of the Agriculture of the County of Kent*, 2nd ed., 1813, p.200.
46. The local historian places it slightly to the north.
47. Arthur Mankelow, 'The Mankelow Family History', unpublished account. I am most grateful to Arthur for a copy of his history.
48. Raphael Samuel, 'Local history and oral history', *History Workshop Journal*, 1, 1976, p.192.
49. My thanks to Alan Mann for his observations.
50. Alan Everitt, *Landscape and Community in England*, London, 1985, p.123; Alan M. Everitt, *Transformation and Tradition: Aspects of the Victorian Countryside*, Norwich, 1985, p.24. Hadlow was also known for its fair share of drunkards as court reports indicate in *Tunbridge Wells Standard and Southborough and Tonbridge Journal*, see, for example, August 1869.
51. Everitt, *Transformation and Tradition*, pp.24–5.
52. See, for example, *The Brick and Pottery Trades Diary and Year Book*, London, 1910. Lists were given of the trademarks of different firms.
53. From Mankelow, 'The Mankelow Family History', Unpublished account.
54. Thanks to Beryl Hatton for a copy of this flier from her personal archive.
55. Beswick, *Brickmaking in Sussex*, pp.40–3.
56. Gerard L. Turnbull, *Traffic and Transport An Economic History of Pickfords*, London, 1979, pp.5–6.
57. Theo Barker, 'Road, rail and cross-channel ferry', in Alan Armstrong (ed.), *The Economy of Kent 1680–1914*, Woodbridge, 1995, p.127.
58. Alan Everitt, 'Country Carriers', *Journal of Transport History*, new series, 111, no.3, February 1976, p.179.
59. Turnbull, *Traffic and transport. An Economic History of Pickfords*, 1979, pp.134–41.
60. Everitt, 'Country carriers', *Journal of Transport History*, new series, 111, no.3, February 1976, p.181.
61. Tonbridge was also the destination of the first turnpike road in Kent in 1709. Peter Swan, 'From turnpikes to trains. Two centuries of transport through Tonbridge', *Journal of Kent History*, September 1999, no.49, pp.9–11.
62. Everitt, 'Country carriers', *Journal of Transport History*, new series 111, no.3, February 1976, p.181.
63. By 1870 Jonathan's work had changed emphasis—he was now an omnibus

driver.

64. According to Winstanley, the decline of brick-making in Kent often led to emigration to Canada. Winstanley, *Life in Kent at the Turn of the Century*, p.174.

65. *London Post Office Directory*, 1875, pp.2384, 2416; *London Post Office Directory*, 1877, p.1144; *London Post Office Directory*, 1883, p.174; *London Post Office Directory*, vol.1, 1886, p.17.

66. Michael Kennedy, *Britten*, London, 1983, p.45.

67. Anna Davin, *Growing Up Poor*, London, 1996.

68. International Genealogical Index.

## 4 Outside the Abyss

1. Gilda O'Neill, *My East End. Memories of Life in Cockney London*, London, 2000, p.80.

2. Mihaly Csikszentmihalyi and Eugene Ruchberg-Halton, *The Meaning of Things: Domestic Symbols and the Self*, Cambridge, 1981, p.17.

3. Grant McCracken, *Culture and Consumption. New Approaches to the Symbolic Character of Consumer Goods and Activities*, Indiana, 1988, p.115.

4. Andrew Mearns, *Bitter Cry of Outcast London*, London, 1883; William Booth, *In Darkest England and the Way Out*, London, 1890.

5. Andrew Mearns, *Light and Shade Pictures of London Life*, London, 1885, pp.116–17.

6. Booth, *In Darkest England*, p.185.

7. Henry Mayhew, *London Labour and the London Poor*, vol.1, London, 1851; Ernest Aves, 'The furniture trade' in ed. Charles Booth, *Life and Labour of the People in London*, vol.IV, *Trades of East London*, London, 1893, pp.157–218.

8. Pat Kirkham, Rodney Mace, and J. Porter, *Furnishing the World: the East End Furniture Trade 1830–1980*, London, 1987; See also Hilda Kean, 'East End stories: the chairs and the photographs', *International Journal of Heritage Studies*, vol.6, no.2, 2000, pp.111–27; Hilda Kean, 'Furniture Makers', *Family History Monthly*, September 2001, pp.32–6.

9. See Raphael Samuel, *East End Underworld. Chapters in the Life of Arthur Harding*, London, pp.94–9.

10. Deborah S. Ryan, *The Ideal Home through the Twentieth Century*, London, 1997.

11. David Esterly, *Grinling Gibbons and the Art of Carving*, London, 1998.

12. Roland Barthes, *Camera Lucida. Reflections on Photography*, London, 1982, p.85.

13. Barthes, *Camera Lucida*, p.115.

14. For an excellent example of the enduring presence of furniture and household items within the family memory of those forcibly removed in the Highland clearances, see Craig, *On the Crofters' Trail*, especially pp.138–9.

15. Csikszentmihalyi and Ruchberg-Halton, *The Meanings of Things: Domestic Symbols and the Self*, 1981, p.61.

16. Kean, 'East End stories: the chairs and the photographs', p.124.

17. *Domestic Economy. A classbook for girls*, new ed., 1877, p.129.

18. *Domestic Economy. A classbook for girls*, new ed., 1877, p.141.

19. John Charles Sallnow senior died at 12 Libra Road in 1869. In the 1930s the Mansfields who lived at 10 Libra Road and were costermongers at nearby Roman Road were active members of the British Union of Fascists. Linehan, *East London for Mosley*, pp.75–6.

20. H0 1540, ff.304, p.46, 1851 census for 4 Abingdon Street; Baptism records of St Matthew's, Bethnal Green, 19 February 1839, for parental details on baptism of John Junior's brother George.

21. Mari E.W. Williams, *The Precision Makers. A History of the Instruments Trade in Britain and France 1870–1939*, London, 1994; W. J. Read, 'History of the firm Negretti and Zambra', *Scientific Instrument Society Bulletin*, no.5, Winter 1985, pp.8–9.

22. H0 1540, ff.304, p.46, 1851 census for 1 and 4 Abingdon Street. Brothers William and George Sallnow lived at 7 and 8 Ann Street respectively in the 1860s, the same street in which John Charles senior had previously lived. Thanks to Linda Sullivan for this information.

23. 1881 census, RG 11/492, f.93, p.50, Usher Road, Bow.

24. 1881 census, Rg 11/1724 f.79 p.25, Park House, Manor Park Road, East Ham, working for James and Hannah Naim, a commercial traveller and his two Scottish boarders who were clerks at the Bank of England. Thanks to Paula Sallnow for this reference.

25. Annie married Joseph Gates, a widower and platelayer, who seems to have some family connection, having been a witness at her sister Eliza's wedding; Nelly Gates was a witness at Ada and Charles's wedding.

26. Derek Taylor-Thompson, *Mildmay. The Birth and Rebirth of a Unique Hospital*, London, 1992, p.10.

27. Davin, *Growing Up Poor*, p.159. The Mildmay Mission Hospital, *The Second Mile*, London, 1943. Since Ada was in service in Bethnal Green I surmise this was to the deaconesses who started the place rather than the 'founders', the Earl and Countess of Tankerville who did not live locally.

28. It was closed as a general hospital; from its official re-opening in 1988 it has specialised in the treatment of patients with AIDS.

29. Davin, *Growing Up Poor*, 1996, p.159.

30. In Britain that is. See various discussions on www.RootsWeb.com for discussion of the family origins in Germany.

31. The actual quote is, 'The History that showed things "as they really were" was the strongest narcotic of history'. Benjamin (translated, Howard Eiland and Kevin McLaughlin), *The Arcades Project*, 2002, p.463.

32. Here near the eastern end there had been a Roman settlement excavated in the 20th century. See Peter S. Mills, 'Excavations at Roman Road/Parnell Road,

Old Ford London E3', *Transactions of the London and Middlesex Archaeological Society*, vol.35, 1984, pp.25–36.

33. The Hertford Union canal was also known as Ducketts cut. Bob Gilbert, *The Green London Way*, London, 1991, p.23.

34. Information drawn from 1891 census indicating number of rooms occupied. H0 12/315 ff.81–90; 12/316 ff.46–57; 12/317 ff.26–32.

35. As quoted in Donald J. Olsen, *The Growth of Victorian London*, London, 1976, p.274.

36. Crory, *East London Industries*, 1876, pp.65, 139.

37. Reprinted *Old Ordnance Survey Map, Hackney 1893*, Godfrey Edition.

38. Assessment of Will Thorne as discussed in Marc Brodie, 'Artisans and Dossers: the 1886 West End Riots and the East End Casual Poor', *London Journal*, vol.24: 2, 1999, p.41.

39. Mary Mills, *The Early East London Gas Industry and its waste products. How were they used?*, London, 1999; James Thorne, *Handbook to the Environs of London*, Part II, London, 1876, p.578.

40. Log book Smeed Road Girls' School, 11 October 1885, LMA. Children were frequently absent, the same head reported, since a combination of poor roads and lack of footwear prevented attendance. Log book Smeed Road Girls' School, 19 November 1886, 17 February 1888.

41. H0 12/318 f.30–48. 1891 census return for Monier Road, FRC.

42. Thorne, *Handbook to the Environs of London*, Part II, 1876, p.578.

43. Revd Arthur O. Jay, *Life in Darkest London. A Hint to General Booth*, London, 1891 (Jay was vicar of Holy Trinity), Revd Arthur O. Jay, *A Story of Shoreditch being a sequel to Life in Darkest London*, London, 1896.

44. Frederich Engels, *Condition of the Working Class in England*, first published in German 1845, first in English 1886; this ed., London, 1987, pp.72–3.

45. Beatrice Webb, *My Apprenticeship*, London, 1926, p.265.

46. Jack London, *People of the Abyss*, 1903, reissued, London, 1998, p.92.

47. J.M. Butteriss, 'Streets within the Jago', *Cockney Ancestor*, no.23, Summer 1984; Peter Ferdinando, 'Child of a child of the Jago', *Cockney Ancestor*, no.1, Winter 1978; T. Harper Smith, 'Re-readings. A child of the Jago', *East London Papers*, vol.2: 1, 1959; Stan Newens, 'Arthur Morrison', *East London Record*, no.19, 1998.

48. Raphael Samuel, 'Local History and Oral History', *History Workshop Journal*, vol.1, Spring 1976, p.199.

49. Gaston Bachelard, *The Poetics of Space*, Boston, 1964, pp.4, 17.

50. Mihaly Csikszentmihalyi, 'Why we need things', in Steven Lubar and W. David Kingery (eds.), *History from Things. Essays on Material Culture*, 1993, pp.25–7.

51. Benjamin, *Arcades Project*, p.461.

52. Alessandro Portelli, 'The Massacre at Civitella Val di Chiana' in Alessandro Portelli, *The Battle of Valle Giulia. Oral History and the Art of Dialogue*, London, 1997, p.157.

53. George Wythes, *The Book of Vegetables*, 1902, pp.73–82, *Soyer's Charitable Cookery or the Poor Man's Regenerator*, London, 1848, p.34.

54. D.E. Allen, 'Regional variations in food habits' in D.J. Oddy and Derek Miller (eds.), *The Making of the Modern British Diet*, London, 1976, p.139.

55. Elizabeth David, *Spices, Salts and Aromatics in the English Kitchen*, Harmondsworth, 1971, pp.22–3, Alan Davidson, *Oxford Companion to Food*, Oxford, 1999, p.134; See Mons Durant, *The Frugal Housewife or Housekeeper's and Servants' guide*, 1840, p.17, for a recipe for caraway cakes.

56. John K. Walton, *Fish and Chips and the British Working Class 1870–1940*, Leicester, 1992, p.87.

57. Thanks to Keren Abse for this information.

58. Thanks to Mary Hayter for other examples. Skate do excrete urea through their body surface and thus careful preparation of the fish is needed.

59. Forster Crozier, *Methodism and 'The Bitter Cry of Outcast London'*, London, 1885; Henry Walker, *East London. Sketches of Christian Work and Workers*, London, 1896; *Primitive Methodist Magazine*; Edward Smith, *Three Years in Central London*, London, 1889; *Methodist Monthly*.

60. J.M. Turner, 'Methodism in England 1900–1932', in Rupert Davies, A. Raymond George, Ernest Gordon Rupp (eds.), *A History of the Methodist Church in Great Britain*, vol.3, London, 1978, p.330.

61. Joseph Ritson, *The Romance of Primitive Methodism*, 4th edition, London, 1909, p.299; Clive Field, 'Methodism in Metropolitan London 1850–1920. A Social and Sociological study', DPhil thesis, Oxford, 1974, pp.10–19; Leslie G. Farmer, *The Bow Story*, London, 1965; Revd Arthur H. Bird, *Outreach, The Story of One Hundred Years of Christian Witness in London's East End. 1870–1970*, London, 1970; William Sampson, *Revd A. McAulay, the Apostle of East London Methodism*, 2nd edition, London, 1896.

62. Turner, 'Methodism in England 1900–1932' in eds. Davies, George, Rupp, *A History of the Methodist Church*, vol.3, 1978, p.312.

63. Bird, *Outreach*, 1970, p.21. Victor was born in 1913.

64. James T. Law, *Law's Grocer's manual*, 2nd edition, London, 1902, pp.418, 983.

65. David Wainwright, *Stone's Ginger Wine. Fortunes of a Family Firm 1740–1990*, London, 1990, pp.25, 38, 42.

66. Wainwright, *Stone's Ginger Wine*, pp.71ff.

67. Fiona Beckett, 'Down in One. Stone's Original Ginger Wine', *Guardian Weekend*, 11 January 2003, p.75.

68. Andrew Wynter, *Curiosities of Toil*, Vol.1, London, 1870, p.228.

69. Henry Sarson, *Family Tradition. The Biography of a Business 1641–1841*, 1941; B/BFY 111–117, London Metropolitan Archives.

70. *Law's Grocer's Manual*, 1902, p.715.

71. David, *Spices, Salts and Aromatics*, 1971, pp.10–11.

72. *Law's, Grocer's Manual*, 1902, p.714.

73. Hatton, 'On a grain of mustard seed', *English Illustrated Magazine*, November 1892.

74. Shaw, *The London Market Gardens*, 1879, p.173.

75. Allen, 'Regional variations in food habits' in Oddy and Miller (eds.), *The Making of the Modern British Diet*, p.146.

76. John C. Horobin, *Domestic Economy for Teachers*, p.441.

77. Anna Pavord, *The Tulip*, London, 1999; Helen G. Nussey, *London Gardens of the Past*, London, 1939, p.69.

78. Martin Hoyles, *The Story of English Gardening*, London, 1991, pp.52–3; Stephen Constantine, 'Amateur Gardening and Popular Recreation in the 19th and 20th centuries', *Journal of Social History*, vol.14:3, Spring 1981, pp.387–406.

79. John James Sexby, *The Municipal Parks, Gardens and Open Spaces of London*, London, 1898, p.553.

80. William Curtis, *A Catalogue of the Plants Growing Wild in the Environs of London*, London, 1774; John Cowell, *A True Account of the Aloe Americana or Africana which is now in Bloom in Mr Cowell's Garden at Hoxton*, London, 1729.

81. Gordon, Dermer and Co., *A Catalogue of Trees, Shrubs, Plants, Flowers, Roots, Seeds, etc, sold by Gordon, Dermer and Thomson, Seed and Nurserymen, at Mile End, near London*, London, 1780; David Solman, *Loddiges of Hackney, the Largest Hothouse in the World*, Hackney, 1995; Kenneth Lemmon, *The Golden Age of Plant Hunters*, London, 1968. See also Mea Allan, *Plants that Changed Our Gardens*, Newton Abbot, 1974.

82. Anne Wilkinson, 'Stoke Newington and the golden flower', *Hackney History*, vol.5, 1999, pp.229.

83. *The Floral Magazine* by Thomas Moore, secretary of the floral committee of the RHS, drawings by Walter Fitch, vol.1, May 1860 and ff.; *The Botanical Register consisting of Coloured Figures of Exotic Plants Cultivated in British Gardens*, London, 1815–28; John Sedding, *Garden Craft Old and New*, new ed., London, 1895; Mary E. Haweis, *Rus in Urbe or Flowers that Thrive in London Gardens and Smoky Towns*, London, 1886; Mary Hampden, *Town Gardening*, London, 1921.

84. 'If it wasn't for the 'ouses in between', sung by Gus Elen, written by Edgar Bateman, London, 1894.

85. Windyridge CDs. www.musichallcds.com.

86. Haweis, *Rus in Urbe*, 1886, p.8.

87. Stephen Constantine, 'Amateur Gardening', p.392; By the author of 'In-door Plants', *Flowers for Window Gardens in Town or Country*, London, 1862, p.4; Jerry White, *Rothschild Buildings. Life in an East End Tenement Block 1887–1920*, London, 1980, pp.38–9.

88. Hampden, *Town Gardening*, 1921, p.81.

89. As Mrs Layton, a working-class woman from Bethnal Green, recalled in the collection describing the lives of members of the Women's Co-operative Guild, in the 1890s people in Bethnal Green had gardens or backyards with animals

out the back or windowsills, on which she as a small child had grown flow-ers. 'Mrs Layton Memories of 70 years', in eds. Margaret Llewelyn Davies, *Life as We Have Known It*, 1931, reissued London, 1977, p.2.
90 Karen Olson and Linda Shopes, 'Crossing Boundaries, Building Bridges. Doing oral history among working-class women and men' in Sherna B. Gluck and Daphne Patai, *Women's Words, the Feminist Practice of Oral History*, London 1991, p.199.

**5 Not Remembering Ann Mankelow and Charlie Kean**

1. Lawrence Stone, *Broken Lives, Separation and Divorce in England 1660–1857*, Oxford, 1993, p.18.
2. Introduction by Marie Mulvey Roberts to Rosina Bulwer Lytton's *A Blighted Life. A True Story*, 1880, reissued Bristol, 1994.
3. Georgina Weldon, *How I escaped the mad doctors*, London, 1879.
4. Entries for 3 September 1894, *Register of Admissions*, 1893–5, Banstead Lunatic Asylum, H22/BAN/B01/014 London Metropolitan Archive.
5. Entry for 20 December 1894, *Admissions of Criminal Patients*, 1881–1908, Banstead Lunatic Asylum, H22/BAN/B01/045 LMA.
6. Entry for 3 September 1894, *Register of Admissions*, 1893–4, Banstead Lunatic Asylum.
7. Reception Order 13 August 1895, *Register of Admissions*, 1893–5, Banstead Lunatic Asylum.
8. Entry for 26 October 1895, Register of Removals, Discharges and Deaths, H22/BAN/B03/033, Banstead Lunatic Asylum.
9. Entry for 31 October 1895, *Burial Register*, 1890–7, Banstead Lunatic Asylum, H22/BAN/B05/003.
10. *21st Annual Report of the Clapton Mission, Primitive Methodist Connexion*, November 1905, Hackney Archives.
11. *The Record of the Tower Hamlets Mission*, June, 1902, p.2.
12. *The Record of the Tower Hamlets Mission*, June, 1902, p.2.
13. The Primitive Methodist Mission in Chatsworth Road also organised specific annual outing for cripples at College Lane school, for example to Theydon Bois. *47th Annual Report of the Clapton Mission*, December 1931, Hackney Archives.
14. *The Tricks of Trade: Adulterations of Food and Physic with directions for their detection and counteraction*, New ed., London, 1859.
15. *Annual Report*, National Association for Promoting the Welfare of the Feeble Minded, 1901, p.6, as quoted in Paula Bartley, *Prostitution, Prevention and Reform in England 1860–1914*, London, 2000, p.123.
16. David G. Pritchard, *Education and the Handicapped, 1760–1960*, London, 1963, reprinted 1998, pp.134–47.

17. Mathew Thompson, *The Problem of Mental Deficiency*, Oxford, 1998, p.36.

18. *Epileptic Children, Report of the Special Schools sub-committee*, LCC, 1908, British Library Official Publications Section.

19. *Annual Report of the Council*, vol.4, Education, p.12, LCC 1913, British Library Official Publications Section; Thompson, *The Problem of Mental Deficiency*, 1998, p.36.

20. General Purposes sub-committee as reported in *Education Committee Minutes*, 2 July 1913, p.3, British Library Official Publications Section.

21. Special schools sub-committee as reported in *Education Committee*, 18 March 1914, p.520.

22. *Special schools for blind, deaf and defective children*, LCC, 1906, p.12.

23. Gordon Holmes, *The National Hospital. Queen Square 1860–1948*, Edinburgh, 1954.

24. William P. Spratling, *Epilepsy and its Treatment*, Philadelphia, 1904, pp.31, 70.

25 Both her paternal grandparents were certified as dying from Phthisis: Harriott Ann Sallnow, 14 July 1872, aged 64, John Charles Sallnow, 5 November 1869, aged 57.

26. Dormandy, *The White Death*, 1999, p.82.

27. *Annual Reports and Balance Sheets*, Alliance Cabinet Makers Association, 1879–85, Bishopsgate Institute.

28. Dormandy, *The White Death*, 1999, p.77.

29. J. M. Turner, 'Methodism in England 1900–32', in Davies, George, Rupp (eds.), *A History of the Methodist Church*, vol.3, pp.313, 330.

30. Clive Field, 'Methodism in Metropolitan London 1850–1920', pp.10–19.

31. J. M. Turner, 'Methodism in England 1900–32', in Davies, George, Rupp (eds.), *A History of the Methodist Church*, vol.3, pp.31, 317.

32. David Williamson, *Ira D. Sankey, The Story of his Life*, London, 1905, p.118.

33. Ira D. Sankey (compiled by), *Sacred Songs and Solos*, London, 1882.

34. *Minutes of Quarterly Meeting of Clapton Primitive Methodist Circuit*, vol.1, 1814–1907, Hackney D/E 234 A1/9; *Annual Report of the Clapton Mission, Primitive Methodist Connexion*, November 1905, Hackney D/E 234 A9.

35. Susan Stewart, *On Longing. Narratives of the Miniature, the Gigantic, the Souvenir, the Collection*, Baltimore, 1993.

36. Susan M. Pearce, 'Collecting reconsidered' in Susan M. Pearce (ed.), *Interpreting Objects and Collections*, London, 1994, p.196.

37. 'Our self definition is often highly dependent upon our possessions' Russell W. Belk, 'Collectors and Collecting', in Pearce (ed.), *Interpreting Objects and Collections*, p.321.

38. Letter from Stan to Win, 8 February 1940, in author's possession.

## 6 Archival Stories and Silence

1. *PO Directory*, vol.1, 1886, p.175. However in the census of 1891 Thomas is still defined as a carrier so he may have obtained employment in this new firm or other growing firms such as Carter Patterson. There is a family story that Carter Patterson had bought out his firm but the archives suggested differently.

2. See Chapter 3, p.78.

3. P&O /76/36, entry no.4899, National Maritime Museum.

4. P&O Information Services leaflet, *Kaisar i Hind* cuttings file, National Maritime Museum.

5. *London and China Express*, 13 September 1878, in *Kaisar i Hind* cuttings file.

6. *Morning Post*, 11 January 1879, *Kaisar i Hind* cuttings file.

7. *P&O pocket book*, 1888, p.71.

8. Peter Padfield, *Beneath the House Flag of the P&O*, London, 1981, p.51.

9. *The Times*, 9 September 1878, *Kaisar i Hind* cuttings file.

10. Agreement and account of crew, *Kaisar i Hind*, 25 July–16 October 1890. Southampton City Archives; Peter Padfield, *Beneath the House Flag of the P&O*, 1981, p.117.

11. H. Campbell McMurray, 'Technology and social change at sea. The status and position on board of the ship's engineer, c. 1830–60' in Rosemary Ommer and Gerald Panting (eds.), *Working Men who got Wet. Proceedings of the Fourth Conference of the Atlantic Canada Shipping Project*, 24–6 July 1980, Maritime History Group, Memorial University of Newfoundland, 1980, p.45. Thanks to Jo Stanley for drawing my attention to this.

12. Cdr R. F.D. Colby, 'The training of marine engineer officers for the Royal Navy', *Past, Present and Future Engineering in the Royal Navy*, Manadon, September, 1989, p.211.

13. Jonathan Zeitlin, 'Engineers and Compositors: A comparison', in Royden Harrison and Jonathan Zeitlin (eds.), *Divisions of Labour Skilled Workers and Technological Change in Nineteenth Century England*, Brighton, 1985, p.187.

14. Robert A. Leeson, *Travelling Brothers: The six centuries' road from craft fellowship to trade unionism*, London, 1979, p.193; Louis Cassier, 'The British Engineers' Strike of 1897–8', *Cassier's Magazine*, April 1900, p.489.

15. He obtained this status by quitting Labour for the Liberals and was generally seen as a turncoat.

16. Alston Kennerley, 'The Nation's Key men: Merchant Seafarers' Education and Training 1890–1990', Paper 2/6/1, *Seapower at the Millennium Conference*, Portsmouth, January 2000, p.2. By 1862 the Board of Trade issued certificates of competency for seagoing marine engineers, effectively licences to practice their craft. J. Cowley, 'Engineering and Education—a marine engineer's viewpoint', *Transactions of the Institute of Marine Engineers*, vol.98, Paper 3a, 1985,

p.1.

17. William Cully Bergen, '*Bergen's Marine Engineer*', 3rd ed., North Shields, 1882, pp.54–6.

18. J. Cowley, 'Engineering and Education—a marine engineer's viewpoint', *Transactions of the Institute of Marine Engineers*, vol.98, Paper 3a, 1985, p.6.

19. Peter Padfield, *Beneath the House Flag of the P&O*, 1981, p.110.

20. Zietlin, *Engineers*, p.204.

21. The documentation for subsequent voyages is missing, destroyed, the National Maritime Museum advises, when the Public Record Office thought that such material was of little interest.

22. She died on 14 January 1970, shortly before her 79th birthday, of pulmonary embolism and deep vein thrombosis, in Whipps Cross Hospital as the death certificate declares.

23. I am aware that some say that this is a relatively recent composition but the nub of the story is still of fancy. www.poetrylibrary.org.uk/poetry/quote/reply.jsp?quote_id=1896. Accessed 21 February 2003.

24. Jean Renvoize, *Innocence Destroyed. A Study of Child Sexual Abuse*, London, 1993, p.148.

25. See chapter two for a discussion of the work of Frigga Haug on this in her *Female Sexualization,* 1987, p.103.

26. Dori Laub, 'Bearing witness or the vicissitudes of listening', Shoshana Felman and Dori Laub, *Testimony. Crises of Witnessing in Literature, Psychoanalysis and History*, London, 1992, p.68.

27. 1891 census return for 42 College Place, Chelsea. RG 12/60 ff.44–52, p.50.

28. One observer has suggested that she may be an orderly rather than an inmate as indicated by slightly different material in her uniform.

29. A recent exception to this is a photography project at Brixton prison. See 'Faisal Abdu'allah in conversation with Anna Robinson', *Notshutup*, issue one, October 2003, pp.26–9, and Anna Robinson, unpublished MA portfolio, Ruskin College, Oxford, 2003.

30. Jeremy Seabrook, 'My life is in that box' in Jo Spence and Patricia Holland (eds.), *Family Snaps. The Meaning of Domestic Photography*, London, 1991, pp.171–85.

31. Paul Montair, *Swelling Grounds. A History of Hackney Workhouse 1729–1929*, 1995.

32. Anne Digby, *Pauper Palaces*, London, 1978, p.164.

33. Digby, *Pauper Palaces*, 1978, p.165.

34. Minutes of the Hackney Board of Guardians, HA/BG 060, 6 May 1891, London Metropolitan Archives.

35. Minutes of the Hackney Board of Guardians, HA/BG/282/2, London Metropolitan Archives.

36. Minutes of the Hackney Board of Guardians, HA/BG/282/2, 1901–2,

London Metropolitan Archives.

37. In 1891 he lived at Redwald Road in Clapton Park within a year he had moved to Dunlace Road, In 1913 he was living at 6 Durrington Road.

38. *Hackney and Kingsland Gazette*, 12 February 1883, p.3.

39. The Vaccination Act of 1840 had been an enabling Act, made compulsory in 1853. F.B. Smith, *The People's Health 1830–1910*, Aldershot 1990, pp.160–1.

40. Dr Garth Wilkinson, Swendenborgian and homeopath speaking at an Anti Vaccination League meeting in 1871, as quoted in Smith, ibid., p.166; Dorothy Porter and Roy Porter, 'The Politics of Prevention: Anti-Vaccinationism and Public Health in Nineteenth Century England', *Medical History*, vol.33, 1988, pp.231–52.

41. Radical Liberal MPs such as Thomas Burt, the Northumberland Miners' leader, or Peter Taylor, and his wife Clementia, both leading London radicals, or Jacob Bright and his wife Ursula or Charles Bradlaugh, the atheist MP for Northampton all supported campaigns against state intervention in family life through vaccination.

42. Supplement to *The Vaccination Inquirer*, 1 April 1899.

43. Minutes of the Hackney Board of Guardians, HA/ BG 056 5 June 1889, London Metropolitan Archives.

44. Anthony S. Wohl, *Endangered lives. Public Health in Victorian Britain*, London, 1983, p.134.

45. This was a source of the production of the smallpox serum which was the rationale of opposition for some protestors. See Kean *Animal Rights*, p.112.

46. Susan D. Pennybacker, *A Vision for London 1889–1914*, London, 1995, pp.10–11.

47. Kean, *Animal Rights*, p.164.

48. It has not been possible to ascertain whether all his children had been exempt.

49. Geoffrey V. Blackstone, *A History of the British Fire Service*, London, 1957, p.324.

50. Correspondence from Post Office Telegraphics, 20 January 1904 to Hackney Board of Guardians. Miscellaneous letters re maintenance Board of Guardians, HA /BG/191, London Metropolitan Archives. Regulation 55B of Defence of the Realm Act, 1 October 1917, gave powers to order any fire brigade including works brigades to come to the assistance of London or other fire brigades. Blackstone, *A History of the British Fire Service*, 1957, p.332.

51. Victor Bailey (ed.), *Forged in Fire the History of the FBU*, London, 1992, p.4.

52. Frederick H. Radford, *Fetch the Engine*, London, 1951, p.35. The leader of the Fireman's trade union, Jim Bradley, was a local man, a former park keeper in Victoria Park and a secretary of the Bethnal Green Municipal Employees Association. Victor Bailey, *Forged in Fire*, p.29.

53. Annual reports in London Metropolitan Archives, Fund-raising committee report in St Bartholomew hospital archives.

54. Anne Digby, *British Welfare Policy. Workhouse to Workfare*, London, 1989, p.52.

55. See for example *The Engineering and Boiler House Review* that in 1932 declared itself to be (on its masthead) 'the practical journal for all steam users throughout the English-speaking world'.
56. John A. Fleming (ed.), *The Electrical Educator*, 2 vols, London, 1926.
57. John A. Fleming, *A Hundred Years of Electrical Engineering*, London, 1927, p.29.
58. Fleming, *The Electrical Educator*, vol.1, 1926, pp.31, 57.
59. Minutes of General Purposes Committee, 22 December 1917, Hackney Board of Guardians, HA/BG 113, pp.207–8.
60. Minutes of General Purposes Committee, 22 December 1917, Hackney Board of Guardians, HA/BG 113, p.208.
61. Board of Guardians minutes book, 23 January 1918, p.238, HA BG 113.
62. General Purposes Committee, 6 February 1918, p.299, HA BG 113.
63. Now called Kenworthy Road.
64. General Purposes Committee House committee, 17 April 1918, p.52, 17 April 1918, p.63, HA BG 114.
65. Buildings Committee, 30 October 1918, 19 February 1919. HA/BG 115. See also Miscellaneous letters re maintenance file, 1891–1914, HA/BG/191.
66. Early electrical installations in the power-house at Hackney hospital donated by Group Engineer (Jones) 1968. Hackney archives reference P 3690(ii).
67. From *Within Living Memory. A Collection of Norfolk Reminiscences*, 1973, pp.134–7, as quoted in Anne Digby, *Pauper Palaces*, pp.159–60.
68. Digby, *Pauper Palaces*, pp.159–6.
69. There were four daughter: Sarah, Ivy, Winifred and Lily and one son Fred. All survived into retirement.
70. Felman and Laub, *Testimony, Crises of Witnessing*, 1992, p.69.
71. Felman and Laub, *Testimony*, 1992, p.58.
72. Louise A. Jackson, *Child Sexual Abuse in Victorian England*, London, 2000, p.26.
73. Felman and Laub, *Testimony*, 1992, p.58.
74. Alexander, *Becoming a Woman*, p.225.
75. One of her two nephews has predeceased her in recent years.
76. Letter from Stan Kean to Winifred Mankelow, 1 July 1940. Letter in author's possession.

## 7 Personal and Public Archives

1. Jean Sebastien Marcoux, 'The 'Casser Maison' Ritual: Constructing the Self by Emptying the Home', *Journal of Material Culture*, vol.6: 2, 2001. Thanks to Antony Buxton for drawing my attention to this article.
2. James T. Whitehead, *A Historical Sketch of the Congregation now meeting in the New Gravel Pit Church Hackney*, London, 1889, p.18; J. Davies, *An Account of the Old Gravel Pit Meeting House*, 1853; Albert Peel, 'Clapton Park Congregational Church as seen in its minutes 1804–1929', *Transactions of the*

*Congregational History Society*, 1929.

3. Whitehead, *A Historical Sketch of the Congregation*, 1889, p.25. Priestley was supported locally by Congregationalists though was not a member himself. See also Jack Fruchtman Jnr, 'The apocalyptic politics of Richard Price and Joseph Priestley: a study in late eighteenth-century English Republican Millennialism', *Transactions of the American Philosophical Society*, vol.73:4, 1983.

4. Between 1769–1850 an academy run by the Congregational Fund Board was established in Homerton training young men for the ministry. it subsequently moved to Hampstead as the New College. William Page (ed.), *Victoria History of the Counties of England, London*, vol.1, London, 1909, p.399.

5. See Bruce Wheeler, 'Language and Landscape in the Construction of Place in an East London Borough' in Kean, Martin, Morgan (eds.), *Seeing History*, pp.105–26.

6. Alan Bullock, *Building Jerusalem, A Portrait of my Father*, London, 2000, p.4.

7. Edward G. Herbert, 'The Congregationalist Character', *Congregationalism. Religious Republics*, 1869, p.96.

8. Marcoux, 'The "Casser Maison" Ritual': *Journal of Material Culture*, vol.6: 2, 2001, p.231.

9. Mihaly Czikszentmihalyi, 'Why we need things', Steven Lubar and W. David Kingery (eds.), *History from Things. Essays on Material Culture*, Washington, 1993, pp.25–9.

10. See Sally J. Morgan, 'My father's photographs: the visual as public history', in Kean, Martin and Morgan (eds.), *Seeing History*, as discussed in the introduction p.3.

11. Licinius, *Vote Labour? Why?*, Victor Gollancz, 1945. He had also purchased (and kept) in the same series, Celticus, *Why not trust the Tories?*, 1944, George Catlin, Vera Brittain, Sheila Hodges, *Above all Nations*, 1945, Cassius, *Brendan and Beverley* 1944, Sir Robert Mayer, *Young People in Trouble*, 1945.

12. J.M. Turner, 'Methodism in England', in Davies, George and Rupp, *Methodism*, vol.3, p.331.

13. The Hackney housing officer, in those pre-equal opportunities time, declared 'your daughter will have to get her husband to cater for her'. Even they knew by then that one way or another filial marriage was not on the cards.

14. He was also a member of the white collar local government union NALGO and kept the membership card of the first year of membership under nationalisation. Alec Spoor, *White Collar Union. Sixty Years of Nalgo*, London, 1967, pp.311–12.

15. *35th City of London Battalion Home Guard, May 1940–May 1943*, London, 1944, pages unnumbered.

16. S. P. Mackenzie, *The Home Guard: A Military and Political History*, Oxford, 1995, p.184.

17. *35th City of London Battalion Home Guard, May 1940–May 1943*.

18. Alessandro Portelli, 'Oral History as Genre' in Mary Chamberlain and Paul Thompson (eds.), *Narrative and Genre*, London, 1998, pp.26–7.

19. Eric Lomax, *The Railway Man*, London, 1996, pp.210, 216.

20. For discussion of the relationship between personal and public time see Hilda Kean, 'Continuity and Change: the Identity of the Political Reader', *Changing English*, vol.3, no.2, 1996, pp.209–18 and 'Searching for the Past in Present Defeat: the Construction of Historical and Political Identity in mid-war British Feminism', *Women's History Review*, vol.3:1, 1994, pp.57–80.

21. Bomb damage map 22/31 LMA. A similar fate befell Ada's childhood home in Monier Street where over half the houses were seriously damaged. Bomb damage map 22/41.

22. J. B. Priestley, *British Women go to War*, n.d. (1943); Susan Kingsley Kent, *Gender and Power in Britain, 1640–1990*, London, 1998, pp.312–15.

23. John Gross, *A Double Thread. A Childhood in Mile End and Beyond*, London, 2002, p.136.

24. Michael Billington, *The Life and Work of Harold Pinter*, London, 1996, p.8.

25. Interview with Harold Pinter, 'Between the Lines', *Independent on Sunday*, 13 April 2003, pp.8–9.

26. Krik Kirk and Ed Heath, *Men in Frocks*, London, 1984, p.18.

27. Marjorie B. Garber, *Vested Interests, Cross-dressing and Cultural Anxiety*, London, 1992, p.69–70. See also Paul Baker and Jo Stanley, *Hello Sailor! The Hidden History of Gay Life at Sea*, London, 2003, pp.116–44.

28. Ross McKibbin, *Classes and Cultures England 1918–51*, Oxford, 1998, p.282.

29. Herbert, 'The Congregationalist Character', in *Religious Republics*, 1869.

30. *Twenty First Annual Report of the Clapton Mission,* Primitive Methodist Connexion, November 1905. Clapton Park Methodist file, D/E 234 A9, Hackney archives.

31. Minutes of Quarterly Meeting, Clapton Primitive Methodist Circuit, 7 December 1906, Clapton Park Methodist file, D/E 234 A1/9.

32. www.hmc.gov.uk/nra/searches/sidocs.asp?SIR=68572 site visited 13 January 2002.

33. Although Stan's parents were Primitive Methodists he had joined the Glyn Road mission, a satellite of the Round Chapel, when a young man and converted to Congregationalism.

34. George Eliot, *Silas Marner*, 1861, reissued London, 1996, ed. Peter Mudford, pp.177–8.

35. For an account of library provision in Hackney see Hilda Kean, 'The Transformation of Political and Cultural Space', in Joe Kerr and Andrew Gibbon (eds.), *London: from Punk to Blair*, London, 2003.

36. Minutes of the Deacons' Meetings Clapton Park Congregational Church, 28 February 1950, Hackney Archives.

37. Minutes of the Deacons' Meetings Clapton Park Congregational Church, 14

November 1952.

38. Minutes of the Deacons' Meetings Clapton Park Congregational Church, 21 September 1953.

39. Minutes of the Deacons' Meetings Clapton Park Congregational Church, 25 July 1955.

40. J.M. Turner, 'Methodism in England 1900–32' in Davies, George and Rupp (eds.), *A History of the Methodist Church*, vol.3, 1978, pp.309–61; Currie, *Methodism Divided*.

41. Elie Halévy, *The Birth of Methodism in England*, ed. B. Semmel, Chicago, 1971.

42. Turner, 'Methodism in England 1900–32' in Davies, George, Rupp (eds.), *A History of the Methodist Church*, vol.3, 1978, p.322.

43. Currie, *Methodism Divided*, 1968, p.131.

44. Article in *Grapevine*, Loughton Methodist Church, n.d. (1990).

45. Charley Wesley, 'And can it be', *Methodist Hymn Book*, no.216, 1999.

46. Jacques Derrida, *Archive Fever. A Freudian Impression*, 1996, p.36

47. Obituary of Stan Kean, *Grapevine*, July 1989, Loughton Methodist Church.

## 8 A Conclusion

1. Carol Ann Duffy, 'The Captain of the 1964 Top of the Form Team', *Meantime*, London, 1994, p.7.

2. Samuel, *Island Stories*, 1998, pp.222–3.

3. Published annually (and without concurrent answers) in the Christmas Eve *Guardian*.

4. Bertolt Brecht, 'Questions from a worker who reads' as printed in Raphael Samuel (ed.) preface to *Village Life and Labour*, London, 1975.

# SELECT BIBLIOGRAPHY
## OF BOOKS AND ARTICLES

Sally Alexander, *Becoming a Woman*, London, 1994,

Victor Bailey (ed.), *Forged in Fire the History of the Fire Brigades Union*, London, 1992

Roland Barthes, *Camera Lucida. Reflections on Photography*, London, 1982

Walter Benjamin (translated Howard Eiland & Kevin McLaughlin ), *The Arcades Project*, Harvard, 2002

Geoffrey V. Blackstone, *A History of the British Fire Service*, London,1957

John Burnett, *Idle Hands.The Experience of Unemployment 1790–1990*, London, 1994

Anna Clark, *The Struggle for the Breeches. Gender & the Making of the British Working Class*, London, 1995

Alec Clifton-Taylor, *The Pattern of English Building*, London, 1962

William G. Crory, *East London Industries*, London, 1876

Mihaly Csikszentmihalyi & Eugene Ruchberg-Halton, *The Meaning of Things. Domestic Symbols and the Self*, Cambridge, 1981

ed. C. R. J. Currie, *A History of the County of Middlesex: Early Stepney with Bethnal Green,Victoria County History,* vol. XI, Oxford, 1998

eds. C. R. J.Currie & C. P. Lewis, *A Guide to English County Histories*, Stroud, 1997

Stephen Daniels, *Fields of Vision. Landscape Imagery and National Identity in England and the United States*, Chichester, 1993

Rupert Davies,A. Raymond George, Ernest Gordon Rupp (eds.), *A History of the Methodist Church in Great Britain*, vol. 3, London, 1978

Edward Dobson, *A Rudimentary Treatise on the Manufacture of Bricks and Tiles*, London, part one, 1850

George Dodd, *Days at the Factories*, Series 1, London, 1843

Thomas Dormandy, *The White Death. A History of Tuberculosis*, London, 1999

Barbara Drake, *Women in Trade Unions,* 1920, reissued London,1985

Richard Evans, *Telling Lies about Hitler. The Holocaust, History & the David Irving Trial*, London, 2002

Alan M. Everitt, *Transformation and Tradition: Aspects of the Victorian Countryside*, Norwich,1985

Alan Everitt, 'Country Carriers', *Journal of Transport History*, new series,111, no. 3 February 1976

Shoshana Felman and Dori Laub, *Testimony. Crises of Witnessing in Literature, Psychoanalysis and History*, London, 1992

Hector Gavin, *Sanitary Ramblings being sketches and illustrations of Bethnal Green*, London, 1848

M. W. Greenslade, *Victoria County History of Staffordshire*, vol. XX, reprinted 1989

Elizabeth Hallam & Jenny Hockey, *Death, Memory and Material Culture*, Oxford, 2001

ed. Frigga Haug, *Female Sexualization*, London, 1987

Humphrey Jennings, *Pandaemonium 1660–1886. The Coming of the Machine As Seen by Contemporary Observers*, (eds. Mary-Lou Jennings & Charles Madge), New York, 1985

Ludmilla Jordanova, *History in Practice*, London, 2000

Hilda Kean, Paul Martin & Sally J. Morgan (eds.), *Seeing History. Public History in Britain Now*, London, 2000,

Hilda Kean, 'East End Stories: The Chairs and the Photographs', *International Journal of Heritage Studies*, vol. 6. No. 2, 2000

Hilda Kean and Bruce Wheeler, ' Making History in Bethnal Green: Different Stories of Nineteenth-century Silk Weavers', *History Workshop Journal*, vol. 56, 2003

Francis D. Klingender, *Art and the Industrial Revolution*, revised edition, London, 1968

Hilary Lees, *English Churchyard Memorials*, Stroud, 2000

Steven Lubar & W. David Kingery (eds.), *History from Things Essays on Material Culture*, 1993

Jean Sebastien Marcoux, 'The "Casser Maison" ritual. Constructing the self by emptying the Home', *Journal of Material Culture*, vol. 6: 2, 2001

Charles F. A. Marmoy, *The French Protestant Hospital. Extracts from the archives of 'La Providence' relating to inmates and applications for admission, 1718–1957, and to recipients of and applicants for the Coqueau charity, 1745–1901*, London, 1977

Peter Padfield, *Beneath the House Flag of the P&O*, London, 1981

Susan M Pearce (ed.) *Interpreting Objects and Collections*, London, 1994

William Pitt, *General View of the Agriculture of the county of Stafford*, London, 1794

Alfred Plummer, *The London Weavers' Company 1600–1970*, London, 1972

Geoffrey Roberts, *The History and Narrative Reader*, London, 2001

Raphael Samuel, *Theatres of Memory*, London, 1994

Raphael Samuel, 'Local History and Oral History', *History Workshop Journal*, 1, 1976

Carolyn Steedman, *Dust*, Manchester, 2001

Michael P. Steinberg, *Walter Benjamin and the Demands of History*, New York, 1996

Susan Stewart, *On Longing. Narratives of the Miniature, the Gigantic, the Souvenir, the Collection*, Baltimore, 1993

Mark Taylor and Dietrich Christian Lammerts, *Grave Matters*, London, 2002

Mathew Thompson, *The Problem of Mental Deficiency*, Oxford, 1998

James Thorne, *Handbook to the Environs of London Part II*, London, 1876

Gerard L. Turnbull, *Traffic and transport. An economic History of Pickfords*, London, 1979

David Wainwright, *Stone's Ginger Wine. Fortunes of a Family Firm 1740–1990*, London, 1990

Frank Warner, *The Silk Industry of the United Kingdom. Its Origin & Development*, London, 1921

Hayden White, *The Content of the Form Narrative Discourse & Historical Representation*, Baltimore, 1990

Michael Zell, *Industry in the countryside. Wealden Society in the Sixteenth Century*, Cambridge, 1994

# INDEX